THE POLICY MAKERS

'It Says Here the Economy Needs Cooling Off.'

JOHN C. DONOVAN

THE

POLICY

MAKERS

PEGASUS   NEW YORK

This book is dedicated with abiding love and great respect to three Tucker ladies, Myrtie, Martha and Nancy, for the quality of their lives.

Acknowledgments   xi

Preface   xiii

Chapter One: Power and Policy Leadership   19

Chapter Two: Leadership in the Institutionalized Presi-
                  dency   35

Chapter Three: The Congressional Coalition: Entrenched
                  Parochialism   57

Chapter Four: The Professional and Social Reform   76

Chapter Five: The Persistence of Policy: Containment in
                  the Sixties   100

Chapter Six: The Budget and National Priorities   118

Chapter Seven: The Military-Congressional Complex: Is
                  there an alternative?   136

Chapter Eight: The Changing Polity   168

Chapter Nine: Ideology and Political Change   188

Chapter Ten: Epilogue—Where Do We Go From Here?   211

Suggestions for Further Research   222

Notes   230

Index   248

The one thing that above all others stands out in my understanding of what has happened in the last eight to ten years is that we have suddenly discovered that we can do anything we set out to do.

W. WILLARD WIRTZ
Bowdoin College May 13, 1969

ALTHOUGH THIS BOOK was substantially written in 1969, it results from a process of reading, teaching, and working which has been going on now for more than twenty-five years, since I first became interested in American politics. It would take more than a brief paragraph to express thanks adequately to all of those who have helped shape my understanding of American politics. I shall limit myself, therefore, to mentioning only those friends and associates who were directly and immediately helpful during the actual writing process. I am very grateful to Everett Ladd, Jr. of the University of Connecticut; J. Clarence Davies, III of Princeton University; Athern P. Daggett, M. Reginald Lewis and Richard E. Morgan, Bowdoin College departmental colleagues and friends, all of whom read the manuscript and offered me the benefit of their critical advice. The cumulative impact of their collective advice has been felt more than they may individually realize. Rep. William D. Hathaway of Maine, Rep. John Brademas of Indiana and Rep. Donald Fraser of Minnesota were kind enough to take the time in the midst of their crowded official lives to read Chapters Three through Seven. I found their detailed comments invaluable. I might say that all three had received favorable mention in my manuscript *before* there was any prospect that they might see a draft manuscript.

Then there are those who suffered with me from beginning to end. Judge Frank M. Coffin not only read the manuscript with his kindly and perceptive editorial eye but also warmed the human spirit when the flesh grew weak. Carey Donovan, now a student in Swarthmore College, helped get my notes in

ACKNOWLEDGMENTS

order; fortunately, she proved to be far more systematic than her father. Lawrence Putterman, class of 1970, Bowdoin College, served with pleasant efficiency as research assistant. Mrs. Gladys McKnight, Mrs. Lucille Sinnett, Mrs. Jean McDougall and Mrs. Jean Hughes typed the manuscript in its various phases. Mrs. McKnight, having assisted me now for the second time in the preparation of a book, has not only earned my deepest gratitude but deserves a special citation for displaying exceptional fortitude under heavy fire. My warm thanks go to John Mong, fine editor and patient friend, who encouraged me to write the book I wanted to write. Beatrice, my wife, suggested the title and proved again to be a skillful editor. Our children, Carey, Christine, Martha and John, have long since grown accustomed to hearing my typewriter banging away at odd hours. So far as I can see, this does not inhibit them in the least. My advice to academic colleagues is to let the youngsters in the study. Otherwise, book-writing is likely to prove as joyful as coal-mining.

JCD

ONE OF THE readers of this book while it was in manuscript form commented that it seemed haunted by the specters of Vietnam and the failure of the war on poverty, and I think this must be true. We are all haunted by these specters, are we not? Even if this were not the case, the author's biases would probably be evident to the reader soon enough. It may, therefore, serve a useful purpose to state the principal biases which seem to me to have affected this work. I regard myself as a Stevensonian liberal, one of a considerable number of Americans who were drawn into political activity in the 1950s inspired by the words and the example of Governor Stevenson. Adlai Stevenson, as those under thirty probably do *not* know, was the first American major politician to attempt the articulation of a liberal creed which would transcend the limits of what has since been pejoratively labeled "interest group" liberalism. I am not quite prepared to write off my own generation (the gap has two sides) as being completely anachronistic nor am I yet convinced that Stevensonian liberalism represented a futile and quixotic search for the impossible dream.

It was, after all, the man who nominated Stevenson in 1960 who later forced the abdication of Lyndon Johnson. One occasionally wonders what the "style" of John F. Kennedy's administration would have been if Adlai Stevenson had not preceded him. Be that as it may, it is hardly to be denied—and scarcely, if ever, acknowledged—that it was the people Stevenson activated in the 1950s who provided a crucial margin (and more) in Kennedy's razor-thin victory over Nixon. Furthermore, the Stevensonian era of Democratic politics produced a number of new liberal leaders who are destined to figure prominently in the politics of the 1970s. Senators Muskie and McGovern are two of the more obvious examples.

Recognizing the history of the Stevensonian impact does not at all imply enormous confidence that the residue of liberalism, Stevensonian or otherwise, is destined to prevail in the face of present turmoil. The pressures put upon it—and us—by events may prove to be too severe. Who can say, for example, what the political repercussions may be if the Nixon administration manages to deflate the economy into a serious recession with all of its grievous impact upon the poor black community? And the prospect grows more ominous as this book goes to press. For this reason alone, I am pessimistic about the possibility that liberalism will be granted the time or that it will find the way to a reworking which might increase its relevance. It may be that we are drifting toward a new ideology, emphasizing science and technology. If so, a detailed picture of this new ideology-in-the-making has not appeared. Perhaps it is too early.

It does seem possible to delineate some of the basic issues such an ideology will necessarily confront. How are we to effect basic reform in the existing institutions of the modern technocracy? In what specific ways is it possible to widen the participation of ordinary people in decisions affecting their daily lives on such matters as work, housing, schools, the use of leisure and so on? How is man to overcome the pervading sense of powerlessness which now increasingly affects the children of affluence almost as easily as it dominates the lives of the poor? These and similar questions relate to a much larger and more profound issue which we are bound to face: man versus machine.

In a sense, this is not a new problem. It is at least as old as the beginning of the Industrial Revolution, but, by this time we have managed to construct a system

of ideas, techniques, and machines that puts us, in terms of power, about where God is, or used to be. And this system evolving steadily, progressively displacing nature, tends increasingly to assert itself as the ultimate reality.[1]

Can man manage and control such a complicated, changing and powerful "system"? This fundamental question underlies politics today and provides the real terror in our lives. If Machine or System comes to win acceptance as the ultimate reality, what then is man?

The American political tradition bears examining on this point: it assumes the autonomy of the individual and warns us to fear concentrated power. In the modern period, in addition to the constraints which constitutionalism imposes, we have come to place a conspicuous reliance on the automatic checking and balancing of powerful groups. These group interests are said to have evolved into a system of countervailing power, as if led by an invisible hand. This "best-of-all-possible-worlds" kind of automaticity is now being seriously questioned, as it should be.

It may appear, therefore, that one takes on a special burden in arguing, as I intend to do, for a strengthening of the Presidential role in policy leadership. Is this not inconsistent with the need to resist the growth of concentrated power? I think not, if we are trying to make power responsible and responsive to the popular will in a constitutional order. The Presidency is our one truly national political institution. It provides a natural locus for policy leadership, and it has the distinct advantage of being highly visible. Certainly, the Congress as an institution is inherently incapable of providing policy leadership for the nation. Congress tends to reflect a diversity of particularized and decentralized constituencies, a not inconsequential role. We should not minimize the functions of Congress, as the popular mentality does. Indeed, the ability of Congress to restrain the use of Executive power ought to be reexamined. It is the *purposes* for which Congress exercises its great powers that we ignore at our peril. Congress has been dominated much of the

[1]Elting E. Morison, New York *Times* book review, March 30, 1969, in a review of *Technological Man* by Victor C. Ferkiss (N.Y.: George Braziller, 1969).

time since 1938 by a coalitional leadership group which has used the powers of the national legislature, a body possessing the greatest independent powers of any national legislature in the Western world, to support domestic parochialism, to perpetuate cold war orthodoxy and to bestow a ludicrously uncritical acceptance on the excesses of the new militarism. On the domestic side, the response of Congress in the face of this dominant coalitional bias has been to minimize the implications of racial crisis and urban pathology. It need not be so. The Congressional oligarchs possess no heavenly mandate. Congress has significant power to make a far more positive contribution to enlightened public policy in the future.

But is there any reasonable prospect that a meaningful change in the control of Congress will take place in the foreseeable future? My analysis suggests that such a change is taking place before our eyes. A new quasi-majority has been gradually coalescing in the Congress throughout the last half of the 1960s. This new political coalition is perhaps easier to recognize in the Senate but similar changes are well underway in the House of Representatives. The new political force as it takes shape in Congress may be expected to embrace a different view of the American world role and of our internal dilemmas than that which has been identified with the Conservative Coalition in the postwar era.

The problem of concentrated power is always a specific one. In our day, the military-industrial-technocratic-educational complex poses the greatest immediate threat not because a power elite has plotted its domination over our lives. Like Topsy it just grew. What should most concern us is the pushing aside of other critical public priorities by the sheer inertial force of the huge complex. Presidential policy leadership is legitimately used in resisting this bureaucratic drift. In any case, Presidential policy leadership seems in no real danger of becoming so effective that it will soon represent, to a perilous degree, the concentrated power of the modern technocracy. Long before this were to occur, one should expect that the forces of change which are transforming the Presidency into a technically sophisticated institution will also have begun to effectuate equally profound changes in the nature, and perhaps the objectives, of Congressional leadership.

A more frightening possibility is that neither Presidency nor Congress will change sufficiently nor soon enough to assert effective control of the technocratic system in all of its pretentious and bewildering complexity.

In the meantime, this book may be viewed as an effort in political analysis, aimed not so much at laying bare the specters of the recent past as it is at locating those lacunae in the process where humane values may perhaps be reasserted. In thus trying to link political science to a more broadly humanistic purpose one assumes, of course, that such values exist and that men will seek to honor them.

JOHN C. DONOVAN

CHAPTER ONE

POWER AND POLICY LEADERSHIP

It is both necessary and desirable that the government of a democratic people should be active and powerful; and that our object should be not to render it weak or indolent, but solely to prevent it from abusing its aptitude and strength.

TOCQUEVILLE

CONTROLLING POWER: AN AMERICAN BIAS

ANYONE BOLD ENOUGH to undertake a serious analysis of how policy is made in the American political system must begin with the realization that he is examining one of the most complex structures ever contrived by man. He must also realize that the "system" under examination has been evolving over at least two centuries—all the while subject to an inexorable process of change—and that he is studying American political development at a time when the process of change seems to be more relentlessly driven than ever before in American experience. One occasionally wonders whether the problems put before the student of politics today are capable of being analyzed in the sense that, let us say, Plato and Aristotle studied the political problems of their civilization. There is not merely the great difference in size—the mammoth American technocratic empire in contrast to the tiny, compact polis of classical antiquity—but so much of what may be crucial to an analysis of the present American political system may not even be visible to the political analyst. Even the office of the Presidency, an institution of high visibility, has now become a complex arrangement of agencies, advisory offices and staff assistants whose presence is barely perceived by the public at large and whose actual functions are understood only by a relatively few specialists.

This study is intended to examine the process of national policy formulation at this critical time in our political life. I am interested in seeing *how* policy is made because I sense that it is not simply a procedural matter. Central to my analysis is the view —the hypothesis—that national public policy formulation involves the intersection of political, managerial, and political preferences, perceptions, and capabilities. The pursuit of this hypothesis will necessitate a rather searching examination of the Presidency and the Congress. In many respects, the nature, scope, significance and persistence of change in these institutions play havoc with the analyst's tools and cloud his vision. The problems of analysis and theory-building are compounded by a philosophical inheritance which tends to minimize the importance of theory as well as by the rapid pace of the transformation of American society.

Nevertheless, the invitation to understand seems irresistible: the problems themselves pose exciting intellectual challenges of a high order; and, furthermore, we must understand what is happening to these institutions if we are to have any chance of controlling what the process produces.

We Americans have inherited a marvelous eighteenth-century invention: a written constitution complete with separation of powers, checks and balances, and an elaborate Bill of Rights. Our constitution borrows heavily from John Locke in seventeenth-century England and from Montesquieu, who was patently *not* thinking of American institutions or American experience. There is also in our inheritance a vaguely Newtonian-mechanistic view of social processes. What possible meaning does any of this have for the late twentieth century, the age of Telstar, Apollo rockets, McLuhan, Sirhan, Oswald and Pinkville? Isn't it naive to assume that the constitution makers of 1787 could have erected constitutional barriers which will control the effects of the American technocracy with its dramatic impact on public policy? Who cares in pragmatic and strife-torn America what John Locke thought about the supremacy of Parliament or the desirability of establishing a fiduciary relationship between people and civil government? Does an eighteenth-century constitution protect us from the tyranny of technology? How do we control those who hold the power of decision within the complex organizations, structures and institutions which presently dominate the American scene?

Perhaps we go back to the formative years of the Republic seeking guidance partly because it is so easy for Americans to do. We have the advantage, if it is an advantage, of having begun our experiment at a fixed point in time. Ours is "the first new nation" and it began in 1776 . . . or was it 1787? In any case, the generation of men who drew up the Constitution of the United States were creatures of the Enlightenment, and the Constitution they brought forth bears the marks of its eighteenth-century birth. In consequence, one might have assumed that the American political tradition, having its starting point in the eighteenth century, would present a warmly optimistic view of man as a rational being full of a potential for goodness, justice and mercy.

After all, our situation was fairly unique, or so we have always thought. We Americans were "born free" as Louis Hartz has so brilliantly shown us.[1] No need in America to throw off the shackles of the *ancien régime;* no need to tear society apart in order to rid ourselves of the institutions and values of a feudal order. We never had feudalism in the first place. We were free to build our own institutions and to create our own values, or to borrow them from John Locke. The ground must have seemed fertile for a Utopia. The commune builders of the New Left would have been ecstatic.

But the men who created the new American nation were neither optimists nor Utopians. They were profoundly apprehensive concerning the dangers of power since their view of man drew far more from their Calvinist forbears than it did from the rationalism of the Enlightenment. The Puritan strain, so easily caricatured in our day, carried with it an imperative sense of man's capacity to do evil, even in the name of good. One thinks immediately of John Adams and his crusty sense of duty. Twentieth-century man encountering John Adams and his fear of the corrupting influence of power might reflect on the significance of the New England conscience. If John Adams sometimes seemed obsessed with the necessity of placing curbs on the exercise of power, he was unfailingly rigorous in searching his own soul, as well as the evidence of history.[2]

The contrast with the typical twentieth-century view of Power could scarcely be greater. We witness the concentration of power in massive forms totally without precedent in all human experience, but we do not seem greatly concerned. Powerful and power-seeking men seldom question the legitimacy of their own roles in our increasingly technocratic Leviathan. Men like Lyndon Johnson and Richard Nixon lead the nation after having invested whole careers in the manipulation of power, and neither appears to have had to struggle with a New England conscience. The personal salvation of either man is not here the issue, but what are the implications in an age of huge organizations when public leaders accept uncritically the role of concentrated power? It is misleading, and possibly unfair, to so personalize the argument. Johnson and Nixon, lacking the restraints of Adams-like introspection, are surely not unusual (in this respect, at least) among contemporary public men. If anything, Johnson and Nixon appear to be rather representative products of the American political process. If they do not seem terribly perceptive about the misuse of massive concentrations of power, who among our political leaders does? What public figure any longer concerns himself with the problem of Power, so central in the thinking and the actions of the men who founded the Republic?

When Senator Eugene McCarthy, as candidate, spoke of firing J. Edgar Hoover, dismantling the CIA, and "cooling" Presidential interventionism, a fairly sizeable group of young faculty, a few writers, and a band of idealistic students responded favorably, but it seems a fair bet that a far larger group of citizens thought the Senator was kidding and some may even have thought him mad. A good many other Americans, of course, were simply not listening. McCarthy's forensic effort, while quixotic, holds a certain interest. The Senator seemed only to be speaking of certain symbols of power, and yet it was novel to discover a man who had been in American national politics for several years who thought that power had been misused and who assumed that perhaps this was worth talking about in the course of a campaign for Presidential nomination. We may be sure that the difference in viewpoint between our eighteenth-century constitution writer and the typical American political leader of the late twentieth century is not simply to be explained away in personal or psychological terms. The centralizing tendencies of modern industrialism have numbed the sensitivities of all of us, and not just our public men, on the danger of concentrated power.

McNAMARA: A CENTRALIZING FORCE

The last public figure to raise serious questions about the dangers of concentrated power was Dwight D. Eisenhower, who waited until his last day in office to do so. It was perhaps an afterthought, yet it was President Eisenhower who first warned the American people about the potential dangers of the military-industrial complex in the years to come—Eisenhower who had lived most of his adult life on one or another of the peaks of power: General of the Army, university president, President of the United States. Ironically, President Kennedy, his successor, had already decided to bring Robert McNamara, President of the Ford Motor Company, to Washington as Secretary of Defense at the time Eisenhower was issuing his warning to the American people. McNamara, as it turned out, was the ideal choice *if* the aim were to centralize further the making of decisions within the military-industrial complex. By the time McNamara had completed his work in the Pentagon seven years later military spending approached $80 billion annually, forward planners in the armed services were convinced this was not enough, and for the first time in the nation's history there was a genuine fear that a permanent military establishment had taken root in our soil.

The usual assumption has been that since Mr. McNamara, an extraordinarily gifted industrial manager and a man of rare personal quality, succeeded in centralizing control of so much power in his own office, a civilian post, the results must be benign. While it seemed true that Secretary McNamara performed administrative miracles in gaining this position of superior influence over the uniformed military chieftains, his

23

triumph would have unnerved John Adams. And with good reason. The significance of McNamara's remarkable accomplishment should not be minimized. He succeeded in establishing a high degree of central control over a massive defense establishment. In doing so, McNamara concentrated military power as never before in the history of this country.

Richard Goodwin,[3] who occupied a privileged observation post inside the Kennedy-Johnson administrations, has this clear perception:

> Robert McNamara not only enlarged our armed forces but rationalized them. Over the resistance of officers of little imagination, he unified the operations of the services, eliminated many old rivalries, and instituted the deceptive techniques of modern computer management. As a result, the military has more influence on public policy than ever before in our history.

We come to the end of the 1960s with a centralized, enormously enlarged and presumably *permanent* military establishment! The old familiar rivalries—the Army, the Navy, the Air Force and the Marines—and the complex relationships they wove with the various centers of Congressional baronial power were often unseemly, and, in part, wasteful; but, there was also at work a rough form of checking and balancing of forces within the Pentagon. And what is now taking its place? Goodwin[4] suggests an answer: "The power that was once held in check by rivalries and folk wisdom is now exerted by a single, fused force on the civilian economy and its decision-makers." We now have the Warfare State.

Scholars who specialize in the study of defense decision-making are likely to feel that Goodwin has overstated the significance of the McNamara managerial revolution. Professor Huntington's analysis of defense policy-making in the 1950s indicates that civilian militants were increasingly in a position to prevail over the uniformed chiefs of staff on vital questions of policy.[5] But surely McNamara carried the centralizing of defense decision-making a step further, and he did so by the use of managerial techniques which strengthened his hand as policy leader within the Defense establishment. The important political point which the specialists may not see, since it transcends the limits of defense decision-making per se, is that McNamara's success as manager of the huge military establishment added to his personal prestige and his policy influence within the Kennedy and Johnson administrations. Hence policy suggestions bearing the McNamara imprint were likely to carry a disproportionate weight. To put the matter crudely, in the struggle over national priorities, as that struggle is reflected in the formulation of the Executive budget, there apparently was no official strong enough to offset the commanding figure of McNamara, unless it was the President himself.

The manner in which Secretary McNamara dominated the budgetary scene has since been at least partially clarified. When Mr. McNamara was at the height of his powers, he would convene two or three budget review meetings in the Pentagon in November and December. In other departments, these review sessions are called by officials of the Bureau of the Budget; the meetings take place in the Executive Office building and are chaired by high-ranking Budget Bureau officials with departmental representatives in the position of defending their budget proposals for the coming fiscal year. At Secretary McNamara's hearing, the Budget Director was a participant— almost an adversary—along with top echelon DOD officials, and the President's national security and science advisers.

A McNamara budget review session has been described as follows:

> Mr. McNamara sat at the head of the table and there was no question who was in charge. He would listen to arguments between the Budget Director and his own controller and try to resolve outstanding differences. He would always point out that any issue could be brought directly to the President. But the Budget Bureau was reluctant to take up an issue if Mr. McNamara was opposed. He had so many facts to bolster his arguments that few wished to tangle in that area.[6]

As the Nixon administration assumed responsibility for defense decision-making, there was the awareness that defense spending had reached the point where the new administration was virtually unable to order its own priorities. Senator William Proxmire,[7] who first revealed that Defense budgets were not subject to Budget Bureau review as other departments are, put the charge with characteristic bluntness: "The military-industrial complex now writes its own budgetary ticket." The Nixon administration was in office only a short time when it reversed the process so that henceforth Defense budgets would come before the Budget Bureau for review in the same fashion as other departmental budgets.

There was a certain fascination in observing Melvin Laird as he grappled with the Defense budget he had inherited. Laird had been a key figure on the Republican side of the small Congressional appropriations elite group which sits in judgment on the mighty defense budget. Laird knew as well as any man that McNamara eventually found himself trapped by his own system as the pressures of the military-industrial (and Congressional) complex forced him, evidently against his better judgment, to proceed with the anti-ballistic missile system which he had long opposed. Laird, a Congressional hawk on Vietnam, soon found that his major task was to effect a major deescalation in Southeast Asia. It was Laird's frustrating assignment to find ways of cutting back on Defense spending. Although the Nixon administration set out to reverse the trend, Defense spending rose to an annual rate of $80.3 billion in July-August-September 1969.

Governments are run by men, not angels, as John Adams and James Madison very well understood. No one should resist the evidence which shows Robert McNamara to have been a brilliant, dedicated, humane, sensitive public servant. McNamara is an extraordinarily gifted man, but he is also fallible, and his fallibility shines through clearly in decisions in which his personal role was crucial: to build the F-111 and to Americanize the war in Vietnam. The McNamara experience suggests that the past may indeed instruct. John Adams and his colleagues bequeathed to us an operating bias which merits a certain respect: too much power concentrated in one place is dangerous even in the hands of good men. Adams also thought he had an answer: in a Republic, one strong institution must be counterbalanced by an equally strong institution or Liberty will be endangered.

Adams' personal contribution was essentially limited to *constitutional* mechanisms: The separation of powers and its corollary, checks and balances. There is also the Madisonian contribution which considers the problem of Power in terms of social processes and which seeks a solution through agencies of social control. The essay we find most helpful is Number Ten of the *Federalist* papers. The reason is clear: it could easily have been written (except for the rhetoric) in the twentieth century. Arthur Bentley's seminal work of 1908 which analyzes the governmental process under the influence of diverse group activities follows directly Madison's brilliant conception as it is set forth in the *Federalist* papers.[8]

Madison's essay deals with the rise and spread of factions in a Republic. A faction, for Madison, is a group of people activated by an interest adverse to that of the community as a whole. We might call it a special-interest group. Madison wrote, of course, before Union had been achieved, before we were sure we had a nation, in what David G. Smith[9] has termed "a disharmonious society." Hence, Madison undoubtedly had in mind the possibility of a disloyal opposition gaining power, a faction which might wish to exploit the conflicts and cleavages of the post-Revolutionary period in order to subvert the Republic. (And it is worth a moment's reflection that Aaron Burr came within inches of the American Presidency.)

A Republic, at any rate, must find a way to deal with factions since their rise and spread is inevitable, their latent causes sown in the nature of man. And man remains an egoistic, contentious creature. When men fail to find something substantial to struggle over, the most "frivolous and fanciful" distinctions will suffice to kindle their passions, so Madison argues. And liberty, the prime political value for Madison's generation, is to faction as air is to fire. If men are free to think, to discuss, to assemble, to agitate, they will form factions.

Then, why not control the *causes* of factions? Could they not be rooted out? Or eliminated by skillful surgery? Yes, this is possible. There is a totalitarian solution which carries with it terrible consequences: Liberty will disappear and the Republic will be destroyed.

Only one alternative is *compatible with Liberty:* the *effects* of factions must be controlled. The controlling of the effects postulates a role for modern government displeasing to those latter-day patriots who erroneously would make the Founding Fathers advocates of laissez faire. Madison prophetically foresees a diverse pattern of interest developing within the new nation: "A landed interest, a manufacturing interest, a mercantile interest, a moneyed interest, with many lesser interests, grow up of necessity in civilized nations and divide them into different classes, actuated by different sentiment and views."

At this point, Madison obviously has moved close to a conception of politics which has had a special appeal in the twentieth century. Audaciously, he makes the forward leap: "The regulation of these various and interfering interests forms the principal task of modern legislation." One notes: Government's *principal* task is to regulate diverse and competing interests. Once Government assumes this positive mediating role in a society permeated by group conflicts, "the spirit of party and faction" inevitably becomes part of "the necessary and ordinary operations of the government." And so it has.

Madison's Tenth *Federalist* accurately predicted the essential relationship between modern government and group activity which is now commonly thought to characterize the American political process. For several decades we have been operating under the comfortable notion that modern government effectively mediates group conflicts. More recently, the notion has been modified considerably: a variety of groups has emerged in which each major group is thought to be sufficiently strong so that no large group is able to dominate its neighbors. In short, this assumes a natural evolutionary process which contains a kind of automatic checking and balancing of one powerful group interest against the other. (Perhaps there was a tendency for something like this to go on in the Pentagon before Mr. McNamara rationalized the process.) And so Professor Galbraith has theorized that the act of concentrating power in one group tends to set in motion forces which lead to a system of countervailing power.[10]

It is a comforting set of notions which some would elevate to theory. If accepted, it might even make empirical analysis unnecessary. Unfortunately, the opposite kind of notion keeps cropping up: quite possibly, the most powerful groups have simply reached a point in their evolution where they prefer coexistence. Perhaps they have found ways of working out their mutual adjustments informally, and, as Commodore Vanderbilt would have it, the public be damned. In this situation one would expect to find that the great groups were content to leave each other's power bases intact. Live and let live is the spirit of the powerful in the Brobdingnagian Utopia, and what's the harm in this if no one comes along to upset the balance?

The complacent pluralist assumptions on which so much of modern American political practice and theory have been based are increasingly subject to critical reexamination by political scientists. First came a line of questioning associated with the thesis that the system of pressure groups has a scope and bias of its own. Following this lead, scholars have called attention to "the other face of power," the hidden face deriving from the fact that the existing structure of organized groups reflects a given version of social conflict while submerging (or ignoring) other possible conflicts. In simple terms, not all interests are organized effectively for the contest. In the struggle of the powerful groups, the weak and powerless are lost sight of.[11]

A second line of criticism holds that the traditional political dialogue between liberal and conservative lacks meaning since both agree fundamentally on the role of government in relation to this group struggle. What emerges is an "interest group liberalism" which sees " . . . as both necessary and good that the policy agenda and the public interest [shall] be defined in terms of organized interests in society."[12] Professor Lowi, the author of this critique, finds the new political ideology little more than a "vulgarized version" of the pluralist model of political science. It is based on three common assumptions: that the organized interests are homogeneous, easy to define, and sometimes monolithic; that they adequately represent most of the sectors of our lives and effectively check and balance one another; and that government's positive role is one of

29

ensuring access for the most effectively organized and of ratifying the agreements and adjustments as they are worked out among the competing groups.

Our current dilemma may be more complex than this. How would we control concentrated power *if* Government were to develop, *within* its own structure, group interests able to combine with both external groups and Congressional power centers to promote public policies—policies which would, in turn, have the effect of further concentrating power beyond anything previously known in recorded history? What would happen in a nation of more than 200 million people, with a Gross National Product rapidly approaching the trillion-dollar mark, if industrial, military and governmental power were to combine? How much reliance should be placed on a written constitution featuring eighteenth-century mechanisms as a control on the immense power of the military-industrial complex, late twentieth-century version? What devices, procedures, and institutions are available if the military-industrial complex is to be held in some degree of sensible control? Is it possible to alter the scope and the bias of the political process so as to protect the interests of the less powerful in the mighty struggle of the great groups? What would the policy impact be if those groups and aspirations which have been quite effectively balanced out of the political process were somehow to be balanced in?

WHO IS IN CHARGE?

Ben Jonson once said: "It is right to prefer the past to the present since by the one we are instructed and by the other overwhelmed." The present clearly overwhelms us. It is not quite so clear that the past instructs us. Perhaps never before have the domestic problems of America been so intimately connected with the past and present dilemmas of our foreign policy. The trauma of Vietnam relates directly to the guilt and the shame of our dark ghettos. Our inability to disengage from the monstrous overcommitment in Southeast Asia limits severely the application of administrative skill and national resources to the problems of poverty, ignorance and urban slums. In consequence the nation finds itself in more serious trouble, at home and abroad, than it has known in a long time. All of us share the anguish and the responsibility. We need to know the sources of the malaise which afflicts this society, whose aspirations for greatness and decency have long been established.

What went wrong? One looks back at the Bay of Pigs, at the Americanization of the war in Vietnam, and at the disappointments, confusions and frustrations of the war on poverty and asks himself: how *did* it happen, how could it have happened? And one realizes that he is not talking about an occasional error in human judgment nor about the misdeeds of evil tyrants. In the case of Vietnam, we have seen three successive national administrations persisting in an American policy in Southeast Asia which has culminated in what surely must rank as the most serious miscalculation in our history: namely the notion that the application of our superior military technology would "settle" another and smaller country's civil war; a civil war, moreover, which had been going on for two decades and about which we knew very little, indeed. (At the time of our involvement in 1954 there were probably not a dozen authentic Vietnam "experts" in the United States.) If this were not sufficiently unnerving, each passing day now makes clearer that this fateful American policy in Vietnam was persisted in *against* a stream of high quality advice, coming largely from knowledgeable individuals outside government, and despite the increasingly unfavorable consequences of the policy at home and abroad.

It is not that we lacked warnings. Consider for a moment the Bay of Pigs incident, April 1961. The Kennedy Administration arrived in Washington filled with energy, initiative, new ideas, enthusiasm, spirit and, presumably, sophistication. Within a matter of weeks, the President-elect found it desirable to sanction the continuation of CIA-led plans for a Cuban refugee invasion of their homeland. The new Administration had been in office only a few more weeks before it had become inextricably enmeshed in an invasion plan so essentially stupid in design that the mind boggles to think that patriotic and intelligent men such as Allen Dulles and Richard Bissell, Jr., were its creators and passionate advocates. The new President was mis-led, as his friendly biographers and former staff assistants, Arthur Schlesinger, Jr., and Theodore Sorensen, have since shown us. But the President's first official act was the reappointment of Allen Dulles as head of the CIA—and J. Edgar Hoover. The new President had doubts, but apparently he failed to challenge the political wisdom or the morality of an American-sponsored refugee-force invasion of Cuba. The new Administration went along with the CIA project so long as it was plausible to pretend that it was not American-sponsored and so long as there was some hope that it might "succeed," although what success would mean in context is impossible to say. And President Kennedy took full responsibility for the debacle—an act of nobility which may be misleading if one really is interested in discovering who was responsible.

In a book which will long remain an important contribution to the Camelot legend, Theodore Sorensen[13] candidly admits that the Bay of Pigs project "seemed to move inexorably toward execution without the President's being able either to obtain a firm grip on it or reverse it." We need remind ourselves that the reference here is to a young, vigorous, highly intelligent, activist President during the first hopeful weeks of a new assertive national administration. Mr. Sorensen is not recording the ineffectiveness of a fumbling octogenarian in the final dying moments of a discredited regime who is unable to get control of this short-sighted and basically stupid project. Nevertheless, it is Sorensen's judgment, after reflection, that "bureaucratic momentum" governed at the Bay of Pigs rather than "policy leadership." One may quibble perhaps about the extent to which President Kennedy asserted himself as policy leader on this occasion. The President did not stop the project at the outset, as he doubtless should have, but the picture of bureaucratic momentum as Sorenson portrays it is frightening. It may be that foreign policy, especially in those unusual situations which involve clandestine CIA-sponsored interventions, presents a special case. We do know that the Bay of Pigs episode alerted President Kennedy, and he promptly attempted a restructuring of the national security decision-making processes.

What do we understand about the making of domestic policy? Recently, the charge has been made by Daniel P. Moynihan,[14] a former official in the Kennedy-Johnson administrations and an important member of the Nixon domestic policy team, that President Johnson's war on poverty was launched in 1964 *by a Government which did not know what it was doing!* Mr. Moynihan levels the charge in reference to the Economic Opportunity Act of 1964, a piece of legislation which was literally written in the first instance by agents of the President in the Executive branch. As a matter of fact, Mr. Moynihan is known to have been one of the architects of the program he now dissects. (In 1965 he won an Arthur Flemming award as an outstanding young government executive and was cited for this precise role.) It was Mr. Moynihan who earlier had made approving reference to the Economic Opportunity Act (which he now regards as having been based upon an erroneous social theory) as by far the best instance of "the professionalization of reform."

One recoils from the implications of Sorensen's assertion that cold-war bureaucrats in the CIA have the ability to prevail in something as potentially dangerous as the Bay of Pigs against the Presidential presence. Yet, in a real sense, Moynihan's charge seems equally grave. Was President Johnson, an unusually powerful and resourceful political leader and possibly the most skillful legislative leader ever to serve as President, initially unaware that his own war on poverty contained a major emphasis on community action coupled with maximum participation of poor people? Mr. Moynihan reports that, upon finding this out, the President's reaction to Community Action was distinctly unfavorable. If this is true, how did Community Action become a major part of a vital piece of Presidential legislation? Ordinarily, one would assume that a Presidential program, especially one so politically significant as LBJ's war on poverty, would not feature a major social innovation which the President personally disliked. Are we to understand that the men who drafted the Economic Opportunity Act for the President misled the President? Or did they have a "better" view of public policy? Have we another disturbing case, this time at the center of domestic policy, in which a socially innovative form of *bureaucratic momentum* has asserted itself against the wishes and the interests of Presidential policy leadership?

If our knowledge of the making of public policy were limited to the two cases as they have been reviewed by Sorensen and Moynihan, we would first be led to wonder: Who is in charge of the vital interests of the nation? What problems were actually encountered in asserting Presidential leadership in the formulation of domestic and foreign policies during the past decade? Certainly, Sorensen's and Moynihan's assertions, based as they presumably are on personal experience in the high levels of national policy-making, are sufficiently provocative to justify a further careful analysis of such data as may be available concerning how these major public policies were formulated. And we seem to have come upon a striking hypothesis which is well worth more attention: *the way in which public policy is made in the United States may affect what specific public policies become. How we make policy may significantly influence the substance of the policies we get.* In other words, there may be a bias in the process.

How real are these problems? In what sorts of circumstances is policy leadership likely to experience serious difficulty in imposing its own priorities? Is bureaucratic momentum a general characteristic of large organizations? If it is, how is policy leadership to be strengthened in a society dominated by large organizations? Or does it make any difference?

CHAPTER TWO

LEADERSHIP IN THE INSTITUTIONALIZED PRESIDENCY

*By now, I've come to see that the way Government
operates determines the nation's policies.
The operation is the policy, I suppose
Marshall McLuhan might say. . . .*
SENATOR EUGENE MCCARTHY, *Look*, April 1, 1969

*The real problem of the Executive office is potential
rather than actual: the danger that the President
might be buried under his own machinery.
The institutionalization of the Presidency could be
carried so far that the man who occupies it
would become a prisoner in his own house,
a victim of too much and too rigid organization.*
CLINTON ROSSITER, *American Presidency* (1956)

THE FIRST PLACE to look for policy leadership in the American governmental system is the Presidency. This is the great office, the one truly national office in the whole system. The Presidency is our "bully pulpit"; an office in which a man is free, in law and conscience, to be as big a man as he can. This is where we turn in time of crisis.

But the office of the Presidency is subject to institutional development. We now have an "institutionalized" Presidency. Two young scholars who served briefly as White House staff members during the 1960s have published a collection of essays dealing with the Presidential Advisory system underscoring the reality that "as expanding external expectations on the

Presidency have escalated, so too has a growing bureaucracy within the Presidency."[1] The Presidency is no longer one man. Presidential decisions are increasingly systematic group decisions.

Occasional glimpses of the iceberg below the surface reveal Presidential policy leadership as it contends with bureaucratic momentum. While the Bay of Pigs episode, the launching of a Presidential war on poverty, President Nixon's decision to proceed with a modified version of an ABM system, all suggest the extent to which Presidential decision-making has become a group process, they also illustrate the increased difficulty for Presidential policy leadership to assert itself against its own supportive machinery. We have come to expect that the President will find himself struggling with bureaucracies elsewhere in the vast Executive establishment of modern American government. This is part of what David Truman described as "the ordeal of the Executive." A more rigorous examination of decision-making as it now takes place within the Institutionalized Presidency will reveal that the contemporary President, if he is to prevail in policy leadership and protect his own power stakes in policy initiative, must be prepared to contend with *bureaucratic forces located within the institution of the Presidency itself.* In terms of Richard Neustadt's interpretation of Presidential power, this would seem an inevitable development once the Presidential office reaches a certain stage of institutional complexity. This stage appears to have been reached at some point during the 1960s, if, indeed, it was not reached earlier.[2]

THE FDR YEARS

The gradual institutionalizing of the Presidency has been taking place since the late 1930s. Franklin Roosevelt entered the White House in 1933 following an era of monumental passivity on the part of the Federal government. The Presidency, when Roosevelt took office, was still the instrument of a single man, assisted to be sure by a few clerks, secretaries, and a household staff. There was always the possibility of adding a Kitchen Cabinet, an informal circle of cronies, court jesters and political lieutenants. On a more substantial and sustained basis, twentieth-century "strong" Presidents had felt the need to have one intimate and steady confidant with whom to share, if possible, the loneliness and the awesome dilemmas of power. One thinks immediately of President Wilson and Colonel House. FDR was later to develop a similar relationship with Harry Hopkins.

By 1936 Franklin Roosevelt decided that he needed a staff of White House assistants. It was clear by then that a changing society had brought into play a relationship between the President and the great Executive departments quite beyond the administrative capacity of any one man to control. President Roosevelt appointed a President's Committee on Administrative Management, headed by Louis Brownlow, to study the problem and to make recommendations. The report was ready in January, 1937. In less than a week the President sent a special message to Congress endorsing the Committee's report. The President's message said in part:

> The committee has not spared me; they say, what has been common knowledge for twenty years, that the President cannot adequately handle his responsibilities; that he is overworked, that it is humanly impossible, under the system which we have, for him fully to carry out his constitutional duty as Chief Executive, because he is overwhelmed with minor details and needless contacts arising directly from the bad organization and equipment of the Government.[3]

Roosevelt and Brownlow presented the problem as one of "organization and equipment." Presumably a solution would be found by improving management and administration. I prefer Richard Neustadt's view. Although the Brownlow report was prepared under the then prevailing theory which set "administration" apart from "policy" and "politics," FDR knew what he was after. His purposes were "emphatically, essentially political." "He wanted to enhance his own capacity to rule." Franklin Roosevelt was primarily concerned "for his position as *the* man in the White House. If he began the institutionalized Presidency, he did not for a moment mean that it should make an institution out of him."[4]

Thus, the Institutionalized Presidency was started by a strong, political President very much aware of his own power stakes. And Roosevelt, after all, did not have a sizeable Presidential staff to master. By 1939 Congress had authorized six administrative assistants so that the President might have a sufficient group of able assistants in his own office to keep him in closer and easier touch with the widespread affairs of administration, and to make the speedier clearance of the knowledge needed for Executive decision. Congress in 1939 provided something else of enormous potential for the growth of the institutionalized Presidency: the Bureau of the Budget was shifted from its innocuous and obscure niche in the Treasury Department, where it had been hiding since 1921, to the Executive Office of the President. In time, the Bureau of the Budget was able to transform itself into the principal Presidential staff agency, an elite corps of permanent civil servants, having basic powers over budgetary, legislative, administrative—and, hence, *policy*—matters.

The rise of the Institutionalized Presidency parallels the enormous growth in the size, scope, and complexity of public policies associated with the evolution of the Welfare State and the Warfare State. President Roosevelt evidently thought in 1936–37 that he was experiencing extreme difficulty in administering the vast responsibilities of modern government. Actually, judged by present standards, one would have to say that the Federal government at the height of the New Deal was relatively small. Federal expenditures in Fiscal '37 totalled $9 billion; receipts stood at $7 billion. There were some 945,000 people in the Federal civil service. At the present time $9 billion would keep the Federal government going for less than three weeks. The Defense department *alone* employs more civilian workers than there were in FDR's entire New Deal-inflated bureaucracy.

THE POSTWAR PRESIDENCY

What stands between the two periods, of course, is the impact of modern warfare on the contemporary state. It was World War II, not the New Deal, which first brought us Big Government (a wholly inadequate term) as we understand and experience it today. It was also the World War II level of spending which demonstrated the full economic implications of massive Federal expenditures. Daniel Bell has summarized the situation nicely:

> From 1931 to 1935, in the depth of the depression years, total federal budget expenditures of all kinds averaged 5.2 billion dollars. In the next four years, 1936 to 1940, it reached a new high of 8 billion dollars. (Income during this period was about 60% of expenditures.) Four years later, the federal government was spending, yearly, a staggering total of over 95 billion dollars and accumulating a national debt which more than quintupled the debt of the previous decade. The figures are in constant dollars.[5]

The American Welfare State remained a distinctly minor appendage until Lyndon Johnson came to power. *It was President Johnson, after all, who deemed it possible for the nation to support a Welfare State of significant proportions in addition to a permanent Warfare State.* We tend to brush the slogan, "guns and butter," aside, and in doing so we may miss the significance of Johnson's audacious effort. (This is a matter to be examined carefully in a later chapter.)

Franklin Roosevelt started the process which leads to the Institutionalized Presidency. The Brownlow report was by all odds one of the most influential Presidential committee documents in our history. But Harry Truman was the first President with a full opportunity of working within the context of the Institutionalized Presidency. Truman was a hard-working and systematic President who used his White House staff, and, after some early signs of reluctance, Truman came to rely more and more upon the Bureau of the Budget. Truman was the first President to have the National Security Council and the Council of Economic Advisers to assist him in the making of policy decisions within their respective areas of competence.

President Eisenhower was a "natural" to head the Institutionalized Presidency. His long military career had predisposed him to rely upon staff assistance. Eisenhower not only utilized the various agencies which were now well-established parts of the White House decision-making process; he installed Sherman Adams in the White House as a kind of chief of staff, thus following the standard Army organizational pattern. Eisenhower brought a science adviser to the White House for the first time. He had a staff to handle legislative liaison. Interagency committees proliferated especially in the area of national security policy.

Those who would like to see a strong Presidential hand in the "politics of policy-making" will feel that Eisenhower overrelied upon the White House staff. Professor Schlesinger reports that President Kennedy tended to be critical of Eisenhower's effort to institutionalize the Presidency. Actually, Eisenhower did not add so much to the institutions within the Presidency. Most of the institutionalizing had taken place before Eisenhower took office. He did use what was there, possibly for more than it was worth.

KENNEDY: PERSONALIZING PRESIDENTIAL CONTROL

At any event, President Kennedy was determined "to restore the personal character of the office and recover Presidential control over the sprawling feudalism of government." What was intended to be "a central theme" of the Kennedy years soon became "a central frustration," as well. Arthur M. Schlesinger, Jr., a Kennedy White House assistant, views the struggle during those years as a sharp clash between Presidential policy leadership and the entrenched forces of the bureaucracy:

> The Presidential government, coming to Washington aglow with new ideas and a euphoric sense that it could do no wrong, promptly collided with the feudal barons of the permanent government, entrenched in their domains and fortified by their sense of proprietorship; and the permanent government, confronted by this invasion, began almost to function . . . as a resistance movement.[6]

If there was to be an epic struggle with the feudal barons of the Executive establishment, President Kennedy, in his drive to be sovereign, commanded a small, loyal, and battle-hardened battalion of his own. Though outnumbered, these New Frontiersmen were alert and aggressive by nature, and they could be counted upon to make the struggle an interesting one no matter how uncertain the outcome. Since President Kennedy was determined to establish personal control of the Executive initiative, it seemed a natural thing for him to elevate the role of the Presidential staff assistant. This is not to suggest that this was the first time a Presidential staff assistant had been able to carve out a position of preeminence in the community of Washington influentials. We have had reason to note the presence of Colonel House, Harry Hopkins and Sherman Adams in earlier administrations. FDR's New Deal featured the sparkling team of Cohen and Corcoran. Clark Clifford first came to prominence as President Truman's special counsel. There are many precedents. What makes the Kennedy experience different, and almost unique, is that so many Presidential assistants functioned in ways which indicated preeminence over a number of Cabinet officers. Sorensen, Salinger, O'Donnell and O'Brien emerged rapidly as influential figures even though Sorensen and O'Donnell, two of the most powerful aides, seemed to have "a passion for anonymity." In certain cases, Kennedy's White House assistants seem to have been transformed into at least minor political celebrities in spite of their own best efforts (at least during those years) to remain in the background.[7]

John F. Kennedy came to the Presidency with an explicit pledge to use his powers of leadership in what he had described as "the great office" so as to get the country moving again. This was to be an assertive, vigorous Presidency, roughly comparable in spirit to that of Theodore Roosevelt.

But there is much to suggest that the Bay of Pigs fiasco, coming as early as it did, nearly traumatized the new Administration which wanted so badly to lead—and not be pushed around by—bureaucratic forces. Schlesinger, one of the few White House special assistants who participated in the decisions which led to the Bay of Pigs (Sorensen did not participate), reports noting shortly thereafter "a general predisposition against boldness in all fields." The Bay of Pigs disaster was, in Schlesinger's view, "a clear consequence of the surrender of presidential government to the permanent government."[8]

But a Bay of Pigs syndrome would not explain the rather modest legislative achievements of the Kennedy administration. The Area Redevelopment Act, which had previously been passed by Congress on two occasions and was twice vetoed by Eisenhower, sailed through Congress early in 1961 and Kennedy, a Senate co-sponsor in the earlier period, happily signed it. A somewhat similar bipartisan effort produced the Manpower Development and Training Act of 1962, aimed at bringing job training to the chronically unemployed. A full year of intense legislative effort preceded the enactment of the Trade Adjustment Act and the ratification of the Nuclear Test Ban treaty. In addition to these important legislative accomplishments, Kennedy offered the Congress the most substantial body of domestic legislation it had seen in many years. But most of his program—Federal aid to education, Medicare, the reform of vocational education, civil rights legislation, even Walter Heller's multi-billion dollar tax cut —was stalled on Capitol Hill at the time of the assassination.

Despite the rhetoric of the 1960 campaign and for all of his personal charm and grace, President Kennedy proved, on balance, to be a rather cautious Chief Executive, and this was especially noticeable in the way he dealt with Congress. The clash, so much stressed by Schlesinger, between policy leadership and the forces of resistance to such leadership, was lessened in the legislative arena, one suspects, by Kennedy's natural caution. Kennedy did not surrender to the Congressional barons; he simply avoided pitched battles whenever possible. There was a political factor which reenforced his caution: the Kennedy administration lacked a decisive popular mandate. The narrow margin of his victory over Nixon left twenty fewer liberal Democrats in the House, and Kennedy was acutely conscious of the strength of the opposing Congressional coalition.[9]

These were glowing years for the President's White House assistants—as they were for the articulate spokesman for the New Economics who dominated the Council of Economic Advisers and for a number of key men near the top of the Bureau of the Budget hierarchy—as President Kennedy concentrated much of his fire on the Executive branch. Congress was another matter, another battleground. One is tempted to draw a lesson, however tentative it may be, from this experience of the Kennedy years with the attempt to personalize Presidential control of policy-making at the highest levels of the Executive branch. The Kennedy experience, taken as a whole, may suggest that a central preoccupation with the real problems of asserting and maintaining policy leadership within the agencies of the Institutionalized Presidency may so absorb the time, interest and attention of the Chief Executive and his principal aides as to leave the Congressional side of the policy struggle relatively unattended. If so, the resulting imbalance seems consistent with President Kennedy's own preferences.

Kennedy made one major addition to the Institutionalized Presidency. Lacking any real confidence in the capacity of the State Department to serve Presidential policy-making needs, President Kennedy established his own small select National Security Staff in the White House under the direction of McGeorge Bundy. Bundy possessed the intelligence, the clarity of mind, the ambition, and, not least important, the supreme self-confidence necessary if one is to build a new institution at so high an elevation in the national-security decision-making process and expect it to have any effectiveness. President Kennedy used the agencies within the Institutionalized Presidency with rare discrimination. He invented one new agency, transformed others, and, increasingly, turned each of them to the purposes and (within limits) to the style of his Presidency. Kennedy enlarged and elaborated upon the offices of Science and Technology and Legislative Liaison which he inherited from Eisenhower. When he was through, they appeared to be Kennedy innovations. Never was the Council of Economic Advisers drawn so closely to Presidential policy as it was during the Kennedy era. Even the Bureau of the Budget found ways of sending men to Cabinet-level interagency meetings who looked and talked astonishingly like members of the New Frontier.

My impression is that President Kennedy came close to success in attempting to personalize his control of the agencies within the Institutionalized Presidency. He was not given much time, but he appears to have made a more determined and intelligent effort to control the Executive initiative in policy than any other twentieth-century President, before or since—with perhaps the single exception of FDR, who had the advantage, as Neustadt reminds us, of starting with the slate clean. Kennedy was determined to lead the making of policy in the Executive branch. The shattering experience at the time of the Bay of Pigs which demonstrated the danger of bureaucratic drift probably served to strengthen Kennedy's determination to personalize the Executive initiative. As a result, Lyndon Johnson, coming to the White House as he did following Kennedy's assassination, inherited a White House decision-making team which was unusually sensitized to the objectives, the needs and the style of another—and quite different—President. Mr. Johnson's background and experience seemed to presage a drive toward mastery of the mysterious and cumbersome legislative process.

LBJ: MASTER LEGISLATOR

Lyndon Baines Johnson brought to the White House more relevant Washington political experience and a greater background in Congressional leadership than any President in our history. Presumably, Mr. Johnson was familiar with the location of most of the levers of power in the complicated Washington governmental machinery. Johnson had been a participant in Big Government for a third of a century, and a leader among the select group of Washington influentials for more than a decade before he became President.

If the Kennedy presidency seemed preoccupied with the problem of controlling the Executive branch, the Johnson presidency could be expected to concentrate on the Congress and domestic policy. Lyndon Johnson arrived in the nation's capital as a young Congressman at a crucial moment in the life cycle of the New Deal, when FDR's Court-reform proposal was under heavy fire. Mr. Johnson, who had previously served as a Congressional assistant, had won a special off-year election to a House seat following a campaign in which the neophyte politician supported Roosevelt on the Court issue. Little wonder that the President took a special interest in the tall young man from west Texas, and smaller wonder that the young Congressman flourished as a Roosevelt protégé. In later years, after Johnson had gained prominence as Senate majority leader, attention often focused on him as a product of one of our toughest schools of politics: Texas and Oil. But Lyndon Johnson was also a product of the New Deal, a man who had lived close to poverty during his early years. As a young man he briefly taught in a country school with poor Mexican-American youngsters in his classes. In one of his first important public jobs, Johnson served as an NYA administrator in Texas.

There was an authentic connection between the Johnson presidency and Roosevelt's New Deal. Johnson hungered to be ranked with FDR as a great progressive President with a domestic legislative program reaching far beyond the social reform programs of the New Deal. To miss this point about Johnson is to fail to see the true measure of his early triumphs in the White House and the poignancy of his ultimate failure.

During his first two years in the White House, Lyndon B. Johnson of Texas, utilizing all of his exceptional skills as a master of the Congress, provided the drive which brought into being the most expensive and far-reaching program of social reform legislation since FDR. It was a virtuoso performance which impressed the community of Washington influentials. Mr. Johnson, onetime charter member of the Senate establishment, managed to get most of the Kennedy legislative program through the Congress: the Vocational Education Act, Federal aid to education, Medicare, the massive tax cut. Not content, Johnson followed this remarkable accomplishment with an even broader program of his own in the fields of medical care, health research, education, community action, the war on poverty, Model Cities. In the meantime, Lyndon Johnson won the office of President in his own right in a landslide victory rivaling FDR's historic triumph of 1936. Lyndon Johnson strode the American scene in Texas-league boots; he was a legislative miracle worker. Where Kennedy perhaps succeeded in winning personal control of the Institutionalized Presidency, Johnson succeeded in mastering the Congress. By the end of 1965

45

President Johnson's place in history as a classic twentieth-century strong President seemed almost assured.

The President went before the Congress in January 1966 and presented a program which promised both guns and butter. The budget assumed an additional $10 billion expenditure in Vietnam, the military escalation having begun the previous summer; and yet, the Johnsonian expansion of health, education and welfare services was not to be impaired. Whereas Franklin Roosevelt had finally to concede the necessity of Dr. New Deal giving way to Dr. Win-The-War, LBJ was to do his mentor one better.

Something went wrong! A growing sense of frustration marked the last two years of the Johnson administration as the application of awesome military firepower and the use of more than half a million American soldiers failed to bring Hanoi to its knees—or even to the bargaining table. Humiliation, as in the case of the Tet offensive, followed frustration, and finally came the President's dramatic announcement that he was through at the end of his term. What caused this proud and sometimes arrogant man to quit the Presidency when both his foreign and domestic programs were under severe attack, their very worth in question? I have written elsewhere about the effect of the escalation and the Americanization of the war on President Johnson's domestic programs and upon his political power base. The United States found itself bogged down in a neo-colonial war being fought by a conscript army, a war not easily rationalized once it was subject to sustained public debate. The fighting of the war drastically altered national priorities. Part of the failure of 1967–68, as it came to affect the Presidency of Mr. Johnson, can be explained by the disproportionate allotment of high-level executive time, energy and thought—to say nothing of national resources—to the war, a war increasingly opposed by many of the most articulate segments of our society. The Vietnam involvement became an obsession which caught hold of the nerve centers of the Institutionalized Presidency and hurt Mr. Johnson grievously. Not least important was the effect the war had in turning the President's attention away from the raging crisis in the black ghettos.[10]

LBJ AND JFK'S NATIONAL SECURITY TEAM

Why did President Johnson take the steps which meant Americanizing the war at the very moment his own Great Society domestic programs most needed the commitment of additional resources and the vital leadership which the President alone was capable of providing? President Johnson decided to Americanize the war in Vietnam not because he had intended to make his mark in Southeast Asia (he was a domestic and legislative-minded Chief Executive if ever we have had one) but rather because his key national security advisers saw the imminent collapse of the Saigon regime and the policy which they had created. McNamara, Rusk and Bundy, the three principal figures, were, of course, Kennedy appointees who were retained by Johnson. All three men were deeply committed to the Vietnam engagement, and their continuing advice encouraged the President to make the decisions to escalate military action thereby transforming the war into an overtly American operation. President Johnson escalated the Vietnam war, which eventually was to frustrate his dream of surpassing Roosevelt as a reform President, largely because the advice he received from his inherited national security team greatly encouraged the making of such a decision. At the crucial moments in 1965 there was no powerful voice within the top advisory group which said: do not escalate; this way lies political and moral disaster.[11]

The nature of the advice President Johnson received, especially in a crucial series of decisions taken in 1965, is so important that we shall return to this point and to a more thorough examination of it in Chapters Five and Six.

The experience contains an intriguing paradox. Lyndon Johnson was a power-wielding, thoroughly experienced Washington politician who wished to dominate the making of policy in his own administration; yet, when the stakes were highest, Johnson ratified group decisions which undermined the basis for his own policy leadership. It is conceivable that the force of bureaucratic momentum in our Asian policy-making machinery proved too strong for Lyndon Johnson. There is a journalistic notion that Johnson was simply following his own hawkish instincts in escalating the war. This is patently a gross oversimplification of reality which ignores the irony of the situation. Lyndon Johnson, who as a Senator in 1954 advised against a limited American military intervention at Dien Bien Phu when John Foster Dulles recommended such a course of action to Eisenhower, eventually ordered half a million American men to fight in Vietnam. Johnson, who was opposed to a small naval air strike in 1954, assumed the responsibility for unleashing the mighty Air Force a decade later. If it took a rather long time for the policy of Secretary Dulles to carry the day, we are about to discover that policies tend to persist in an age of group decision-making. The Johnson administration accepted uncritically the bankrupt containment doctrine of the past. This was a major mistake. President Johnson kept intact the national security advisory team he had inherited from his fallen predecessor. The ultimate futility of the Vietnam intervention proved too large a political liability for Johnson to bear, and he quit.

A President who intends to be effective as a policy leader must guard his leadership against the departmental bureaucratic forces whenever they resist his leadership. The struggle between Presidential leadership and the negative power of Congressional barons goes on constantly. These things we tend to understand as part of the conventional wisdom of modern political science. The experience of the Johnson Presidency highlights an additional issue. The Institutionalized Presidency now contains a fairly complex set of small but potent bureaucratic structures. The President may, therefore, have to guard his own policy leadership, his own power of initiative, against the biases and dogmas of his own White House technicians. The more specialized their technical expertise, the less likely it will be to make ample allowance for the President's broader political position. This is, of course, a clear disadvantage for the President, but it is also vital in terms of national policy-making since the Presidency is the one institution from which we expect to get national leadership that is accountable to popular controls.

There is an obvious danger in overgeneralizing on the basis

of a Vietnam experience which may be unique, although it must be said that the persistence of the American involvement in Vietnam through three national administrations suggests something important about the nature of national security decision-making in recent decades. But one does not have to rely on the Vietnam case alone in order to question the nature of leadership in the Institutionalized Presidency during the last decade. The Johnson war on poverty also reveals how complex the relationship between the expanding White House bureaucracy and Presidential policy leadership may become. I have written elsewhere in some detail about the origins of the Economic Opportunity Act of 1964. There have been a number of recent contributions to our understanding of the antipoverty program. One basic point on which all of these studies seem to agree: President Johnson *intended* that the war on poverty should be *his* war. He wanted the Economic Opportunity Act to occupy a central place in his program of domestic reform. The legislation was Presidential to an extraordinary degree.[12]

THE WAR ON POVERTY: WHOSE PROGRAM?

Where did the new President turn for the formulation of this new legislative program, the first program which was to be distinctively his own? The agencies of the Institutionalized Presidency were headed at the time by Kennedy men who had been key participants in a special kind of personalized Presidency, as we have seen. One would have thought, therefore, that President Johnson might have preferred having his own men design the Presidential war on poverty. Instead, Johnson created a White House task force to draw up the program under the leadership of Sargent Shriver, a member of the Kennedy family establishment who staffed the project with Eastern intellectual-political activists.

This is troublesome. Why was Lyndon Johnson apparently so little concerned about the Presidential power stakes in the coming war on poverty, if it was to be his war? Did the President assume that he could control the outcome? Was it necessary to rely on Kennedy technicians at this early point in the transition between administrations? The Bureau of the Budget would have had no difficulty in drafting an Economic Opportunity Act for the new President. Indeed, the Budget Bureau is now known to have played an important role in putting the program together, even though Shriver had the authority and reported directly to the President.

As soon as Mr. Johnson took office as President, he learned of the staff work well underway within the Institutionalized Presidency which might lead to a new program aimed at attacking poverty. Immediately, the new President instructed Walter Heller, Chairman of the Council of Economic Advisers and an influential figure in the Kennedy White House, to move ahead with the planning. "This is my kind of program," the President said. Within a matter of weeks the Johnson war on poverty included Community Action and maximum feasible participation of the poor. Were these new program concepts consistent with Lyndon Johnson's kind of program? The President's attitude toward Community Action, according to Daniel P. Moynihan, appears to have been one of "instant suspicion and dislike."[13] *How, then, did Community Action combined with participatory democracy get into the President's new program?*

Community Action and maximum feasible participation appear in the Economic Opportunity Act because they were conceived and aggressively supported in the early negotiations which produced the war on poverty (negotiations which took place within the Executive Office of the President) by men loyal to Attorney General Robert Kennedy, not a notable Johnson admirer. David Hackett, executive director of the President's Committee on Juvenile Delinquency and a close personal friend of Robert Kennedy since prep school, prepared a memorandum for the Bureau of the Budget in which he proposed a series of comprehensive community action programs; they were, in effect, the juvenile delinquency programs taken just a bit further in scope and resources.[14]

Hackett's proposal was accepted. Why? Sargent Shriver was reported cool toward the concept because it required a long lead time. The President, presumably, would have had serious doubts. In what manner was the thinking of the Juvenile Delinquency staff able to achieve so much influence in the making of the Johnson anti-poverty program?

The Economic Opportunity Act was put together by the men and agencies which were part of the Institutionalized Presidency, including the Bureau of the Budget and the White House staff still manned, in key spots, by Kennedy staff assistants. Moynihan[15] accounts for the acceptance of Hackett's proposal which led to Title II as follows:

> It responded fully to the concerns, fears, hopes, expectations of the quasi-permanent presidential staff "across the street" from the White House and was quickly adopted by his personal staff in the West Wing—which, it may be noted, continued for some time under Johnson to be made up largely of Kennedy men. Theodore C. Sorensen, Myer Feldman, and Lee C. White, who were successively Special Counsel to the President and in turn handled the anti-poverty legislation, were all Kennedy appointees.

In the light of this analysis, suggesting the critical role played by Bureau of the Budget professionals and Presidential assistants, Moynihan's notion that social science theory propounded by Professors Ohlin and Cloward played a large role in shaping Community Action seems a little overdrawn. Professor Ohlin exerted a considerable influence on Hackett and the JD committee staff during an earlier period. The technicians "bought" Ohlin's line of thinking long before the Economic Opportunity Act saw the light of day. Community Action, as it appears in the Act, probably owes more to Paul Ylvisaker, prestigious Ford Foundation social planner, than it does to Lloyd Ohlin. The relationship between social theory and government program appears to be indirect and less than clear, at least in this instance.

THE BUDGET BUREAU AS POLICY-MAKER

A more fruitful approach leads us to the Bureau of the Budget, if one is seeking significant influences on the making of Presidential programs. After all, it was not Professor Ohlin who allocated $315 million for Community Action in the first fiscal year. In an earlier study of the Johnson war on poverty, I suggested that high officials in the Bureau of the Budget supported Community Action as a program concept. Now Moynihan has identified several of these BOB officials: among them, Charles Schultze, at this time an Assistant Director and later appointed Director by President Johnson, and William Cannon, an able young BOB careerist. One may ask why BOB professionals found Community Action so attractive, containing, as it did, a potential for encouraging poor people to challenge City Hall and to shake up such torpid urban bureaucracies as those dealing with welfare and schools. Surely Moynihan is right in suggesting that part of the BOB's technical concern is to find means of achieving the *coordination* of overlapping programs, and it was possible to view Community Action, at least partially, in this light. Undoubtedly men like Schultze and Cannon were also looking for something "new." The old-line departments had produced singularly few innovations. The Bureau of the Budget had a new boss, and they did not want the President's first new program to be simply a rehash of earlier legislative bits and pieces. In this sense, Schultze, Cannon, *et al.,* were trying to serve the President's interests. They were acting professionally, and perhaps they did not see the *political* implications of Community Action and maximum feasible participation. One expects technical competence in the advice received from BOB experts, not political sagacity.

But men like Schultze and Cannon were sophisticated beyond their professional fields of specialization. Moynihan[16] has characterized these men, so influentially placed within the institutionalized Presidency, as follows:

> Close to universities, intellectual by bent, familiar with social science beyond the confines of economics, in them the sponsors of community action could not have hoped for more perceptive arbiters.

The key question in our analysis is: *were they also perceptive arbiters for the President?* Did the men in the Bureau of the Budget perceive the conflicting theories of Community Action which Moynihan and others found to be present from the beginning? Did the Bureau of the Budget professionals make the conflicts clear to the man they serve, the President of the United States? These questions must be faced up to. Moynihan[17] wrote some time ago: "It was never clear that the persons to be in charge of the program perceived these differences, and no hint of them emerged in the Congressional hearings." It has now been established that Community Action moved from tentative concept in the first task force draft of the proposed Act to an Act of Congress with scarcely a semicolon altered.

The war on poverty was patently not designed only to introduce new social welfare techniques; it also had important *political objectives.* Writing in 1966, after he had left his Washington post which was located on the edge of the Institutionalized Presidency, Moynihan[18] described the Shriver Task Force view of Community Action: "The Task Force wanted a program that would pass the Congress, help to win the Presidential election, and eliminate poverty, in perhaps that order." The men most directly responsible to the President for putting the program together evidently viewed their role as being guided by the principle of *political effectiveness.* This moves us close to the issue of Presidential policy leadership. Unfortunately, Moynihan's book, which appeared in 1969, omits this line of analysis.

President Johnson's war on poverty, announced with full publicity early in his administration, contained one significant new program concept: Community Action and its remarkable corollary, "maximum feasible participation" of the poor. Individual members of the Shriver Task Force continue to insist that they thought "maximum feasible participation" was aimed at assisting Southern Negroes, walled off from participation by segregation. Perhaps so. (This does raise a question, however, about the qualifications of the Task Force as judges of political reality.) In any event, the staff of the Juvenile Delinquency committee, who were initially responsible for putting the language in the Act, knew better than this. Most of their experience had been in the Northern urban slums. They knew, and men like Schultze and Cannon *should have known* (they had only to ask David Hackett or Richard Boone) that Community Action, once it was combined with "maximum feasible participation," carried with it real potential for social reform; if the program worked, it might even effect a redistribution of political power in our troubled cities.

In the Kennedy era, the staff of the President's Committee on Juvenile Delinquency had something on the order of $10 million a year which they used as "seed money." The Johnson administration provided $315 million for Community Action in its first year. An allocation of such a large sum of money at a time when President Johnson was still presenting himself to Senator Byrd as an "economy-minded" president must surely have carried a favorable recommendation from the Bureau of the Budget. The Deputy Director of the Bureau at the time was Elmer B. Staats, the quintessential BOB professional. Mr. Staats enjoyed an excellent reputation with the new President. It seems highly implausible that the Economic Opportunity Act would have gone to the Presidential desk without a careful review by Mr. Staats. He is too superbly professional not to have examined a major legislative proposal, the first major legislative proposal on which BOB professionals had worked for President Johnson. The irony is that in 1969, Mr. Staats, now Comptroller General of the United States, (with the blessing of Lyndon Johnson) was responsible for a General Accounting Office evaluation of the Economic Opportunity Act which was highly critical of antipoverty programs.[19]

The Bureau of the Budget, elite Presidential staff agency, was involved in a major way in the development of President Johnson's war on poverty. The Bureau held out for the inclusion of Community Action as the most important new element in the Economic Opportunity Act against the doubts and skepticism of Sargent Shriver, the man who would direct the program. Community Action was allocated a large sum of money thanks to Budget Bureau support. While it is not entirely clear what the President's expectations were for his war on poverty, there is little doubt that the program originally was designed in a way which would give high visibility to the LBJ brand. What the President got was a program which transferred Federal dollars and the Federal presence directly into urban slum neighborhoods there to stimulate poor people in the fine art of protest. That this was policy-making in a vital area of public concern seems quite clear. Whether it was Presidential policy-making is a far more difficult issue to untangle.

President Johnson was one of the most successful Congressional leaders in our entire history. He spent most of his adult life learning how to make the Congressional system work (no easy matter as the next chapter will show). But Mr. Johnson's lifelong preoccupation with the Congress ill prepared him for the nuances of Presidential power. He was a power-driven man who often squandered power. Evans and Novak[20] found Johnson "largely disinterested and dispassionate" about the struggles between Shriver and the established departmental bureaucracies for control of the antipoverty program. But these struggles were important to the President if this were to be his program.

At least this much seems fairly clear: a President who willingly turns over his own key program to an opposing group in his own party (the Kennedy establishment, in this case) and asks them to design it for him has a curious view of his own stakes in the program. Those interested in understanding the decline and fall of Lyndon Johnson might look more closely at how policy was made in the Institutionalized Presidency during the early months of 1964 as his war on poverty took shape.

There is, one realizes, the possibility of a wholly different interpretation of Mr. Johnson and the war on poverty. Mr. Johnson, wise in the ways of power-manipulation, Washington-style, might have been tempted to seek more than one objective. His opposition within the party had drawn up the program; they dare not criticize it and they had better make it work. A Kennedy brother-in-law, an able and visible public personality, was to have responsibility for the administration of the program. If the program were to falter or were later to get into serious difficulty, Shriver could take the heat while the President kept busy with his other responsibilities. The President might pretend that the program was not his. This might even work in Congressional politics where program parentage is a confused business.

But poor people in our dark urban ghettos who tend to know a good deal about local political manipulation are likely to have less appreciation for the subtleties of Washington infighting. For better or worse, they reached out in desperation for the promise of Community Action, offering as it did a chance to overcome their customary powerlessness. In this fashion, the war on poverty tied the Presidency directly to the hope for fundamental reform within the ghetto. The President did not retreat when the connection was made. On the contrary, Lyndon Johnson went to Howard University in June 1965 and made the strongest pledge in the history of the Presidency to equality for black Americans. Unfortunately, the President failed to follow through with a program backing his commitment, as Vietnam rapidly took form as a national obsession.[21]

CHAPTER THREE

THE CONGRESSIONAL COALITION: ENTRENCHED PAROCHIALISM

*All forms of political organization have a bias
in favor of the exploitation of some kinds of conflict
and the suppression of others because organization
is the mobilization of bias. Some issues are organized
into politics while others are organized out.*
E. E. SCHATTSCHNEIDER, *The Semi-Sovereign People*

THE PRESIDENT and the Congress represent two quite different constituencies. This is part of the conventional wisdom of contemporary American political science.[1] The Presidency, thanks in part to the special role which nine large industrial states play in the unique arithmetic of the Electoral College, responds more directly than the Congress to the needs and aspirations of our increasingly complex urban, industrial, cosmopolitan, megalopolitan society. The Congress typically casts its gaze inward, as it were, toward the smaller cities and towns, to the diverse sections of the nation, to the nostalgia of a bucolic past, to the insular, to the parochial interests of Main Street, USA. These are also aspects of American reality. As the Presidency has been transformed into the great office to which the nation instinctively looks for leadership, the Congress has emerged as the institution which reflects the local, parochial, particular, decentralized, fractionalized interests of a restless nation of more than 200 million energetic people.

If, therefore, it is true that Congress plays a lesser and lesser role in the making of legislation—and such an assumption needs critical reexamination—this conceivably may be fortunate, considering the nature of the issues the nation now faces. An institution devoted to protecting the nation's most parochial interests may have great difficulty in responding effectively to the stresses and strains of the megalopolitan sprawl. In any case, a basic political separation now marks the divide where the Founding Fathers erected a separation of governmental institutions as a means of maintaining a proper balance in society. The political gap is further complicated by ideological contrasts between a Presidential view of society and the essential parochialism of Congress. Not surprisingly, the contemporary relationship between President and Congress appears often as one of deadlock or stalemate rather than as one of balance.

The Founding Fathers, fearful of a tyrannical majority, cast their most apprehensive glances in the direction of the House of Representatives. Their fear was that the House might become *too* representative. A legislative chamber with which the People identified might be encouraged to launch confiscatory assaults on the rights of property. Little did the Fathers imagine that in less than fifty years a strong war-hero President, himself by nature a kind of Border conservative, would effect the first close identification of the President as tribune of the People with the cause of popular democracy. Such a conception of the Presidency was destined to transform the Congress into an agency of opposition.

Jacksonian democracy brought us a new national party system, replaced King Caucus with a delegate convention system of nomination, opened political offices to a broader range of talent and energy, encouraged a new kind of bourgeois capitalism. And it did something else: it began the process, later to be greatly accelerated, by which the nationalizing, centralizing, and the democratizing forces were concentrated in the Executive. Thus, contemporary Americans have inherited a system in which the Presidency functions as the one truly national—and cosmopolitan—policy-making office while the Congress has long since established itself as the principal guardian of American parochial and provincial interests.

A few years ago Andrew Hacker[2] published an essay in

which he found the approaches of United States Senators and business corporation presidents to public questions rooted in "disparate images of society." The Senators were provincially oriented; the corporation presidents proved to be more "metropolitan" in their thinking. The contrast would sharpen and take on greater significance if we were contrasting the image of society of an average member of the House of Representatives and the President of the United States—any President of the United States. This difference between the parochial and the cosmopolitan view is reflected in the national policy-making process. Hacker found a serious tension between our major political and economic institutions, tension based on a lack of understanding between two elites. The finding is important, but it is more important to understand that a similar tension exists between the modern Presidency and the Congress.

Little wonder our great national elections display a tendency to produce results which often seem slightly ambiguous. Presidents find it necessary to push forward. This is true even for those Presidents who may prefer a somewhat more passive role. Eisenhower was in office only a few months when he found himself elevating Health, Education and Welfare to Cabinet status. Congress, on the other hand, has in recent years displayed a special fondness for holding back, as long as possible, to the lines of the familiar and to the orthodoxies of the status quo. The usual assumption is that "we" want it this way, and presumably many of us do. A controlling fact, I should judge, is that Presidential politics has been highly competitive in this century while Congressional politics, viewed as a national system, has been far less competitive. Candidates of the two major parties contest one another in perhaps 100 of the 435 Congressional districts, if one is talking about real contests. Much of the rest is shadowboxing. At least three out of every four House seats must be considered "safe" on a long-term basis. In 1969 there were 362 safe seats and 73 which appeared to be marginal. With a new census imminent in 1970 and with the prospect of more redistricting, it is obvious that these figures will change, but not considerably.[3]

1966: RESTORING THE BALANCE

The Congressional election of 1966 was easily the most important "negative" election since 1938. The Republicans scored heavily, changing the composition of the House in a way which brought the Great Society period of legislative initiative and innovation to an abrupt halt. Yet the Republicans gained this major political victory by winning back 47 House seats. And who were the casualties? By and large, they were young, one-term, liberal Democrats who had been swept into office in the Johnson anti-Goldwater landslide of 1964. They were marginal political men, here today, gone tomorrow. But their presence in the Eighty-ninth Congress made all the difference in the world.

None of this is unusual. What was unusual was the nature of Johnson's triumph over Goldwater which gave Johnson, as virtually an unearned increment, the largest Democratic majority any Democratic president had enjoyed since 1936. Congress represented essentially the same balance of political forces for the greater part of thirty years following the rejection of further New Deal reform in the Congressional elections of 1938. And the balance which was to be seen most clearly in the House of Representatives was weighted on the conservative side of domestic policy.

TABLE A

House of Representatives, Party Representation, 1958–1968

YEAR	CONGRESS	DEMOCRATS	REPUBLICANS
1958	86th	283	154
1960	87th	263	174
1962	88th	259	176
1964	89th	295	140
1966	90th	246	187
1968	91st	243	192

The visitor from another planet or, for that matter, most

Americans faced with the figures in Table A would conclude that the Democratic party, holding a clear majority throughout the decade, dominated House legislative action. In reality, the Democrats enjoyed a viable House majority large enough to support an activist President's full legislative program only during the Eighty-ninth Congress, the period of Great Society activity following the Goldwater presidential debacle. Four years later, another Presidential year, more than seventy million Americans voted and yet they managed to bring about the reelection of virtually the same Congress which had been in office for two years. The 1968 election highlights two features of our present Congressional system: first, the balance of forces in the House tends to remain unchanged; and second, there is all too little effective political competition in that portion of the system which produces the House of Representatives. Rather than becoming too representative, as John Adams might have feared, the House of Representatives has been in danger of losing touch with the most troublesome issues of our times.

In 1968 when the voting was over a remarkable fact emerged: the House of Representatives had changed hardly at all. Three hundred ninety-four incumbents were reelected; 173 Republicans and 221 Democrats. Ten Republicans succeeded Republicans who were not running for reelection for one reason or another, while 16 Democrats succeeded Democrats. Of the 435 House seats, 420 did not change party designation in 1968. Professor Huntington,[4] noting the tendency for Congressional tenure in office to increase throughout this century, reported that by 1961 close to 90% of the House members were "veterans" of more than one term. In 1968 this increased to 97%. No wonder we hear so little about the shortcomings of the seniority system from Congressmen. All Congressmen are senior, more or less.*

The actual day-by-day pattern of House voting differs significantly from the figures shown in Table A. There are two bipartisan coalitions which ordinarily contest for power in the

*A group of Congressmen who are members of the Democratic Study Group may be expected to push for modification of the seniority rule in the 1970s.

Congress. The first coalition, composed of leading southern Democratic oligarchs and solid midwestern Republicans, forms the normal operational majority. The second coalition of liberal Democrats and a tiny band of moderate Republicans from the metropolitan areas forms the minority legislative party, a minority which would support a liberal and activist President's domestic program. The experience of the Kennedy Administration is illustrative and instructive on this point. Table A suggests that President Kennedy faced a comfortable Democratic majority in the House throughout his administration. In fact, as we noted in Chapter Two, the Kennedy Administration was largely ineffective in getting Congressional support for its rather expansive legislative program because it did not have the necessary votes in the House. The conservative Coalition was strong enough to weaken or stall most of Kennedy's domestic program. If President Kennedy had been fortunate enough to inherit Eisenhower's last Congress (the Eighty-sixth) the Kennedy era, short as it was, might have been legislatively almost as successful as the first two Johnson years. But this was not to be. Kennedy's razor-thin victory over Nixon in 1960 cost the Democrats twenty precious seats in the House. These were twenty northern liberal votes which were lost. Hence Kennedy faced a House having a nominal Democratic majority of about 260. But the 260 House Democrats included *as an absolute minimum* 60 southern Democratic votes which were automatically to be cast against virtually any item of the President's domestic legislation. In order to put together a majority in the House (218 votes), Larry O'Brien and Kennedy's other legislative lieutenants were forced to scrounge through Capitol corridors seeking at least twenty House Republicans who might perceive some advantage in helping bring about the enactment of a key Kennedy domestic program. Needless to say, it was never easy to find those twenty Republican votes.

LBJ SPLITS THE COALITION

It is not exactly a coincidence that Lyndon B. Johnson, during the 1950s a skillful leader of the dominant Congressional coalition, proved to be far and away the most effective *legislative* President since Franklin D. Roosevelt. Johnson's success began early in 1964, months before the anti-Goldwater outpouring in November gave him the kind of swollen majority which only FDR before him had enjoyed in recent history. It is to be remembered that Johnson inherited the same Congress, the Eighty-eighth, which had made Kennedy's last year in office a study in frustration. Coming to the Presidency after the assassination of his brilliant predecessor, Mr. Johnson faced a House with a nominal Democratic majority of 259. Applying the special arithmetic demanded by the reality of Congressional coalition politics, President Johnson knew, better than most, that the normal southern defection on most domestic issues would leave him with fewer than 200 votes in the Democratic House. And yet President Johnson dared to declare war on poverty in his first State of the Union address. President Johnson in January 1964 appeared to be short between twenty and thirty votes in the House if he were to push successfully a domestic program of his own, but nevertheless he announced a remarkable program of reform that could hardly have been more controversial. Did he know something that we do not know?

Three of our most knowledgeable Washington political journalists, Rowland Evans and Robert Novack, the columnists, and Alan Otten of the *Wall Street Journal,* have since concluded that Johnson accomplished very little in the Congress in 1964 which JFK would not have accomplished sooner or later.[5] Their judgment seems to me not only "iffy" but just plain wrong, in this case. Johnson knew that he had for a time the psychological advantage of coming to power as he did. He also was not the kind of politician who was likely to underestimate his own enormous legislative tactical skill. Lyndon Johnson was the most experienced national legislator *ever* to occupy the White House. And President Johnson was able to do something which President Kennedy had not been able to do. He knew how to entice a considerable number of southern Congressmen to vote for his program.

Consider the Economic Opportuntiy Act of 1964, the legislative vehicle for the Johnson war on poverty, which was drawn up in the White House in January and February 1964. When the time came to introduce this astonishing piece of legislation in the House, Mr. Johnson carefully hand-picked a Southern Representative, Mr. Landrum of Georgia, as floor leader of the bill. Throughout the complicated legislative maneuvering which accompanied the bill during the next few months, Johnson skillfully built a base of southern support for his war on poverty which would be combined with the normal northern liberal voting power. In August, when the critical votes were about to be taken, Sargent Shriver, in consultation with the White House, agreed to sack Adam Yarmolinsky, his principal anti-poverty deputy, as the price of support of at least some members of the North Carolina delegation. This would appear to be rather hard bargaining by any standard. When the final fateful votes were taken, some sixty southerners voted with the Administration in support of the Economic Opportunity Act with all of its Community Action, maximum feasible participation of the poor, and other forms of social reform. And the President had the legislative vehicle for his attack on poverty. For one brief moment, the powerful conservative Coalition was split in two by a determined legislative President who knew more about the Coalition than most of its incumbent leaders.

In the next Congress, which gave him a majority, minus the Southern hard core, Mr. Johnson, of course, was in the best position since FDR to work the Presidential legislative will. Anyone who has the time to survey the legislative accomplishments of 1965 will discover that Lyndon B. Johnson may well have outpaced FDR, his mentor. But 1965 was also the year in which the Johnson Administration took the steps, one by one, which transformed the war in Vietnam into an American military operation. By 1966 the Great Society initiative was weakening, as much from lack of day-by-day attention as anything else. And the November 1966 Congressional election restored the balance. The Coalition was back in business on a business-as-usual basis.

THE CONGRESSIONAL BARONS

The Coalition is powerful. The Coalition is conservative. The Coalition resists Presidential leadership, especially in matters of social reform. But who are the leaders of the Coalition? Where do they come from? Are they agents of the Establishment? The Power Structure? Wall Street?

The leaders of the Congressional Coalition are well known to those who participate in the workings of the Congress: legislators, lobbyists, journalists and staff personnel. Yet the Coalition chieftains have been studied hardly at all by American political scientists. Professor Huitt established a considerable academic reputation as a student of the Congress by writing two essays, one dealing with Lyndon Johnson's methods as majority leader in the 1950s and the other making perhaps a bit too much of Senator William Proxmire's early Senate career as a nonconformist. Of the Coalition leaders whose names appear in this chapter, only one, Wilbur Mills, has had his influence assessed in a systematic way by a political scientist. And we are discussing a group of men who have dominated the making of Congressional policy throughout most of the postwar period.[6]

The dominant figures in the conservative Congressional Coalition are Southern conservatives (white supremacists to a man) and midwestern Republicans. In the Senate of the United States all of the informal lines of power run to the so-called Inner Club whose alleged virtues were lyricized more than a decade ago by William S. White, LBJ's own poet laureate. The Coalition leaders are charter members of the Inner Club. They decide who gets into the club and who does not. Paul Douglas and Estes Kefauver were among those who did not. Hubert Humphrey did. The leaders of the Coalition control the important committees and the most important chairmanships in both Houses of Congress. The key to their control of Congressional power lies in the principle of seniority which ought to be called in this case by its proper name: longevity. Rigid adherence to seniority in parceling out pieces of Congressional power is a twentieth-century development, as both Professor Huntington and Representative Richard Bolling have pointed out. The

Coalition chieftains cannot compromise the principle of seniority without surrendering their power, and oligarchs seldom, if ever, surrender power willingly.[7]

Under the workings of the labyrinthine Congressional procedures, whose details they lovingly master, a predominant role has been preempted by the Coalition leaders as a group. The Coalition leaders and their allies, the other committee chairman, are in control of the Congress—not the majority party. Woodrow Wilson discovered, nearly a century ago, that the committee chairmen constituted what is effectively Congressional government. But even Wilson did not anticipate the possibility that a smaller coalitional leadership bloc might emerge within the nucleus of the committee chairmen. (This is perhaps another form of atomic power.) Locally elected, claiming the power centers of Congressional decision-making as their own baronies, the Coalition leaders appear to be responsible largely to their own view of the public interest. Whether they are responsible even to their small local constituencies remains unclear because the Congressional barons represent areas in which there is virtually no political competition for the seats they hold. They, of all American politicians, are the least likely to have been exposed to political alternatives. The Congressional barons are at least as secure in their power seats as are upper-echelon civil service bureaucrats—and these senior Congressmen appear to have been drawn from a far narrower and more provincial social base.[8]

The conservative Coalition would probably like to dominate all Congressional committees, but this is not quite feasible. Hence, the power of the Coalition centers in the most important committees, three in the Senate and four in the House. The Senate committees are Appropriations, Armed Services and Finance; the House committees are functionally the same, Ways and Means, Appropriations and Armed Services, with the Rules committee serving a peculiar function as the traffic cop for House legislative activity. Since the Democrats have controlled the Congress almost all of the time since 1938 when the Coalition first took shape, the senior partners in the Coalition normally are Democrats. *Southern* Democrats who are conservative on domestic matters have proved to be the best legislative tacticians in the modern Congress.*

The Senate Coalition leaders, on the Democratic side, during the 1960s were Richard Russell of Georgia, Chairman of the Senate Appropriations Committee, and John Stennis of Mississippi, who inherited the chairmanship of the Armed Services Committee when Russell assumed the chairmanship of Appropriations. The southern barons believe in defense in depth where essential Congressional power is involved. Russell Long of Louisiana, on the basis of seniority, automatically succeeded the late Harry Byrd, Senior, of Virginia, as chairman of the Senate Finance Committee, although Long's views on a number of important issues are far less rigidly conservative than were Byrd's.

Key House committee chairmen and leading coalitionists during the past decade were: Representative George Mahon of Texas, who chaired Appropriations; Mendel Rivers of South Carolina, head of Armed Services; William Colmer of Mississippi, chairman of House Rules following the defeat of Judge Howard Smith (Virginia) in a 1966 primary; and Wilbur Mills of Arkansas, veteran Ways and Means potentate who many believe ranked as the single most important legislator in the House of Representatives by the end of the 1960s.

Each of these seven gentlemen was a long-time representative of the Deep and Segregated South; all, except Long, were conservative on domestic issues, although Mills, essentially a conservative, was the principal Congressional architect of Medicare (after opposing it for a decade). Furthermore, all were able legislators with the possible exception of Rivers who, whatever else may be said about him, was not to be slighted when it comes to pork-barreling his own district.[9]

The Republican counterparts on the seven key committees were Senators Margaret Chase Smith of Maine, Milton Young of North Dakota and John J. Williams of Delaware, and Rep-

---

*On issues relating to race it is rare to find a southern coalitionist who is not a reactionary. Lyndon Johnson was such an exception, let it be noted here, during his Senate career.

resentatives Frank T. Bow of Ohio, the late William Bates of Massachusetts, who died in 1969, John Byrnes of Wisconsin and H. Allen Smith of California. If most of the Republican names seem somewhat less familiar than several of the Democratic barons this is undoubtedly due to the fact that since 1938 the Republicans have constituted a formal majority of the Congress for a total of four years, 1947–48 and 1953–54. Why the Republican party has been content to leave the formal control of the Congress in other hands remains uncertain, but it is a fact that the Republicans in Congress provide most of "the troops" in the conservative Coalition while the southern Democrats have developed most of the "generals." If the aim of most Congressional Republicans since 1938 has been to limit the effectiveness of activist Presidents, it may very well be that the partnership with the southern oligarchs better serves their purposes than would outright Republican control. This way it is almost impossible for the ordinary American citizen to have any clear notion as to who is responsible for public policy.

THE PROVINCIAL BASE

The essentially parochial and nonurban bias of the Congressional Coalition is suggested simply by listing the individual leaders and their respective home communities as published in the Congressional Directory:

SENATE

Richard Russell	Winder, Georgia
John Stennis	DeKalb, Mississippi
Russell Long	Shreveport, Louisiana
Margaret Chase Smith	Skowhegan, Maine
Milton Young	La Moure, North Dakota
John Williams	Millsboro, Delaware

HOUSE

Wilbur Mills	Kensett, Arkansas
Mendel Rivers	Charleston, South Carolina
George Mahon	Lubbock, Texas

William Colmer	Pascagoula, Mississippi
William Bates	Salem, Massachusetts
H. Allen Smith	Glendale, California
John Byrnes	Green Bay, Wisconsin
Frank Bow	Canton, Ohio

Mike Mansfield, Senate Majority leader, and the late Everett Dirksen, who served as two key brokers in the system of coalitional legislative politics in the period we are examining, listed their home bases as Missoula, Montana and Pekin, Illinois.*

The Coalition leaders are not by background a group finely attuned to the stirrings of megalopolis. Nor are they notably young. And it goes without saying that they are white. Richard Russell and William Colmer first entered Congress in 1933. George Mahon came to the House originally in 1935, four years earlier than Wilbur Mills. Mendel Rivers is a relative newcomer having first arrived in 1941. The average Congressional service of the seven Democratic leaders mentioned in this chapter is thirty years. On the Republican side the average tenure for members of their leadership group approximates twenty years.

No one should be too surprised if closer examination were to reveal that coalitional leadership reflects a less than cosmopolitan view. Such a leadership group might be expected, at a minimum, to experience some difficulty in relating the functions of the modern legislature to the needs of our restless technocratic empire with its large organizations and its complex bureaucratic structures. And it would be remarkable if the Coalition leaders showed any special sensitivity towards the cry of despair rising from the dark ghettos.[10]

The leaders of the dominant Congressional Coalition have proved to be conservative in more than one sense. They instinctively fear social reform which, if carried very far, may succeed in activating new political groupings, as FDR's New

*When the Senate Republicans chose the urbane Hugh Scott of Pennsylvania to succeed Dirksen the change was a sign of a profoundly important transformation taking place in the Senate, as we shall see in Chapter Seven.

Deal encouraged the growth of the labor unions, thus altering the political balance in the Congress and weakening the Coalition's power base. The southerners among the group are ultra-conservative on matters of race. Products of the politics of segregation, they would be the first to go, presumably, if southern blacks were to develop their full political potential. At this point the fundamental connection between the noncompetitive nature of southern Congressional politics and the vital importance of the seniority principle in maintaining southern leadership in the Coalition must be noted. Undoubtedly, the Coalition leadership group holds certain views on public policy issues but, additionally, the Coalition has a primary interest in conserving the Congressional system *as it is.*

There is a difference between the policies a contemporary President will pursue as chief legislator and the public policy preferences of the leaders of the particular Congressional Coalition under examination. The Presidency, *as an institution,* now represents those forces in American society which seek social reform. Even Richard Nixon, having been elected by a combination of forces distinctly not seeking social reform and while catering to the silent majority, found it desirable to introduce a major proposal for welfare reform, calling for a minimum guarantee of family income, during his first year in office. The Congress, on the other hand, so long as it is in the control of a leadership group which is essentially conservative, nonurban, nonreformist in its bias, may be expected to resist social reform. (The question which we must return to in a later chapter is: what are the chances that this Congressional leadership bias may be altered in the foreseeable future?)

The broad scope of Presidential initiative in legislative policy-making has become almost a cliché in modern political analysis. It is now said that the Presidential initiative in legislation has been largely "institutionalized." Through the State of the Union message, especially through the annual Budget message, the message which accompanies the annual Economic Report, and sometimes dozens of special messages, as in the Kennedy-Johnson administrations, the Presidential program, enunciated in elaborate detail, establishes the agenda for legislative business. Vital pieces of legislation, aiming at social reform, may actually be written first in the Executive branch with only one question remaining: will Congress ratify? Something like this seems to have occurred in the writing of the Economic Opportunity Act in 1964.

Perhaps the Congressional role in legislation is increasingly a minor one, and, if so, the power of the Coalition may be partly an illusion. I think not. The Congressional role in the shaping of the Economic Opportunity programs has not been minor over the longer range. And one has only to go back to the Kennedy era to find Congress in a strong position to develop key legislation of its own inspiration. The Area Redevelopment Act of 1961 was conceived and written in Congress in the 1950s. In fact, the original Presidential view was unfavorable; Eisenhower vetoed the bill twice. The Manpower Development and Training Act of 1962 was at least as much Congressional in conception as it was Executive. This is not to suggest that Congress ordinarily shows the initiative in legislative policymaking. More typically, the Coalition leaders guide the Congress in the direction of restraining the Executive in the area of domestic reform.

ANTICIPATING THE REACTION

A great deal of what appears on the surface as Executive legislation has been developed only after the most intimate consultation with the appropriate Congressional committees. Much that may pass as Executive legislation is actually conceived, fretted over, modified and either shelved for the time being or pushed forward to a priority position on the Presidential agenda with a nervous Executive eye fixed on the Congress. The law of anticipated reaction has not been repealed.[11]

Think of how long it took to get Medicare. Some observers think that Medicare was held up for a decade by Chairman Wilbur Mills of Ways and Means. They assume that Mr. Mills' essential conservatism and his power as chairman combined to slow down this major social reform. But Chairman Mills is also careful to bring to the floor of the House only those large measures which he has reason to believe have an excellent

71

chance of passing. Fortunately, in terms of our analysis, it is not vital that we sort out the variables at this point—that is, Mills' personal value preferences versus his tactical judgments. In any event, the practical effect was: *Congress set the pace for this momentous reform.* When the votes were available on the floor of the House, Chairman Mills skillfully engineered a major social reform. Medicare was drafted and redrafted by HEW technicians time and again in intimate consultation with Chairman Mills.[12]

CONTROL OF ADMINISTRATION

The Congressional influence is by no means limited to shaping the substance of the specific legislative proposals which seemingly emanate from the Institutionalized Presidency. Congress also displays a continuing interest in the administration of Executive programs. An impressive sanction supports this aspect of Congressional power: Congress controls the purse strings. We now have the benefit of a definitive analysis of the Congressional appropriations process by Professor Richard Fenno[13], and there is no longer any reason to question the reality of this Congressional power. The single most effective technique for detailed Congressional control of administration of public policy is exercised by the appropriations subcommittees of the Congress in their annual review of departmental money requests. The review has its weaknesses, and they have been carefully evaluated by Fenno and others. Nonetheless, the appropriations subcommittees of the Congress subject the Executive agencies of the government (especially on the domestic side) to a more detailed review of administration than that which occurs in any other western parliamentary system.

The chairmen of the appropriations Committees, Senator Russell and Representative Mahon, are thirty-year veterans of Congressional coalitional politics. Under their leadership social welfare programs are likely to receive a more detailed scrutiny than are those items marked "national security."

During the period, 1962–65, I served for two years as Executive Assistant to the Secretary of Labor of the United States and for one year as the administrator of the Labor Department's manpower program. It would be impossible to exaggerate how much high-level executive time, energy and attention and how much detailed professional staff work went into the matter of maintaining an effective relationship with our appropriations subcommittees. These committees exerted a control on the administration of the policies of the Department which was felt by the men at the top of the Department. The annual review sessions with the subcommittees indicated that the leading committee members (and their staff) were remarkably well-informed about our programs and our problems, sometimes in embarrassing detail. This was especially true in the case of our House appropriations subcommittee, as Fenno's analysis would suggest. In the effort to reorganize the Department—a high-priority item at the Secretarial level—the attitude of the House appropriations subcommittee toward the reorganization plans was invariably influential; and at certain points, it appeared to be perhaps the most important limiting factor. The late Representative John Fogarty of Rhode Island was the chairman of the subcommittee during those years. Representative Melvin Laird of Wisconsin was his Republican counterpart on the House subcommittee. This was the subcommittee which reviewed the appropriations requests of the Departments of Labor and Health, Education, and Welfare, and of the Office of Economic Opportunity. In short, the most important human welfare programs were subject to legislative oversight, a process in which the House appropriations subcommittee plays the predominant role. Both Fogarty and Laird were veterans of the appropriation system, and they were determined to maintain as strong a Congressional control as possible.

Fogarty and Laird were a force to be reckoned with. Chairman Fogarty's power to affect the administration of public policy was respected in the Department. This is not a minor point. When a House appropriations subcommittee is led by an able and determined chairman (and most of them are at least that), the men in key positions in the Executive agency concerned face a potential control device which they recognize and respect.

73

Thirty years ago Harold Laski wrote a book about the Presidency in which he concluded that the American President, was not exactly an embarrassed phantom in the struggle for power. Neither is the Congress of the United States. When the Congress is subject to the strong influence of a conservative Coalition, as it has been most of the time for the past thirty years, we should expect to find that major domestic policies will be shaped in accordance with the Coalition's policy preferences. Likewise I am confident that systematic analysis of the Congressional role in national security policy-making since World War II will reveal that Congressional thinking on world issues had a dogmatically anticommunist and pro-military bias which has helped establish the limits of executive-branch national security actions. It is comforting to imagine that Lyndon Johnson might have turned aside the virtually unanimous advice of his national security advisers in June 1965 and declared: "Enough is enough. The United States is unwilling to go further in shoring up a regime in South Vietnam which is close to political and military collapse." But this is hypothetical. Where in the summer of 1965—which seems to have been the critical period, as a later chapter will attempt to show—was the Congressional support for such an alternative to be found?

Thus far our analysis has shown that the Presidency as an office for national policy leadership has been subjected for thirty years to a steady process of institutionalization which has now reached the point where it is appropriate to wonder how the President is to make effective his assertions as the national leader. The modern administrative state appears to have developed a bureaucratic inertial force which sometimes limits Presidential policy initiative, as it also tends to keep policy moving in the direction it has been moving.

This chapter has explored the nature of the conservative Congressional Coalition which has been the dominant force in the legislative body during the same thirty-year period which has produced the institutionalizing of the Presidential policy initiative. We find another major political and institutional force (one might also call it a "system") whose character is ambiguous at best. In domestic matters, its bias is fundamentally antireformist: first, because the Coalition is led by conservative and provincial men; and second, because social reform, if it were to gain momentum, would almost certainly turn its attention to the problem of the anachronistic, obligarchic system which pervades the Congress. Hence, a modern President who attempts to deal with the demands of a national (or cosmopolitan) urge for social reform must expect to encounter a basic resistance from the Congressional Coalition. In national security matters the Coalition has been approximately as dogmatic and rigid in its anticommunist orthodoxy as the Pentagon. Indeed, the Congressional Coalition has been careful to solidify its leadership position on those few key Congressional committees which deal with the development of military strength and the expenditures of public funds which support that development. As a military-industrial complex takes shape in the United States, we may be certain that the Congressional Coalition forms a vital part of it.

Our analysis up to this point may help to explain the emergence of a military establishment as part of postwar American society. It does not, however, adequately explain the emergence of the Welfare State. How are we to account for the very substantial increase in human welfare program activity in recent years? Is the Coalition less conservative on welfare issues than we have suspected? Less provincial? Or are there other forces at work in politics, in the Congress and in the policy-making process which have the capacity of overriding the resistance of the conservative Coalition? In an age of urban crisis and youthful rebellion, are there countervailing forces within the American society with the vitality and the strategic location necessary to offset the influence of the Congressional Coalition?

In the next chapter, we shall examine the possibility that social reform may itself have become institutionalized, at least to some extent. And in a later chapter we shall inquire further into the possibility that even the Congress may not be invulnerable to the winds of change.

CHAPTER FOUR

THE PROFESSIONAL AND SOCIAL REFORM

> *The ideological debates of the past began*
> *to give way to a new agreement on the practicalities*
> *of managing a modern economy.*
> *There thus developed in the Kennedy years*
> *a national accord on economic policy—*
> *a new consensus which gave hope of harnessing government,*
> *business and labor in rational partnership*
> *for a steadily expanding American economy.*
> A.M. SCHLESINGER, JR., *A Thousand Days*

ABRUPT CHANGES in American public policy do not occur frequently; a great deal of modern government consists in doing just what has been done in the past. The President has a hard time leading, and at the same time Congress has been dominated by men who wish the world looked more like the small towns in which they grew up fifty years ago.

Then, we have the inertial force of the bureaucracy. "The bureaucrat's constant concern is to keep the system moving, and he, more than anyone else, is aware of its enormous inertia, and the difficulty of changing course or starting up again if it is stopped even momentarily." So writes a man who knows the Pentagon and the Institutionalized Presidency well.[1]

Many of our social problems arise from the nature of modern industrialism. They are, in part, the social results of rapid technological change in a society in which institutions change only slowly. The basic issues of domestic policy have been with us for long periods of time: social security, medical care for the aged, support for an expanding system of public education, the maintenance of full employment, the conservation of resources, the renewal of our decaying cities.[2]

But Presidential leadership, Congressional control, bureaucratic inertia, in whatever combination, face this stubborn fact: somehow we must shape public policies which will make the modern industrial system work. The real issue today, we are often told, is the management of the industrial society, a problem not of ideology but of administration. President Kennedy, a dramatic political personality, had been in office only little more than a year when he told a distinguished gathering of corporation executives, labor leaders and economists:

> The fact of the matter is that most of the problems or at least many of them, that we now face, are technical problems, are administrative problems. They are very sophisticated judgments which do not lend themselves to the great sort of "passionate movements" which have stirred this country so often in the past.

"How can we look at things as they are," the President wanted to know, "not through party labels, but as they are, and figure out how we can maintain this economy as it moves ahead."[3]

President Kennedy was speaking at a White House Conference on National Economic Issues in May 1962. A high rate of unemployment continued to bedevil the new Administration more than a year after the shining inauguration. The White House Conference, the first step in a series of incremental moves, pointed the way to a Presidential decision, greatly influenced by Walter Heller and the Council of Economic Advisers, to seek a massive tax reduction rather than an increase in Federal domestic spending.

Speaking at the Yale Commencement in June 1962, President Kennedy developed the theme further:

> The central issues of our time relate not to basic clashes of philosophy or ideology but to ways and means of reaching common goals. What is at stake is not some grand warfare of rival ideologies which will sweep the country with passion but the practical management of a modern economy.[4]

The Kennedy Administration may have been beguiled into thinking it had found a way, an unpassionate, nonideological, managerial, administrative, technical, professional way to manage the economy. It is a short step, intellectually, to the next position: that social reform itself is a technical matter best handled by the professionals who understand the esoteric nature of the problems being dealt with. Thus, Nathan Glazer, the noted sociologist, wrote shortly before the assassination of President Kennedy:

> Without the benefit of anything like the Beveridge report to spark and focus public discussion and concern, the United States is passing through a stage of enormous expansion in the size and scope of what we may loosely call the social services—the public programs designed to help people adapt to an increasingly complex and unmanageable society.[5]

And yet Glazer noted the absence of anything like the powerful political pressures and the long-sustained intellectual support which produced the New Deal. The new force, which Glazer identified, was the growth of a large body of professional persons and professional organizations with what might be considered a professional interest in social welfare reform.

THE PROFESSIONALIZATION OF REFORM

What we are moving toward, according to Daniel P. Moynihan, is "the professionalization of reform," of which The Economic Opportunity Act seemed to Moynihan by far the best example we have had to date. And he predicted that we would get more. We now have a group of professionals in government whose business it is to devise new programs, including programs aimed at social reform. Moynihan himself served for three years during the Kennedy-Johnson period as an Assistant Secretary of Labor in charge of policy planning. He has since served as Counsellor to President Nixon, planning across a vast range of urban problems. Moynihan was one of the first to warn us that the professionalization of reform might lead to a certain loss of moral exhilaration in politics. This seems too bad in a society in which the reformers have always been passionate individuals who looked forward to the joys of combat. Mr. Moynihan personally is very much in this good old-fashioned American tradition, and I, for one, should hate to see social reform turned over to the generous minds of, let us say, the Children's Bureau. So would Mr. Moynihan.

But is it true that politics, passion and moral exhilaration have lost relevance in the making of public policy? How much initiative do the professionals have in their hands? Do they launch programs of social reform unmindful of their political consequences? Do social reform programs go through the Congress in some mysterious, *unpolitical* way? If people are no longer to be stirred by great "passionate movements" as in the past, how are they to be moved?

This much is certain: the rise of modern industrialism has everywhere been accompanied by the development of the modern administrative state—that is to say, by the growth of bureaucracy. In this country perhaps the most significant development, *within the administrative state,* these past twenty-five years, has been the fairly rapid proliferation of specialized agencies which now constitute the Institutionalized Presidency. *Technical expertise has invaded the office to which we look more than any other for political leadership.* But political leadership in a democracy requires more than technique.

Some of the more recent arrivals, the Council of Economic Advisers, the Office of Economic Opportunity, the new Urban Affairs Council, and now a Council of Environmental Advisers, represent an attempt to relate the Presidency more directly and more professionally to some of the most difficult and troublesome issues which the American industrial system poses for public policy decision-making.* No one doubts that these is-

*This book was in the press when President Nixon announced his plan to reorganize the domestic side of the Institutionalized Presidency, effective July 1, 1970. The creation of the Domestic Council to parallel the National Security Council and the establishment of the office of Management and Budget to replace the Bureau of the Budget obviously constitute a potentially significant change in Presidential decision-making machinery.

sues—full employment, economic growth, a decent minimum standard of living, educational opportunity—have a technical side. Of course they do, and to deal with them at all adequately requires all of the technical competence we can muster. But, just as surely, the policies which are devised to solve social problems are not merely technical in nature. Judgments must be made about the size and scope of the new programs. To embark upon a new program requires a commitment to use certain resources for this purpose rather than for that. Once made, commitments tend to persist, as we have seen. Choices must be made; dollars appropriated and spent. And people's lives are affected; their hopes and expectations encouraged. People may even be stirred.

THEORIES OF SOCIAL ACTION

Recently there has been considerable interest, at least among social scientists, concerning the relationship between social theory and public policy. Shortly before he joined the Nixon White House team, as its leading social-theorist-in-action, Daniel P. Moynihan[6] published a short book, largely a critique of the Community Action phase of the Johnson war on poverty, which was highly critical of the part certain social theories had played in influencing the new program. Moynihan was especially harsh on the views of Professors Lloyd Ohlin and Richard Cloward of the Columbia University School of Social Work whose earlier studies of juvenile gangs in urban slums led to a broader thesis of how the sense of powerlessness which pervades the urban ghetto might be overcome. Professor Ohlin was a major contributor to the thinking of the small staff of the President's Committee on Juvenile Delinquency, a special project under the personal guidance of Attorney General Robert Kennedy during the Kennedy era. The PCJD experience formed the basis for Community Action as it found its way into the Johnson war on poverty. Hence, it is possible for Moynihan and others to trace the influence of Ohlin's theories into at least a few of the projects financed by the Economic

Opportunity Act. Moynihan has come to feel that the social theory sponsored by Professors Ohlin and Cloward was the "wrong" theory; and for reasons not made clear, has been harsher in his treatment of Cloward, although, of the two, Ohlin was probably the more influential with PCJD staff members.

What Moynihan seems to imply is that the two Columbia professors misled the innocent staff members of the Juvenile Delinquency Committee; that the professors sold the staff an erroneous theory; and that they ought to have told the government technocrats that there were other social theories relating to poverty and powerlessness which would have greater utilitarian value. Carried very far, this line of analysis leads to the conclusion that Ohlin and Cloward were responsible for a great deal that went wrong in the Johnson war on poverty.

Moynihan is correct in suggesting that there were other theoretical approaches to the problems of juvenile delinquency. There are, indeed, other social theorists with notions about how to go about overcoming the sense of powerlessness among the poor and the downtrodden. Saul Alinsky is an old-time radical organizer, and the Woodlawn Organization in Chicago may be the best know example of a local organization based on Alinsky's theory of social conflict. Moynihan treats Alinsky with deference and respect, although, oddly enough, a national war on poverty which was based frankly and openly on the Alinsky model would assuredly not pass the Congress. Whether a particular social theory is "right" or "wrong" depends in part on what one expects from the theory once it has been suspected of having influenced an operating program. Needless to say, expectations about these great public programs vary greatly from one individual to the next and from one group to the next. As a result, speculation about which theory has been more influential than another theory may go on endlessly. In the meantime, the administrative and political weaknesses, unrelated to theory, are likely to remain unexamined.

There is a further difficulty of which Mr. Moynihan must be

aware, since he personally experienced it in a painful way. In 1965—Moynihan was then an Assistant Secretary of Labor in the Johnson Administration—a government report was prepared in Mr. Moynihan's office entitled simply, "The Negro Family." The report was an "inside" document apparently intended only for key officials within the Institutionalized Presidency, and it was based upon certain social theories about the poor Negro family. Its findings were not unlike those of E. Franklin Frazier, a black sociologist who had written a sociological classic on the Negro family in 1939, and Kenneth Clark, the Negro psychologist, whose studies of the contemporary dark ghetto are crammed with socioeconomic data about the poor fatherless ghetto family.[7] But Mr. Moynihan's report was written by a white man (actually it was written by Mr. Moynihan's staff), and it shortly became, through a series of misadventures, a public document. Hence, the social theory implicit in the report became the subject of intense and bitter public controversy. The Moynihan report, as it was henceforth to be known, seemed to be saying that the poor black ghetto family, typically fatherless and welfare-dependent, was a vital part of a "tangle of pathology" (the phrase originated with Kenneth Clark) in the urban slums. The report hinted that the malignancy might be feeding upon itself. The social theory in the Moynihan report, if indeed it was a social theory, appears to have had a great deal of validity. Nevertheless, a variety of individuals and groups, with their own perceptions and interests, some of them inside government, many of them on the outside, took noisy public exception to the findings of the Moynihan report.

There is probably no clearer example of one kind of interaction between social theory and modern public policy than the controversy over the 1965 report on the Negro family. The controversy has been examined intelligently and perceptively, and with a view to its implications for social science, by Professors Rainwater and Yancey.[8] Their study confirms what might be postulated on the basis of common sense: that social theory, when it gets close to actual social conflicts which are "live," will inevitably become part of the ongoing conflict. The theory becomes part of the political struggle. At this point, theory is likely to lose some of its purity, and, incidentally, those who would like to trace the impact of that theory on the making of public policy have their work cut out for them.

THE END OF IDEOLOGY

Another social theory gained widespread currency during the early 1960s, asserting that we had finally come, after centuries of the human struggle, to "the end of ideology." The theory was constructed around a striking hypothesis: that most of the social problems of the industrial society, or better still, of the post-industrial society, are largely technical and administrative in nature. Such problems, so the notion suggests, are peculiarly responsive to the "endless nibbling" of the technocrats. If only we were able to discover the proper mix of, let us say, economic growth (affluence), full employment, and a reasonably stable price level, a new Utopia would presumably be near at hand. Much of the activity and program-planning which took place in the agencies of the Institutionalized Presidency during the 1960s leaned heavily on this general intellectual framework.[9]

The end-of-ideology theme proved far more influential at this level than any ideas which owe their existence to the writings of academic social-action theorists, such as Cloward, Ohlin or Clark. As we noted, President Kennedy made explicit use of the theme in two important addresses. While President Johnson seems not to have had any interest in the issue, one way or the other, his uncritical acceptance of the virtues of economic growth provided no defense against those who did. Before many months had passed, Johnson was seeking a grand consensus in which apparently there were to be no serious ideological conflicts but one national partnership of government, labor, and business. This is not to suggest that President Johnson lacked political objectives of his own. These were, as we were to learn, rather broad. His administration fashioned a combination Warfare and Welfare State which would police the earth, conquer space, and eliminate poverty. President Nixon has shown a clear preference for the nonideological. His administration, a team of managers and technicians, may have no generally shared purpose in view other than to make the system work.

WALTER HELLER'S ECONOMIC ADVICE

The tendency for the technician to invade the policy sphere is perhaps most clearly demonstrated in the case of the Council of Economic Advisers, now one of the oldest and, in the 1960s, one of the most influential units within the Institutionalized Presidency.[10] The Council is the creature of the Employment Act of 1946 with its statutory pledge to make full employment a reality in this country. This is obviously a central objective in every modern industrial system. One might even suggest that full employment has become the nonideological objective of modern industrialism.[11]

The Council of Economic Advisers is a small agency by any standard: forty people, of whom fifteen are economists. The Council itself has three senior economists, invariably men of academic distinction, selected by the President whom they are collectively to advise. It is obvious that if the CEA is to be influential its impact will not be due to its weight as a bureaucratic empire. But the Council has something far more enticing: its conviction that modern economics is able to show the President how to make the modern industrial system operate at a point of maximum efficiency and maximum productivity. (Does anyone seriously doubt that the theory of "maximum productivity" has a greater potential for influencing Presidents than, let us say, "maximum feasible participation"?)

The CEA, under the leadership of Professor Walter Heller of the University of Minnesota, an able, articulate and persuasive practitioner of the New Economics, unquestionably played a significant role in influencing President Kennedy. Kennedy won the Presidency at a time when the modern American industrial system was not working as it should; it was not functioning at a point of maximum efficiency. The 1950s featured three economic recessions, each one leaving us with a higher plateau of chronic unemployment than its predecessor.

The third of these "recessions" reached its peak just as Kennedy prepared to move into the White House. The national average rate of unemployment on Inauguration Day 1961 stood virtually at 7%. (In the early 1950s the comparable rate was closer to 3%.) The patient had a thermometer reading of about 106 degrees. Unemployment was as serious a problem as it had been for a long time in West Virginia and in Washington County, Maine; but unemployment in January 1961 was extremely serious in Pittsburgh and Detroit, as well. There was sluggishness—and worse—in the economy, and the President was pledged to get the country moving again. What was needed was a higher rate of economic growth. The President presumably understood all of this, quite apart from anything the Council might have to say. But how was the expansion of the economy to be stimulated?

The Council knew that an appropriate blending of fiscal and monetary policy would lead the way out of the morass. It was possible, Heller argued, to achieve a significantly higher rate of economic growth, maintain reasonably stable prices and effect a sharp reduction in unemployment. The Administration set for itself an interim goal: by the end of 1963, the overall rate of unemployment should be lowered to 4% by a considerable expansion of the economy. Getting there was in large part a technical matter on which the advice of the experts was to be crucial. This is not to suggest that the technical, expert advice of Council did not necessitate problems of choice for the President. But the President, with the support of a Congressional majority where Congressional action was required, would be likely to move the nation toward the interim goal whenever he found it politically and administratively possible to follow the Council's largely technical advice.

The record of the Kennedy Administration in the field of economic policy is as interesting as it is impressive. By the end of 1963 the overall rate of unemployment stood at 5.6%, a notable improvement over the 7% figure inherited from the Eisenhower period but distressingly remote from the interim goal of 4%. Economic growth was another story. President Kennedy inherited a $500 billion economy; at the time of his tragic assassination Gross National Product had increased to an approximate annual rate of $600 billion. The annual growth rate which had hovered between 2.5% and 3% in the 1950s now exceeded 5%. And prices remained relatively stable. This is the record of achievement of the Kennedy administration. It is a remarkable record, and the Heller CEA deserves much of the credit for its "theory" as well as for the influence the Council had on Presidential decision-making.

Was Heller's CEA offering merely technical advice? Heller[12] has written since that it was not. He insists that the kind of advice offered by the Council necessitates value judgments in the giving as well as the receiving. It seems quite clear, for example, that the CEA target goal of a 4% unemployment rate implies certain *values*. It assumes that a 4% rate of unemployment is socially (and politically) to be preferred to a 7% rate of unemployment. But it is also a technical matter since the 4% rate assumes a fuller and more efficient use of human resources. Another *value* question was implied, and in a sense, hidden, when the 4% unemployment rate was postulated as in interim goal. As a practical matter, many economists believe that the 4% rate represents "full employment" in the United States. It is the point at which the technical experts begin worrying about the pressure on prices to rise. In short, below 4% unemployment, the threat of inflation becomes real. Below 4%, one encounters the trade-off in which any further decrease in unemployment is likely to be achieved at the expense of a rising level of prices.

This balancing of prices and jobs presents an exceedingly important and complex technical problem in the economics of modern industrialism; its resolution plagues all western industrial nations. One ought not minimize the difficulties of choice nor is there any reason to doubt that a President should seek expert advice in charting his economic course. But a President should also keep his wits about him. The problem is political and moral, as well as technical, although the values are always in danger of being obscured in the technical formulations of the problem. Walter Heller* has put the moral issue with simple clarity: "Involuntary unemployment is a sign of economic waste, but the fundamental evil of unemployment is that it is an affront to human dignity."

The Kennedy administration, following the technical advice of the CEA, managed to lower unemployment to a level of about 5.6%, a level which the administration itself regarded as unsatisfactory. By this time, Heller, still seeking an expansionist goal, had convinced President Kennedy and his political assistants that the nation needed a large dose of tax *reform* (actually, it turned out to be mostly a massive tax *reduction*) if the unemployment rate were to be driven down toward 4%. The Kennedy Administration accepted this advice. A large part of the Administration's legislative effort in 1963 was devoted to the task of selling the massive tax cut to Wilbur Mills and his colleagues on the House Ways and Means Committee and to the late Senator Harry Byrd of Virginia and his fellow Senators of the Finance Committee.

The fact that Heller recommended following the tax-cut route to full employment, rather than presenting a program for increasing federal expenditures which would expand social service programs, indicates that the advice of the Council of Economic Advisers was in part political. There were others who urged programs which would improve the quality of our social services, but the Council came out firmly for the tax cut, and this view prevailed. There was, of course, almost no hope in 1963 of winning Congressional support for increased domestic spending, a point which Chairman Wilbur Mills made with unconcealed delight in presenting the case for the tax cut. President Kennedy made the political choice following Heller's advice.[13]

The tax cut was to produce an additional two or three million jobs, and it may have done so. Unfortunately, the evidence is not as clear as one might wish. The tax cut finally passed the Congress in 1964 only after President Johnson apparently con-

*The sentence quoted above appeared originally in the Annual Economic Report for 1962, p. 37. It is repeated in Heller's book *New Dimensions of Political Economy*, (Cambridge: Harvard University Press, 1966).

vinced Senator Byrd that his Administration would hold the line on Federal expenditures. (If such a deal was made, Senator Byrd had reason to stir in his grave.) It is difficult to measure the impact of the tax cut because the Johnson Administration not only failed to hold the line on expenditures but soon brought into being the largest expansion in social welfare programs in this century. This expansion carried with it a sizeable increase in the level of Federal spending. So the decision of the Kennedy Administration not to travel the route of increased expenditures was quietly reversed by the Johnson Administration. In effect, President Johnson's drive for full employment had the benefit of *both the massive tax cut and a sizeable increase in the level of domestic expenditures.*

After the summer of 1965, the Johnson Administration added an additional factor of great weight: it substantially increased the level of Defense spending by a series of decisions which escalated and Americanized the war in Vietnam. Within a remarkably short time, the annual rate of expenditure for Vietnam alone exceeded $20 billion; eventually, it reached an annual rate of $30 billion. The search for "growth" and "full employment" was assisted by a massive increase in Vietnam expenditures which approached a cumulative total of $100 billion before President Johnson left office. The purpose of the additional expenditure may not have been exactly what most liberals had had in mind, but no one could deny that the pump was being primed.

While the military escalation in Vietnam has made it difficult to measure the impact of the 1964 tax cut, it is perfectly clear that the American economy finally achieved "full employment," as the Council of Economic Advisers defined it, in 1966, a year in which the rate of unemployment averaged 3.8%. For a time thereafter the Johnson policies produced more growth than any one had dreamed possible back in the more cautious days of 1961 and 1962. In any event, by 1966 we had reached the point where the guild of economists worried far more about inflation than it did about those fellow citizens who remain without work or hope.

FULL EMPLOYMENT: FOR WHITES ONLY

This analysis suggests that the pursuit of the elusive goal, full employment, brings into play technical expertise which is continually spilling over into those areas where human values are critically at stake. A man out of work in the modern industrial order has lost more than a job; he has lost his opportunity to share in whatever the society has to offer. His children are also denied the same opportunities unless society finds another way of sustaining them. Policies which put men out of work or perpetuate joblessness, therefore, have moral significance.

Yet the technical theory of full employment is prepared to accept a certain amount of unemployment.* The layman finds this difficult to understand. The theory of full employment, as it is understood in modern neo-Keynesian economics and as it has been articulated by the Council of Economic Advisers, accepts the necessity of some unemployment, although not among economists, one may be sure. Paradoxically enough, full employment, as a technical objective, recognizes that some people will be unemployed. Their dignity—indeed, their survival in a complex, interdependent system—becomes a problem which must be dealt with, one has to assume, on some other basis.

In terms of human welfare, there is a point beyond which affluence, growth, full employment and the New Economics has not been able to take us. That point was reached soon after the American economy achieved the 4% unemployment rate. During the final four years of the 1960s the United States

*Unemployment, as a technical concept measured in the official US statistics compiled by the Bureau of Labor Statistics, has its inherent defects. It includes only individuals who are actively seeking work. It does not attempt to measure those who are grossly underemployed. Partly to overcome these limitations, the US Department of Labor at the insistence of Secretary Willard Wirtz undertook in November 1966 an intensive survey of the employment problems found in ten of the nation's largest urban slums. This special study found in these areas an unemployment rate which was nearly three times the national average rate. Furthermore, one in every three of the slum residents was found to have a serious employment problem. The Wirtz study observed: "Unemployment—or subemployment—in the city slums is so much worse than it is in the country as a whole that the national measurements of unemployment are utterly irrelevant."

experienced what most economists were willing to call full employment. The average rate of unemployment in 1969 was 3.5% Very good! Yet, in no *real* sense had the nation reached full employment; that is to say, not in any sense beyond the purely technical definition. The rate of unemployment for all nonwhite Americans in 1969 was 6.4%, a rate which, if it were to appear as the average for all Americans, would send the Administration in power off in pursuit of new policies. A typical rate of unemployment in an urban slum in 1969 was 10%. The unemployment rate among Americans who are young, black, and ghettoized remained close to 25% as the overall rate dipped to 3.5% Technical full employment was reached and was maintained for four long years, and yet nearly one in every four young urban blacks was without work. All of this took place in the context of "full employment" and inflation.

The technical goal of full employment has been defined in a way which excludes the reality of black despair. If any economist or fellow social scientist knows a technical, nonideological answer to the problem of finding meaningful work for a fourth of our black youth, he ought to make his views public. Such a social theory deserves to be influential. In the meantime, however, the nation may expect to experience more protest, more passion, more rebellion, more ideology, more politics in the activities of young people in the ghettos and their natural allies. The integrity of our society is placed in serious doubt by a technical definition of the full employment goal which excludes so many young black people. It is not clear that any individual owes loyalty to a society which denies his manhood. Even John Locke provided the right of rebellion against a tyrant. Why not against a tyrannical definition?

The policy-making process of modern government adds another dimension to its already complicated form when social science is applied in a serious way in the making of policy judgments. The narrow instrumentalism of modern social science, the preoccupation with methodological elegance, the fascination with the manipulation of esoteric data may have seemed innocuous when encountered in the turgid prose of scholarly journals. Once the techniques of social science invade the agencies of government where public policy is being shaped, there is reason to be apprehensive about the cult of scientism. There is the prime danger that we may come to believe that only that which we can measure is "real," while the unmeasurable remains unreal. It has been suggested that anyone who does not appear as a statistic in contemporary society is in grave trouble. One nonwhite male in every six between the ages of twenty and thirty-nine was missing from 1960 census data.

The limitations of the analytical methods of social science should be placed alongside some of the more extravagant claims put forth by propagandists for the New Economics. The failure of economic policies of expansionism to find the solution to the job problem of young blacks surely has at least as much to do with social conflict in urban America as do the theoretical constructs of men such as Professors Ohlin and Cloward. How many young militants have read the learned works of Ohlin and Cloward? A few perhaps, but every black militant in the land has experienced the frustration of being ghettoized in a society which insists that it has full employment and freedom. In this basic sense, the alienated young black American is the victim of faulty analysis based upon an inadequate doctrine. Raising the interest rate may cool the economy but it will not pacify the militant, nor bring social justice to our city slums.

THE PRESIDENT AND SOCIAL REFORM

A President interested in leading the nation toward social reform will find it necessary, of course, to look beyond his own office for influential allies. He must seek to build a legislative majority to support a reform program, not any easy matter when Congress is led by a conservative bipartisan coalition, as it has been so often since 1938. Chapter Seven will suggest that there are certain groupings taking shape in Congress which promise an increased measure of support for social reform in the 1970s. Under the most hopeful circumstances, however, a reform-minded President has his legislative work cut out for him if he is to construct a solid Congressional majority.

There is another source of support within the structure of government for Presidential leadership aimed at reform: the technicians in the executive bureaucracy. Taken as a group, the civil service bureaucrats are probably more broadly representative of the changing American society than are the leading members of the conservative Coalition in Congress. The high-ranking civil servant's view of the world is likely to be relatively sophisticated. In any event, there are men in the executive bureaucracies in positions of influence who may wish to see progressive change in particular parts of the "system." The difficulty is that they may be anonymous to all but their closest associates. One of the reasons a President needs a talented staff of political assistants in the White House is precisely to help in locating these nearly anonymous technicians so that Presidential leadership may enlist their skills and their influence in the policy struggle. Some of them may even be among the Washington influentials of whom so much has been made in Neustadt's interpretation of Presidential power. Surely he is correct in stating that a President who would lead must carry them with him.

This is not to suggest that the President who wishes to prevail as policy leader will necessarily find the technicians an unmixed blessing. While the best among them know a good many mysterious and esoteric things, some of which may prove helpful in managing a complicated economy, they also have their own technical dogmas to which they are committed. (It goes without saying that they also are often tied to bureaucratic interests.) It is a rare technician who is prepared to question the presuppositions of his own occult art. The technical mind is often curiously unquestioning when it comes to the assumptions on which its own specialized knowledge is based. In certain situations, this all-too-human defect may mean that some of the hardest questions may not be sharpened for Presidential judgment. For example: why does full employment, as an operational concept, include chronic joblessness for thousands of Americans? Or: how effective is the application of military technology in containing revolutionary change?

Unfortunately, relatively little is yet known about the role technicians may be playing in the policy-making processes of modern government. The social scientist dedicated to interviewing the most obvious power brokers is probably destined to miss the strategically placed technician, unless the interviewer is extremely lucky or unusually perceptive. At the present time, one has to learn about the technicians as best one can. One of the principal sources is the written report of the participant-observer who has been sufficiently immersed in the procesps to be able to identify who has been influential in shaping a particular policy or program. Studies which are able to identify other than highly visible principal actors are exceedingly rare.

One example of the nearly anonymous technician as policy-shaper follows. There is no reason to suppose that similar cases could not be multiplied many times.[14]

MANPOWER TRAINING: STRUGGLE BETWEEN THE TECHNICIANS

The Kennedy administration decided early in its first year to seek support for a legislative proposal which would provide Federal funds to state and local authorities for training and retraining unemployed workers. Since Congress had initiated the original bill which finally became the Area Redevelopment Act of 1961, it was assumed that substantial legislative support for the training program could be organized. Senator Joseph Clark, Democrat of Pennsylvania, was prepared to provide leadership in the Senate. Another Pennsylvania Democrat, the late Representative Elmer Holland of Pittsburgh, was anxious to perform a similar role in the House. The story of the origins of the Manpower Development and Training Act of 1962 is complicated. It has been presented in rich detail in James L. Sundquist's book, *Politics and Policy*.[15] Mr. Sundquist is an appropriate person to capture the realism of the legislative struggle since he was a participant in it, having served for several years as Administrative Assistant to Senator Clark.

A special aspect of the story deserves emphasis here: two largely anonymous technicians played important roles in shaping the new piece of legislation destined to become the second major Kennedy program aimed at alleviating structural unemployment. One of these technicians was a career professional employed in the Bureau of the Budget. He was a permanent staff member of the Institutionalized Presidency. The other was a staff member with a Senate committee and was shortly to become special legislative assistant to the Secretary of Labor. Michael March was the BOB professional, Samuel V. Merrick the other staff assistant. Each man had strong views of his own concerning basic features of the proposed legislation. Each occupied a special vantage point in the policy-making process. Each had allies in the struggle to shape the new program.

Merrick's long experience in the Washington policy-influencing community included an earlier tour of duty as assistant to a member of the National Labor Relations Board. By the late 1950s he was a Capitol Hill staff man. Merrick served as chief counsel to a special Senate subcommittee chaired by Senator Eugene McCarthy and created in 1959 by Lyndon Johnson, the Senate majority leader, to undertake the first systematic Congressional assessment of the new persistent unemployment phenomenon. Merrick next served as professional staff assistant to the Senate Labor and Public Welfare Committee. This was his location in 1961 when the struggle to write the Manpower Training Act commenced. Merrick's experience on Capitol Hill had persuaded him of the necessity for compromise on tactical points, and he was mindful that the enactment of major new legislation usually requires support on both sides of the aisle. March, on the other hand, as a veteran career employee of the Bureau of the Budget, was far less sensitive to the stresses and strains of legislative politics and far more inclined to write a bill which would reflect the best professional thinking within the Executive Branch.

Merrick worked closely with legislative draftsmen in the United States Department of Labor, then under the new leadership of Secretary Arthur Goldberg. In addition to the support he could expect to find among northern Democratic representatives, Merrick soon discovered that certain Republican legislators had an interest in manpower training legislation. He decided further to adjust the proposal to accommodate the views of the powerful American Vocational Association, whose Washington spokesman, Mr. M. D. Mobley of Georgia, was reputed to be one of the most resourceful lobbyists in the nation's capital. What the AVA wanted principally was a bill which would insure that the training of unemployed workers take place within the existing public vocational education system with basic control remaining at the state level.

March had a significantly different view of the matter. His view, not uncommon at the higher levels of the Executive establishment, was that the vocational education system needed fundamental reform. Federal intervention was needed. March hoped to keep the new manpower training program as free as possible of entangling alliances with the vocational education establishment. His policy preference was for maximum utilization of on-the-job training programs within industry. It is a safe assumption that March had influential allies at the highest levels of the Bureau of the Budget.

In any event, the lines of the battle were soon drawn. Merrick with his allies in the Labor Department, on the Congressional committees, and Mr. Mobley shaped a draft bill *their* way. As soon as the draft reached the Bureau of the Budget where Mr. March was the reviewing officer for this particular proposal, the situation changed. The Bureau of the Budget rewrote the bill along lines indicated by March's preferences. Needless to say, the Bureau of the Budget version triumphed in the Executive branch. It was in this form that the manpower training bill was sent to Capitol Hill by the Kennedy administration. March had won the support of political assistants in the White House.

Once the bill had been formally introduced in the Congress, Merrick and Mobley were in a far more favorable position than March to shape the bill's final substance. The bipartisan coalition which enacted the Manpower Development and Training Act of 1962 was in no position, apparently, to thwart the will of the vocational educators. The new program was to be administered at the state level in a fashion which would not unduly disturb the existing vocational education system.

But March was not easily pushed aside, either. Nor was he

alone in seeking reform of the public system of vocational education over the longer haul. In the Johnson years which followed, two major bills were enacted, each aimed at bringing the lagging vocational education system more completely into the twentieth century. The full story of the legislative struggle to enact those bills has not yet been written. It is a fair assumption that Michael March, BOB professional, was on the alert to help shape the new legislation in accordance with the best thinking within the Bureau of the Budget. Policy persists (and changes) in part because key actors, not always visible, persist at it.

There are many Mike Marches and Sam Merricks in the Washington legislative community and more than a few group spokesmen such as M. D. Mobley. A President who seeks to construct a program of his own which will change basic institutions—such as vocational education—must carry many of these men with him. His task will be complicated by this hard fact: even the technicians are usually found on both sides of tough problems. The technicians themselves are part of the political process. This is true whether they are eminent, visible professionals at the higher reaches of the Presidential establishment or long-time, career staff technicians, not visible even to the attentive public but, nevertheless, with views of their own and with bureaucratic-political interests to advance and protect.

DIVERSE PATTERNS

Presidential leadership in policy-making is no simple matter. The patterns of such leadership, relating the Presidency to technical and professional advice, are bound to be complex. We have observed three different situations in this analysis. In effect, we have been examining three different levels of technical advice.

The process of gestation which produced the Manpower Training Act illustrates the policy-influencing role of the lone career technician with distinct policy preferences of his own. In this case, the Budget Bureau specialist needed the support of high-echelon officials in his agency, to whom he reported, in order to have his version accepted as the Budget Bureau's proposed bill.

The Budget Bureau is the oldest and the most prestigious Presidential staff agency with principal responsibility for putting together a President's legislative program. Michael March was not simply another career bureaucrat. He was a strategically placed specialist in an elite agency within the Institutionalized Presidency. His views on matters within his area of technical responsibility were potentially "Presidential," assuming they had the support of his agency superiors and, ultimately, the support of the political assistants in the White House. A President who embraced the cause of reform in the system of public vocational education had an ally in Mr. March. A Presidential legislative proposal bearing the imprint of March's thinking on the technical aspects of the subject was also bound to encounter strong resistance in the legislative arena where other forces were assembled to resist such views. In short, March's technical advice was loaded with political significance.

The appearance of Community Action as a vital new program in the center of a Presidential war on poverty illustrates the role of social theorists outside government who influence public policy through their relationship with agencies inside government. In the case of Community Action, Professors Ohlin and Cloward originally influenced the thinking of David Hackett, the executive director, and other staff members of the President's Committee on Juvenile Delinquency. The President's Committee, although located administratively in the Justice Department, was part of the Institutionalized Presidency. It was, after all, a Presidential committee; but, more important, the Committee functioned during the Kennedy era as a personal project closely related to the interests and activities of Robert Kennedy. At a later stage, as President Johnson's war on poverty was taking shape, Community Action gained the support of high officials in the Bureau of the Budget. In this fashion, program concepts which may be traced in part to socially concerned professors of social work came to form vital portions of Presidential reform legislation through the intervention of agencies within the Institutionalized Presidency. The President in proposing Community Action as part of his attack on poverty was taking on considerably more than a technical concept from modern social science. It is by no means clear that the political significance of Community Action was subject to critical examination by the White House at the time it first gained Presidential endorsement.

The third example, the role played by Walter Heller's Council of Economic Advisers in advancing a program of economic expansion, reveals still another pattern of relationship between the technicians and the contemporary President. This is not a case of a specialist in the Budget Bureau who must work through his superiors in the hierarchy nor that of social scientists outside government who gain a hearing for their pet concepts through influential government agencies and agents. The Council of Economic Advisers is a permanent agency of the Institutionalized Presidency. Its influence may vary from one President to the next, but no President, activist or otherwise, finds it possible to ignore the economic issues of industrial capitalism. The Council is armed with special analytical methods which are most useful when dealing with matters having to do with the management of aggregate demand. The CEA is institutionally and politically close to the center of Presidential attention much of the time. The relationship between professional advice and the Presidency in this case is a direct and continuing one in an aspect of public policy in which presumably it is relatively easy for Presidential leadership to prevail. The President having appointed the Council members either accepts or rejects the Council's advice, along with the advice of the Treasury and other sources he respects, and that is it.

Is it quite so simple? We know that Walter Heller set out to "educate" President Kennedy in modern economic analysis, and Sorenson has said that the President was a willing student. But was it only *economic* doctrine which Heller came to teach? Surely the whole "science" of modern economics is built upon certain value premises, among them the notion that growth in Gross National Product is a desirable thing. (It is undeniably a marvelously measurable thing, hence desirable for those who especially enjoy measuring.) This particular value premise is subject to some skepticism when we see how much a trillion-dollar GNP leaves that is undone and unlovely. Since there are economists who ask why the endless proliferation of "goods" is presumed good, there is reason to hope that policy advisers at the Presidential level will be encouraged to raise similar questions. Unless they do, the President is limited by the presuppositions he uncritically accepts. Just because Keynes felt that political leaders were destined to follow ideas whose time had passed, this does not preclude the possibility of creative and critical thinking in contemporary policy leadership.

What the President most needs is an immediate staff of political assistants, not comprised of the kind who ride herd on Capitol Hill but of men who have the technical sophistication and the intellectual capacity to apply rigorous *political* analysis to program proposals brought forth for Presidential endorsement. The President as the chief political activist in the White House must be alert to the possibility that technicians, professionals, senior civil servants, and, yes, professors, who come bearing conceptual gifts done up as program packages, are also political activists. They are activists seeking Presidential support for their ideas. The President will want to incorporate into his program those ideas he believes show some promise of serving the purposes he has in view. In the future even more than in the immediate past it seems probable that program ideas which are founded in social science will carry implications for effecting changes in society's institutions. The President should be the first to realize this if he is to help in guiding the process of change. The President who would lead the nation in meeting the immensely complex challenges of a technological society in the throes of rapid change must first find ways of evaluating the certitudes of the technicians.

If the Presidency is viewed as essentially an office of economic management rather than a center of political and moral leadership in the policy struggle, where are we to look for policy leadership?

CHAPTER FIVE

THE PERSISTENCE OF POLICY:
CONTAINMENT IN THE SIXTIES

*The determinism of which I speak
is the determinism of process or of procedure—
sometimes operating independent of ideas
and sometimes as an uncritical
projection of ideas.*
SENATOR EUGENE MCCARTHY *Harvard Commencement
Address* New York *Times,* June 11, 1969

POLICY TENDS to resist abrupt change. Policy, once made, tends to persist whether it is a policy having to do with welfare, Vietnam or the ABM. One should not expect to find great quantum leaps taking place in the formulation of public policies. Harry Truman launched the campaign in behalf of medical care for the aged. Lyndon Johnson and Wilbur Mills finally brought Medicare successfully through the Congressional labyrinth in 1965. Policy moves slowly step by step, stage by stage, committee by committee, budget by budget, Congress by Congress. Policy, it is said by the social scientists, moves in increments. Aaron Wildavsky,[1] who has made a pioneering study of the politics of budgeting at the Federal level, has stated it simply: "The largest determining factor of the size and content of this year's budget is last year's budget. Most of the budget is a product of previous decisions." Professor Charles Lindblom[2] of Yale, the principal academic student of incrementalism, explains the concept more broadly: "Usually—though not always—what is feasible politically is policy only incrementally, or marginally, different from existing policies. Drastically different policies fall beyond the pale."

A review of the setting in which Presidential policy leadership develops, the inertial force of the great Federal bureaucratic structures, and the entrenched bastions of Congressional baronial power, makes it a little easier to appreciate why policy does not easily depart from existing policies.

Professor Lindblom is also the creator of what might be called the "endless nibbling" theory as a means of illuminating the behavior of some of the principal actors in this kind of system. He observes that we Americans nibble endlessly at taxation, social security, national defense, conservation, foreign aid, and so forth. The ordinary assumption is that these basic problems are never "solved," and, hence, men who are in a position to influence policy-making "hold themselves in readiness to return to them again and again." Yet this kind of persistence in nibbling away at basic problems has transformed the society, Lindblom would argue. As he sees it, we have gone through one revolution after another in this fashion: the industrial revolution, the organizational revolution, an economic revolution (from laissez faire to regulation), a family revolution, and so forth. All of these impressive social changes have come about through "policy sequences so undramatic as to obscure the magnitude of change."[3]

As a means of demonstrating the persistence of policy, the theory of incrementalism has cogency. Policy-making does appear to be an endless process peculiarly subject to marginal changes. But policy also persists because men in key positions persist at it. These men have views of the world, their own images of society, views of themselves and of their special roles in the process which produces policy. Policy may persist not merely because "policy analysts" (a favorite Lindblomian concept) nibble away everlastingly, but also, because men in positions to influence the making of policy find themselves committed to certain policy positions, some of which may have become enormously bureaucratized positions. No one man can easily alter them. And then, too, there are ego involvements (this was almost surely a far-from-minor factor in the Vietnam decisions in 1964–67) which count—and may sometimes count heavily.

CONTAINMENT: A VIEW OF THE WORLD

The American involvement in Vietnam appears to be a classic example of incrementalism. Viewed superficially, a case can be built that President Johnson made two or three key, specific decisions in 1965 which effectively Americanized the war in Vietnam. But this is surely an oversimplification. The American dilemma in Southeast Asia represents the culmination of a policy—bipartisan and coalitional in nature—based upon a certain view of the world and of our role in it, a view which has been dominant since the end of World War II. The policy persisted through the Truman, Eisenhower, Kennedy and Johnson administrations. During this long period, the national security decision-making machinery operated within the limits of an official doctrine. Apparently, there was very little internal (i.e., within the Executive branch) dissent against the doctrine.[4]

If we ask ourselves what we have been doing as a world power since 1947, we shall find that we have spent an incredible amount of time and an incalculable amount of money and have sacrificed a good many lives, not all of them American, in pursuit of the doctrine. We have been busy, for three decades, containing communism. Since 1954 we have taken upon ourselves the major assignment of containing communism (or so we imagined) in Southeast Asia. Since the days of the Truman Doctrine, now more than two decades old, American national security policy has been in the hands of men who have had a view of an opposing world force called communism, which for a long time they *thought* was monolithic and which they believed was expansionistic, with a driving mission to dominate the world unless checked by a superior power. And that superior power, of course, was to be supplied by the new American technocratic empire.

We tend to forget, even those among us who reflect on these matters, that the Truman Doctrine was formulated more than twenty years ago in response to a special set of circumstances at the far end of the Mediterranean Sea, an area which had been a traditional sphere of British influence, much to the annoyance of Russia, for a large part of the previous century. Suddenly, one harsh winter day, the British realized they were broke. A decision had to be made. The British withdrew from Greece precipitously. The United States Department of State was caught napping. The Truman Doctrine was the result of hasty improvisation on our part. The American system not only nibbles away at its problems but is also capable, now and then, of acts of improvisation. In the process, we improvised our way into the philosophy of containment. We decided to contain monolithic communism, by which we meant Russian power (since Mao had not yet triumphed in China) in the eastern Mediterranean. Mr. George Kennan, the first head of the new Policy-Planning Staff which General Marshall was creating at the State Department, became the official philosopher of containment. So that the attentive public would better understand, an essay was prepared explaining the containment doctrine. The article signed by Mr. X appeared in *Foreign Affairs* Magazine.[5] We all soon learned who Mr. X was.

It is a curious fact which tells something about the American style that the Truman Doctrine, aimed specifically at Greece and Turkey, was expressed in sweeping, universal language. The rhetoric seemed to be saying that whenever a local regime *anywhere* felt itself threatened by a communist-led insurgency, it had only to call upon the rich United States and aid would be forthcoming. Now, twenty years later, Mr. Kennan is writing his memoirs and in them we learn that the containment doctrine, in his view, was limited to Europe; it was indeed a doctrine growing out of a special set of European-Mediterranean circumstances in 1947–48. Mr. Kennan personally opposed stating the Truman Doctrine in universal language. That Doctrine, as Kennan understood it, was never intended, and certainly it was not designed, to apply in Asia. This was his perception. And yet, it is obvious that containment has been applied in Asia; first in Korea in the days of Truman-Acheson, then in Vietnam after 1954.[6]

Mr. Kennan's view of the way in which containment gained

the status of "doctrine" is as curious as it is interesting. He notes that his Mr. X article was soon picked up and widely distributed through certain popular journals, most notably *Life* magazine and *Reader's Digest.* He adds this poignant observation.

> The term "containment" was picked up and elevated, by common agreement of the press, to the status of a "doctrine" which was then identified with the foreign policy of the administration. In this way there was established—before our eyes so to speak—one of those indestructible myths that are the bane of the historian.[7]

Mr. Kennan seems embarrassed by his part in creating the containment doctrine. The *Foreign Affairs* article, he insists, was written in an innocent and unsuspecting manner. One wonders why a sophisticated man, a career foreign service officer of considerable worldly experience, an advocate of policy-planning in foreign affairs, would have published the article unless he thought some one would read it and take it seriously. Perhaps Mr. Kennan intended the article *only* for the elite readership of *Foreign Affairs.* In any event, there was a Truman Doctrine. Its overt purpose was to contain Soviet power. Mr. Kennan wrote about the doctrine in lucid, almost philosophic, language. Twenty years later we learn that he is troubled by the way in which the doctrine was transformed into rigid orthodoxy. So are many of us.

Containment certainly owes a great deal to the support it received during the Secretaryship of John Foster Dulles. Mr. Dulles' devotion to it was single-minded. With it, he combined a deep sense of mission. In his own way, Mr. Dulles was as presbyterial and as Wilsonian as Woodrow Wilson. This time it was Vietnam which was made safe for democracy, and it is scarcely an exaggeration to say that Mr. Dulles was personally responsible for the United States' taking over the bankrupt French position in Indochina after the French military collapse in 1954. The French attempt to hang on to the remnants of empire in Asia (and Africa) was doomed to fail. Their position was untenable to begin with. In fact, at the end of World War

II the French did not have the physical capability of disarming the Japanese occupying troops in Indochina. The job was assigned to British and Nationalist Chinese forces. What the United States thought it was doing in Indochina, after the French had sensed the utter futility of their own anachronistic position, is quite impossible to imagine, unless we thought we were containing communism (Chinese, presumably). The fact that what we were facing in Indochina was not Chinese communism, but Ho Chi Minh leading an indigenous force as authentic in its own way as Tito's brand of communism, appears to have been totally lost on the makers of American policy at the time.

ANALYTICAL DEFECTS

Americans need to think hard and clearly about the view of the world and of the special American role in it which led to the nation's tragic involvement in Vietnam. Our economic interest in that country was slight. Yet the United States became the last western nation to use large-scale military force as a means of hanging on to the final remnants of empire in Asia. Does history hold a greater irony? The British were out. The Dutch were out. The French were out. And the Americans were in.

Before it was over, we had committed a military force of more than half a million American men to Vietnam. The cost of our "small" war exceeded $100 billion by the end of 1969. Heaven alone knows how many lives were taken, men, women and children. But we were determined to contain communism in Southeast Asia. One reads the official statements, and they always come back to this fundamental. To be sure, there was monumental unclarity—perhaps it was sheer intellectual confusion—as to whether it was Chinese, Russian or "monolithic" communism which was being contained. Any additional rhetoric about helping a brave little nation and so forth may be regarded as so much hogwash or, alternatively, as a messianic Dullesian delusion. Only slowly and painfully did we begin to sense the futility of this effort aimed at imposing a military solution on an enormously complicated political problem in Southeast Asia.

For a very long time, we simply managed to ignore the serious analytical-intellectual defects in the Truman-Acheson-Dulles-Rusk view of Asia, although these defects were known and understood by a number of ranking scholars of Asia, Fairbank and Reischauer among others. But the American cold-war reflex, conditioned by official views of events in Europe, contained a paranoic view of the world mission of expansionist communism. Perhaps the greatest tragedy of the Joe McCarthy period in the long run was that it effectively cut off the kind of policy dissent within government which conceivably might have illuminated these defects in our official view of Asia.

What were the defects in the official view of the United States role in world affairs? Two basic defects are clear. The official view had grossly overstated the monolithic nature of communism, so that even when the polycentric nature of the communist-led portions of the world became obvious, it remained virtually impossible for American policy makers to take advantage of the very real and substantial differences between Russian and Chinese foreign policy interests. The preliminary efforts of the Nixon administration in 1969–70 to explore these differences came as a striking innovation.

The second defect grew from an almost equally gross underestimation of the force of nationalism in Asia. American policy in Vietnam was based on assumptions drawn from the official doctrine. If Ho Chi Minh was a communist, and he was, then he must be serving as the Hanoi agent for Mao—or, alternatively, for the Kremlin. By minimizing Ho's lifelong career as a leader for national independence, official American thinking perpetuated the analytical error which made all of our subsequent calculations about our own military involvement in Vietnam miscalculations.

Why did American policy persist in misreading the will of North Vietnam to resist the application of our vastly superior military firepower? A recent review of the way in which we decided to Americanize the war in Vietnam, a review, incidentally, which looks at decisions inside the Institutionalized Presidency during a critical period, offers this crucial insight:

Either no one close to the President considered the implications of the graduated response should North Viet Nam and the Viet Cong refuse to yield, or American intelligence about North Viet Nam's capacity and will to resist was badly in error.[8]

Surely the point is that it was not simply our intelligence in the field which failed us but the limitations imposed by the stereotyped official view. Ho Chi Minh's effectiveness as a fighter for national independence was consistently underestimated because the doctrinists insisted on seeing him as an agent for an ideological-international expansionist movement. Professor Arnold Toynbee[9] summarized the resulting confusion in American thinking:

Because the Americans believe in this monolithic Communism, to them Ho Chi Minh is a Communist, and Mao is a Communist, and therefore Ho Chi Minh and Mao must be solid with each other, and must be one person, so to speak.

He then offered a less doctrinaire view of reality, a view which official American policy was not prepared to recognize: "But the truth is that Ho Chi Minh is a Vietnamese and Mao is a Chinese. The Vietnamese for two thousand years have been resisting being absorbed by the Chinese."

So American officials decided finally to take over the direct military responsibility for fighting Ho Chi Minh's forces without assessing the staying power of a regime under leadership which had resisted the Japanese and ousted the French.[10] The doctrine assumed that communism was to be contained by the application of superior military force. Ipso facto.

The policy-making process in the Pentagon, in the CIA, in the State Department, in the National Security staff in the White House, and in certain committees of Congress has been committed to the general view which we have briefly outlined. Such evidence as is available indicates that most of our official national-security thinking between 1947–69 took place within the limits which this view—containing serious distortions of reality—established.

Lyndon Johnson as President was responsible for taking the

specific steps which led to the Americanization of the war. They were incremental steps. We were nibbling away at the problem, as we misperceived it. The decisions were group decisions as Eugene Eidenberg discovered in extensive interviews with many of the key national security advisers in the former Johnson administration.[11] The President made the specific decisions to escalate, but his decisions were made because the line of decision coming to the President from his closest advisers worked within the limits established by the official doctrine. In order for President Johnson to have deescalated or to have withdrawn American support of the crumbling South Vietnam regime in 1964–65, he would have had to reject the virtually unanimous advice of his national-security advisory team. More than that, he would have had to abandon or alter the official doctrine of containment. The failure of the Institutionalized Presidency to seek an alternative to containment in the 1960s was a major intellectual, analytical and political failure. It was a failure of the policy-making process which did not pose an alternative. It was a failure on the part of the American people who supported the cold war policies. It was a failure of national leadership which never questioned this mythology, so much more pernicious than the economic mythology which President Kennedy questioned.[12]

SEEKING THE ALTERNATIVE

What was lacking in 1964–65 was an alternative to containment, as it had been practiced in Asia. We needed at the highest levels of the Executive branch a clearer view of the world and the role of America in it, a firmer sense of the limited capacity of American technology to set the world aright. A sense, that is, of the limits of power, a decent respect for the opinions of mankind, a lot more humility and a great deal more humanity. What was needed, one might suggest, was a *better* ideology.[13]

Professor James C. Thomson, Jr., an East Asian specialist who served in Washington from 1961–66 as a young professional within the national-security decision-making apparatus (where he was associated at one time or another with Chester

Bowles, Roger Hillsman, Walt Rostow, William Bundy and McGeorge Bundy), has written about those aspects of the process which make Vietnam, if not less tragic, at least a little more understandable. He has been helpful in identifying certain phenomena which affected the thinking and the behavior of the men who were key participants in national-security decisions during the 1960s: the sense of bureaucratic detachment, the role of executive fatigue, the curator mentality, the domestication of dissent. We need to know a great deal more than we now know about these aspects of the process as they affect decisions being made, but we also need to get at the *thinking* which goes into and comes out of the decision-making process. And here, Thomson[14] is most helpful as he states his concern about

> the rise of a new breed of American ideologue who see Vietnam as the ultimate test of their doctrine. I have in mind those men in Washington who have given a new life to the missionary impulse in American foreign relations: who believe that this nation, in this era, has received a three-fold endowment that can transform the world. As they see it, that endowment is composed of first, our unsurpassed military might; second, our clear technological supremacy; and, third, our allegedly invincible benevolence, our "altruism", our affluence, our lack of territorial aspirations. Together, it is argued, this three-fold endowment provides us with the opportunity and the obligation to ease the nations of the earth toward modernization and stability: toward a full-fledged PAX AMERICANA TECHNOCRATICA.

In this manner, James Thomson ably summarizes what I have been referring to as the official Washington "view of the world." It appears to have been a remarkably influential and persistent view these past twenty years or more.

A basic limitation of the theory of incrementalism as applied to national policy-making is that it does not leave as much room as it might for the views of key participants. In the case of something as global and as significant as foreign policy, it should be possible to discover what those views are. Indeed, they are apt to be stated openly, if unsystematically, in official propaganda.

Once the analysis shifts away from the global, life-and-death struggles of nuclear powers, it becomes far more difficult to assess the role of ideas in policy-making. Yet, even technicians and professionals, insulated though they may seem to be from the pressures of everyday politics, will be found to exhibit strong personal policy preferences which may affect the making of policy. Eidenberg's study reveals how strongly and sincerely William Bundy, for example, held certain policy views relative to Vietnam. Bundy was an influential figure, we may assume, during his earlier career at the higher levels of the CIA and the Defense Department *before* he gained a certain degree of public visibility as a State Department Assistant Secretary during the period of escalation. In an earlier chapter we met men in the higher echelons of the Bureau of the Budget who were anonymous so far as the general public was concerned, but their influence appears to have been decisive in mapping some of the more innovative and politically controversial features of President Johnson's war on poverty. And, at a lower level in the structure, our attention has been called to technicians who were responsible for incorporating the concept "maximum feasible participation" in the Economic Opportunity Act.

We need ways of finding out more about these influential, relatively unseen, actors. It may be that their role makes the process less deterministic than it sometimes appears, and it may raise havoc with a simplistic "power elite" theory. In any event, it is important that we should understand the key points at which such influence is effective in shaping our public policies, and who the men are who occupy these positions.

PPBS: A RATIONAL APPROACH

There is no reason to assume that only students of the process see the need for policy leadership based on sharpened alternatives. Practical men of affairs who must make decisions in government have a natural interest in seeing that their decisions are "rational." It seems almost inevitable, therefore, that those men at the highest levels of government who are at all sensitive to the problem as we have glimpsed it would seek new approaches to making policy-leadership more meaningful. Thus we come to one of the most interesting, most ballyhooed and least understood of the innovations to be credited to the Kennedy-Johnson era: the Program-Planning-Budgeting System (PPBS). PPBS was brought to Washington and installed in the Pentagon by that remarkable man, Robert McNamara, whose imposing presence as professional manager and superb technician reveals so many of the strengths and the weaknesses of the new technocracy. Mr. McNamara assumed office as Secretary of Defense determined to function as policy leader in national security matters. He came to Washington believing that his position as policy leader in vital questions of national security depended upon his ability, as manager of one of the world's most complex bureaucratic structures, to seize control of decision-making, especially those key decisions which lead to the choice of weapons systems. This is, after all, a large part of what the Defense Department is all about: the selection and development of increasingly sophisticated instruments of warfare. They happen also, of course, to be fantastically expensive weapons systems. In an age of swollen budgets and at a time when fundamental public purposes, national security and social security compete for priority position, and for the budget dollar, the manager who is able to relate costs to program effectiveness will be much sought after and admired.

Mr. McNamara's career in the industrial world indicated that he was such a manager. As the Secretary of Defense in the new Kennedy Administration, Mr. McNamara did something at least slightly ironic. He went to the RAND Corporation, the Air Force's special "think-tank," where a new breed of technician was busily experimenting with analytical techniques designed to measure the costs of weapons systems. McNamara hired away from RAND its very best systems analysts (as they were called) bringing their esoteric skills into his office where they were applied to bring the Air Force and the other military services under the centralized control of the new Secretary of Defense. Two key RAND specialists who joined McNamara in this heroic effort were Charles Hitch, who became the Comptroller of the Defense Department, and Alain Enthoven, the quintessential McNamara Whiz Kid who was soon to become an Assistant Secretary of Defense. What McNamara, Hitch and Enthoven brought to the Pentagon was a new system of decision-making called the Program-Planning-Budgeting-System. PPBS, the outgrowth of several years of pioneering work on the part of RAND professionals, was aimed at viewing program objectives in terms of costs and benefits so that comparative and rational judgments could be made by the decision-maker (in this case, the Secretary of Defense) between weapons system A and weapons system B. In a real sense, the installation of PPBS in the Pentagon represented an early triumph of the new professionalization in the field of public policy-making. In another sense, PPBS may also be seen as the instrument McNamara used to try to offset the inertial force of incrementalism. PPBS was McNamara's technique for asserting *his* leadership, a more centralized civilian leadership, and a more "rational" programmatic leadership.

Hitch and Enthoven have subsequently testified that PPBS was first applied to the Defense budget of 1963.[15] Presumably, it was applied to every succeeding Defense budget, at least through Fiscal Year 1970.

The arrival of PPBS as a new and, at least at first, glamorous approach to governmental decision-making coincided with the tendency to centralize further the process of decision-making within the Pentagon. It also coincided with a steady increase in Defense spending from an annual rate of $52 billion when Mr. McNamara took office to an annual rate approaching $80 billion when he left. PPBS also enjoyed its greatest influence, as it was used more and more in weapons-system analysis, at the same time the decisions were made to Americanize the war in Vietnam. PPBS was not used to make the specific decisions which led to the Americanizing of the war, but it was part of the mystique adding credibility to the myth that Secretary McNamara was gifted with some extraordinary quality of judgment. The truly bizarre fact is that President Johnson, who was never famous for halfway measures, imposed PPBS on the entire Administrative branch in August 1965, just as the decisions to escalate in Vietnam were beginning to take effect. In making the decision to universalize PPBS in Federal executive budget-making the Johnson administration apparently assumed that a system which was performing so well in Defense matters ought to be applied across the vast range of public policy. There is, as we have implied, a natural desire among the most conscientious public administrators to use the best techniques available in relating program choices to actual costs. On the other hand, Aaron Wildavsky, a leading student of Federal budgetary practices, was unable to discover any data which would show that PPBS had been evaluated for its effectiveness before it was spread across the broad spectrum of Federal program activity. There was skepticism among some experienced budget officers in the Departments who felt that the Johnson administration was waving a wizard's wand over matters not much given to magical solutions.[16]

THE DOUBLE STANDARD

In all of the extensive, and often controversial, literature which now surrounds the great PPBS debate, only Wildavsky, so far as I can see, has noted what seems to be a crucial point: that PPBS received star billing in the Pentagon at a time when Defense expenditures were sharply increasing. Secretary McNamara intended to control Defense costs, but military escalation in Vietnam greatly increased the costs of national defense and, at one point, came perilously close to sending those costs out of administrative control. On a purely common-sense basis, one would assume that any system of decision-making which attempts to link costs to program "benefits" will probably work better in areas where funds are fairly flexible; just as one might also suppose that the installation of a new budgetary system in a complex bureaucratic organization would perhaps prove troublesome in situations where the dollar constraints were tight.

Apparently, PPBS was installed in the Pentagon on a basis which has rarely, if ever, been provided for a Cabinet officer on the domestic side of government. In the Pentagon under McNamara's system, the process started with a review of strategy and (military) needs. Following this, a proposed program was developed to meet those needs *without regard to*

113

predetermined financial limits. Dr. Enthoven[17] made this clear in testimony before Senator Jackson's National Security subcommittee when he said:

> First and fundamental is the fact that since 1961, the Secretary of Defense has not operated with any predetermined budget ceiling. Rather, he judges each proposal on its merits, considering the need, the contribution of the proposal to increased military effectiveness, and its cost in national resources.

The point Enthoven wished to emphasize was that the systems approach McNamara used marked a significant improvement over previous Pentagon practices in choosing weapons systems. His argument was that prior to 1961 military planning by the Joint Chiefs of Staff was fiscally unrealistic in that military requirements tended to be stated in absolute terms by the various branches of the armed services without reference to their costs. The virtue of McNamara's approach to the Defense budget was that military needs were related to financial realities.[18]

We may assume that Secretary McNamara used PPBS to make choices with respect to weapons systems in a manner which represented an administrative and technical advance over previous practices. But in the larger perspectives of the total Executive budget, Defense was operating with a notable advantage over non-defense programs. In the major human welfare program areas no official had comparable authority to begin with an assessment of need which was then to be viewed in terms of the contribution each program might make to *national* effectiveness and without regard to predetermined financial limits. There was, and is, a double standard in making these assessments. The clearest and most notorious recent example is the Vietnam military escalation, in which fundamental decisions were taken as if costs were immaterial. The contrast between the funding of Vietnam and the war on poverty shows how basic this double standard is and how greatly national priorities are affected by the assumption that military power is the vital ingredient in national strength. In order to see the grave economic effects of this imbalance, we shall return to a more detailed analysis of several annual budgets in the next chapter.

The fact is the PPBS was developed originally to improve the making of decisions in which choices of weapons systems were involved. PPBS was designed to be used in selecting military hardware.* The cost of a missile system was to be balanced against the "benefits" it might provide in terms of increased military effectiveness. Mr. McNamara and his colleagues used PPBS, apparently with some degree of success (at least from their administrative point of view), in making assessments of comparative weapons systems. But Mr. McNamara did not himself use PPBS in all cases. He did not in fact use it for some of the decisions for which he is most famous. The decision to build the F-111 is an important case in which PPBS was not used. The broad decisions which led to the Americanization of the war in Vietnam go beyond questions of military hardware. PPBS was not involved.

In any event, PPBS came to Big Government in the decade of the 1960s because an unusually competent industrial manager, familiar with the new analytical and statistical techniques, saw a way of using PPBS as a means of helping him rationalize (and centralize) his own policy leadership, as Defense secretary, in the area of weapons-systems decision-making. Mr. McNamara was a manager who presumably knew how to use PPBS to his own advantage as Secretary. He also used the PPBS approach in a way which altered the nation's basic strategy. McNamara changed our military posture so that the United States would be capable of a flexible response to diverse military threats. The United States henceforth would have the capacity (the weapons systems) for deterrence of a rival nuclear power, and it would also have the means of fighting a

---

*It should be noted that PPBS will work best where cost data is firm. A General Accounting Office review of Defense Department records in 1969 found that 38 major weapons systems initially estimated to cost $42 billion when they gained Congressional approval were expected to cost $62.9 billion. The additional $20.9 billion was the result, according to the GAO, of cost growth overruns (a marvelous concept in itself) resulting from poor management and faulty estimating as well as an apparent Pentagon tendency to underestimate eventual costs.

more conventional war. It has not often been noted that the McNamara regime, in providing the means for the "flexible response" military posture, helped make military escalation in Vietnam possible. We were in Vietnam, both politically and militarily, before Mr. McNamara became Secretary of Defense, but the success of his methods in changing weapons systems and strategic concepts had a profound influence in making it seem feasible to transform the Vietnam effort from a limited special-forces kind of commitment to one in which primary military responsibility was assumed by American fighting forces. One wonders a little if the RAND-trained analysts were tempted to apply PPBS methodology to an analysis of whether the benefits of the Americanized war justified the costs.

PPBS was used by Mr. McNamara in important but limited ways. Hence, the Johnson administration's decision to universalize PPBS seems premature at best. Surely Wildavsky[19] is correct in suggesting that:

> Policy analysis is facilitated when (a) goals are easily specified, (b) a large margin of error is allowable, and (c) the costs of the contemplated policy makes large expenditures on analysis worthwhile. That part of defense policy dealing with choices among alternative weapon systems was ideally suited for policy analysis.

The reverse proposition would seem to be that in aspects of domestic policy dealing with the contentious issues of poverty, race and urban pathology—where goals are not easily specified, where issues are subject to passionate and noisy public dispute, where Congressional and public tolerance of "error" is slight, and where it is often difficult to get adequate funds for the substance of the program to say nothing of additional funds for analysis—the climate for PPBS may prove to be less auspicious.

Neither the Kennedy nor the Johnson administration challenged the assumptions of the containment doctrine which had persisted since the late 1940s. The policy which had been initiated originally with European problems in mind was gradually modified and expanded to include Asia in the 1950s. The official American world-view eventually perceived American technocratic-military power holding back Communism around the globe. By the end of the 1960s, in addition to Vietnam, the United States had accepted a defense "theory" (or sets of theories) which seemed to call for general-purpose forces to fight a NATO war, to resist a Red Chinese attack in Southeast Asia, and to handle a minor problem in the western hemisphere à la Dominican Republic.[20] Small wonder that the Nixon administration found it necessary to undertake a searching review of the nation's military commitments shortly after assuming office.

We entered the decade of the sixties needing an alternative to containment, but policy analysis in government did not provide it. The critique of American foreign policy based on analysis of the changing realities of world politics, rather than on the residues of a murky past, came largely from outside government. The most publicized procedural innovation relating to government decision-making was the installation of PPBS with reference to weapons-systems analysis, followed by the attempt to apply it to broader areas of public policy. In Defense, where PPBS originated, the methodology appears to have been used primarily in the selection of military hardware. But PPBS also appeared as part of a new managerial mystique which changed the nation's defense posture and in the process helped make the Americanization of the Vietnam war possible.

The failure of policy analysis in the higher levels of the Executive branch to engage the larger issues of policy and doctrine stemming from containment should be seen in a context that relates this to the Congress of the United States, which has a responsibility to examine thoroughly and critically the basic assumptions and concepts underlying the military budget, and has not done so. Congress' reluctance to use its inherent powers of review over Defense policy receives closer attention in Chapter Seven. But the policy-making process, for all of its inertial force, does not exist in a social vacuum. The United States faces the threat of a military-industrial complex in part because most Americans have been perfectly willing to buy anything labeled national security.[21] The silent majority has been conspicuously silent about the new militarism. The critique, such as it is, owes something to the unsilent minority.

CHAPTER SIX

THE BUDGET AND NATIONAL PRIORITIES

*Policy making . . . is what it is
because participants in the policy-making process
behave as they do. Men make policy;
it is not made for them.
They also make the policy-making machinery.
Much of what might be called the "irrationality"
of the policy-making system is, therefore,
the consequence of the irrationality of the participants in it.
It may be serious—even disastrous.
But it represents the quality of man's control
over policy making, not the absence of it.*
CHARLES E. LINDBLOM, *The Policy-Making Process (1968)*

NO ANALYSIS of modern governmental decision-making is complete until it faces the reality of budget-making. The annual budget reflects the powerful inertial force of the ongoing programs. The Federal budget contains the full force of incrementalism as it affects the making of public policy. At the same time, the budget, more than any other device, forces the making of program decisions. Incremental decision-making processes and the development of an expanding national budget as an instrument of economic policy are bound together in relationships which are both intricate and intimate. One feeds the other, and yet only rarely does anyone take the time and trouble to examine carefully the process by which so many national options are effectively closed. For purposes of clarity in illustration, and since the subject matter is familiar to all of us, this chapter will review briefly and chronologically the series of decisions by which the war in Vietnam was transformed into an American military operation; wherever possible, an attempt will be made to correlate these decisions, one by one, with their budgetary effects. The decisions relating to Vietnam which are of most interest here were made in 1965. Nevertheless, we shall go back to 1963 in order to trace the manner in which the Johnson Administration formulated—and changed —its budgetary thinking.[1]

Mr. Johnson came to the Presidency late in November 1963, precisely the time of year when the key budgetary issues for the coming fiscal year, which begins on July 1, make their way to the Presidential desk for final decision. The new budget and the President's annual budget message must go to Congress in late January. Under the circumstances of the transition in November-December 1963, the new President could expect to have only a limited freedom in asserting any new budgetary priorities of his own. President Johnson had at most only seven or eight weeks in which to "get inside" the budget he had inherited from his slain predecessor. The first Johnson budget was destined to appear largely as another Kennedy budget. Mr. Johnson retained Kennedy men at the top of the Bureau of the Budget structure as well as Walter Heller and the other Kennedy appointees on the Council of Economic Advisers. The importance of this fact is that Johnson inherited a budgetary and economic philosophy as well as a budget. The Kennedy administration had been committed to using the Federal budget as an instrument for promoting economic growth; and yet, oddly enough, the inheritance also included a strange mythology which made a fetish of holding a certain line on expenditures. Specifically, the pressure was great in behalf of holding the line of annual expenditures (in the administrative budget) below $100 billion. President Kennedy had been at pains to keep total expenditures below this magic line. One could imagine that the new President in office only a few weeks would not wish to establish himself immediately as the "spendingest" President in the history of peacetime America.

There was still another complication in the inheritance. The Kennedy Administration, following the advice of the Council

119

of Economic Advisers, had devoted a year of intense legislative activity to gain Congressional support for its massive, multibillion-dollar tax reduction proposal. This, also, was part of the strategy devised to increase the rate of economic growth. The tax reduction scheme was stalemated in the Senate Finance Committee whose chairman, the late Senator Harry Byrd, Sr., of Virginia, a leading figure in the conservative Coalition, was opposed to it.

There seemed little room in this complicated situation for the new President to maneuver. But the President had an imperative psychological and political need to establish his own leadership and, if possible, his own program. Lyndon Johnson, a man of vast Washington and Congressional experience, had at least the normal desire to be President in his own right. Besides, 1964 was a Presidential election year. If the President's tactical problem seemed complex, Mr. Johnson soon complicated it still further by declaring unconditional war on poverty in his first State of the Union message. Hence, a new, expensive program of social reform was about to be launched, although the support for such a program in a Congress dominated by the Coalition seemed dubious at a time when expenditures were to be held to an arbitrary limit and taxes were to be reduced. President Johnson was about to give the nation a war on poverty, a reduction in income taxes and economy in government. All in one budget.

LBJ'S EARLY BUDGETS: BEFORE VIETNAM

President Johnson's first budget, submitted to the Congress in January 1964, proposed expenditures totalling $97.9 billion, advocated over $1 billion of new obligational authority to begin an all-out attack on poverty, assumed the enactment of the tax reduction bill which the President estimated would reduce income tax liabilities by $11 billion, and continued military spending at a level of $54 billion. Vietnam was not a major budgetary factor since there were only about fourteen thousand American military personnel stationed there acting as advisers to the South Vietnamese army.[2]

The next budget which Lyndon Johnson sent to Congress,

January 1965, was presumably put in final shape in the weeks immediately following the President's epic landslide victory over Senator Goldwater. Hence, it seems safe to assume that by this time Mr. Johnson felt secure as President in his own right. He had his own program, the war against poverty. The Economic Opportunity Act had been signed into law in August. Congress appropriated $800 million for the initial attack on poverty in October just before the Presidential election. The massive tax reduction bill had also passed the Congress. In the field of foreign affairs, the President's position seemed equally imposing. On August 2, 1964, two United States naval vessels were allegedly attacked in the Gulf of Tonkin. Within a matter of days, both Houses of Congress had given almost unanimous support to the now famous Gulf of Tonkin resolution. The Senate vote was 88–2, the House vote 416–0, in favor of the resolution. The President presumably felt that he had Congressional support to do whatever seemed necessary to prevent the collapse of South Vietnam. Actually, the President's position in January 1965 was even stronger than this brief résumé suggests. The November election had given the Democrats a dominance over the executive and legislative branches unequaled since Franklin Roosevelt's second term following the 1936 landslide. Lyndon Johnson, who came to the Congress as a young admirer of Franklin Roosevelt just as the conservative Coalition was hardening in its opposition to the New Deal program of social reform, now faced one of those rare opportunities when a vigorous, activist President faces a Congressional majority large enough to outvote the Coalition. Nineteen sixty-five was destined to be a year of extraordinary legislative achievement.

If so, very little of this shone through the lines of the budget which went to Congress on January 25, 1965. Once again, overall expenditures as proposed in the Presidential budget were miraculously to be held below the sacrosanct $100 billion line. The figure which the Johnson administration used in its budget presentation, $99.7 billion, seemed close enough to win the cigar! If the precision of the projection seemed a little dubious, the whole budget was perhaps made slightly more credible by the new managerial controls which Secretary McNamara and his PPBS team were exerting over Defense spending, by far the largest item in the budget. Defense expenditures budgeted at $54 billion in Johnson's first budget were now to be lowered to $51.6 in Fiscal 1966. Once again, Vietnam was assumed not to be a major factor affecting the budget. The American special forces in Vietnam had grown to about twenty-five thousand men by this time, but for purposes of the annual budget there was no indication of any plans for a major expansion of the war. Within a month of the budget submission these plans were altered.

1965: YEAR OF INITIATIVE

As it turned out, 1965 proved to be Mr. Johnson's most momentous year as new initiatives of far-reaching significance were taken on both the home front and in the field of foreign affairs. In 1965 President Johnson was determined to serve as policy-leader. He was to be a strong President in the tradition of Wilson and FDR—especially FDR, his one-time mentor. And he had the Congressional majority to support a major domestic legislative program. Before the year was over Congress had enacted legislation which included Federal aid for elementary and secondary schools, Medicare (after a decade and a half of legislative stalemate, thanks to the Coalition), more money and new initiatives in the war on poverty, and the historic Voting Rights Act.[3]

In February, shortly after Congress had received the $99.7 billion budget, Mr. Johnson and his team of national security advisers, including Messrs. McNamara, Rusk, Rostow, and the two Bundys, decided to unleash American bombing power to coerce Hanoi and possibly to bring Ho Chi Minh to the bargaining table. The national security advisory group evidently understood what the February 1965 decisions meant. One of them later put it simply: "The war began in February 1965." If so, there is no evidence to show that the decision-makers made any serious estimate of the costs of bombing as a means of staying in Vietnam.[4]

In April 1965, the President sent United States Marines into the Dominican Republic.

In May 1965, the CIA's leading Vietnam authority reported to McGeorge Bundy at the White House that "the atmosphere of defeat in South Viet Nam is palpable. Unless there is a major increase in the size of the army in the field, there will be a complete military collapse in the South."[5]

By June 1965 President Johnson was facing the question of whether to pull out the approximately thirty-five thousand special forces troops or take the next steps which would Americanize the Vietnam war. Once more, there is no evidence showing that any White House-level calculations were made of the probable costs of staying in Vietnam by Americanizing the war. Ironically, this was approximately the time when the President decided to install PPBS, with its reliance on cost-benefit analysis, as a universal budgeting method to cover the entire range of Federal governmental program activity. If this seems odd, the explanation apparently is that the President and his special team of advisers in the Institutionalized Presidency made a series of group decisions to Americanize the war because they believed we had to stay in Vietnam, *no matter what the costs might be.* Such an approach to public-policy decisions would find little use for a nice calculation of costs and benefits. It is also noteworthy that such an approach is *never* employed when domestic purposes are at stake.

By the end of summer 1965 there were seventy-five thousand American troops in Vietnam, an increase of 300% in approximately six months. The time had arrived for a fundamental rethinking of the assumptions on which the budget had been submitted to Congress in January. William Bundy, whose role in Vietnam decision-making deserves to be studied more thoroughly than it appears to have been, has since said that by June 1965 "it was clear to all the President's senior advisers that we had to up the level of American troops. . . . This is the fork in the road when we came to another kind of commitment."[6] And so it was.

A COMMITMENT TO THE BLACKS

June 1965 was a busy month in the Johnson White House as a restless, activist President made still another commitment of incalculable significance. On June 4, President Johnson drove across the city to Howard University where he delivered a remarkable Commencement address pledging the majesty of the Presidential office to the cause of equality more firmly than any of his predecessors had dared to do. The Presidential address was packed with socioeconomic data about the plight of some ten million American blacks who were being sucked down in poverty's quicksand. The speech was drafted by two young technicians who were carryovers from the Kennedy era. Richard Goodwin, at the time the more visible of the two, had recently authored the Great Society concept. Daniel P. Moynihan, relatively anonymous up to this point in his Labor Department post, was about to gain unusual public attention as the man principally responsible for a government report entitled *The Negro Family.* It is impossible, even now, to read the President's Howard University address and *not* conclude that it intended to elevate the cause of the American Negro to a new level of official concern and action.[7]

If one were to ransack the past seeking particular months having exceptional historic impact, it may be that June 1965 would top the list in recent American history. Before June was over, the President of the United States started making the specific decisions, one by one, which escalated Vietnam into a major American military operation. Decisions were made inside the Institutionalized Presidency—and they appear to have been very much *group* decisions—to utilize hundreds of thousands of American fighting men, billions upon billions of dollars, and unlimited tons of American military hardware in an attempt to force Ho Chi Minh to the bargaining table. At almost the same time, other agencies and individuals within the Institutionalized Presidency encouraged the President to announce his intention of escalating the domestic campaign to win an equal status for millions of American black people. The budgetary implications of these two momentous lines of decision are obviously enormous. There is no evidence that the Johnson administration took any new budgetary action in the summer of 1965. Certainly, it said nothing to the Congress which would have required a fundamental rethinking of national priorities. The nightmarish truth is that the Johnson administration seemed totally unconcerned about the budgetary implications of its own powerful policy initiatives so forcefully taken, at home and abroad, in the middle months of 1965. These were the same months in which the Johnson administration decided to make cost-benefit analysis the basis for all Federal budgeting.

Of course, one can ignore the reality of the budget for only a relatively short time. Major new commitments place demands on resources—men, machines and dollars—which are limited.* The actual Federal expenditures in Fiscal Year 1966 exceeded $106 billion in contrast to the projected magical $99.7 billion figure which appeared in the budget. Defense expenditures projected as a $51.6 billion dollar item turned out in reality to be $54.2 billion. The planned reduction in Defense expenditures did not occur.

The really difficult budget decisions were yet to come. President Johnson's third budget (Fiscal Year 1967) was put in its final form in December 1965 and January 1966, some months after the basic decisions had been made to escalate the war and to push further the cause of equal treatment for black Americans. The budget for Fiscal Year 1967 is almost impossible to understand when viewed retrospectively, and it is almost equally impossible today to appreciate or to recapture the mood of budgetary optimism which pervaded official Washington in the closing weeks of 1965. It seems quite clear that the Council of Economic Advisers' wing of the Institutionalized Presidency was tragically out of touch with the thinking of the team of senior national security advisers. Edwin L. Dale, Jr.,[8] of the New York *Times,* whose reporting on the state of the national economy tended to reflect the prevailing atmosphere at the Council of Economic Advisers, published an article in November entitled "Uncle Sam's $50 Billion Surplus." The problem, it seemed, was how to devise public programs (presumably domestic programs) which would use the budgetary

---

*There are also limits, as Charles Schultze has since suggested, on the nation's psychic energies.

surplus which the new policy of economic growth, based upon the New Economics, was bound to produce in the course of the next few years. "It is now certain," Mr. Dale lyricized, "that, if we avoid a major depression, the Gross National Product in 1970 will be more than $850 billion, meaning we will have more than half as much growth in the next five years as in the three hundred years up to 1950." The problem worrying the economic myth-makers in this view was that a President might encounter difficulty finding ways of spending the growth-created budgetary surpluses. (The moral may be: don't spend your budgetary surpluses before they are created.) Presumably, the expansionist mood of the economic advisers encouraged the Johnson administration as the White House put the final touches on the budget for the coming fiscal year.

GUNS, BUTTER—AND BUST

The budget which the Johnson administration submitted to Congress in January 1966 was a marvelous concoction. Despite the rapidly escalating war in Vietnam—now Americanized to the extent of two hundred thousand men with the number increasing steadily each month—and following what was perhaps the most productive Congressional session in modern history, the White House proposed expenditures of nearly $113 billion (the $100 billion barrier had already been passed). This record level of expenditure was to be accomplished without any increase in income tax rates, and yet the projected deficit in the coming year was to be held to a mere $1.8 billion, the lowest projected deficit in seven years.

Surely a magician had been at work on this budget. The same administration which had found it possible two years earlier simultaneously to declare all-out war against poverty and to lower taxes had now discovered a way to fight a larger and larger American war in Southeast Asia, to continue the war on poverty, and to enact and fund a Great Society domestic program which included Medicare and Federal aid to education among other items—all without increasing income taxes and with the promise of producing the smallest budget deficit in nearly a decade. Seldom have we known this kind of policy

The Mini-and-Maxi Era

Copyright 1969 *by Herblock in The Washington Post*

leadership. The New Economics seemingly had given way to pop-art economics. Some new ingredient had been added to Federal budget-making.

Two principal factors were at work: a reliance on the growth of the national economy, and an unusually flexible attitude in the White House and at the top of the Bureau of the Budget toward budget gimmickry. Although President Johnson bears ultimate responsibility for the budget he submitted in January 1966, it is interesting to note that Charles Schultze, who had played a significant role as an Assistant Director of the Bureau of the Budget in shaping the Community Action portion of the war on poverty, had been promoted by Mr. Johnson to the Directorship of BOB. Mr. Schultze, a friend was reported to have said, "would sell the air rights over the White House if he had to."[9] So far as is known, the air rights were not sold in January 1966, but the cleverness of the budget technicians in projecting the tiny deficit bordered on magic. No one in the national press called the budget-makers on their manipulations. The general attitude of the national press seemed to be one of awe.

Hobart Rowen,[10] respected economic writer for the Washington *Post,* came as close as anyone to calling the play. And he put it rather gently: "President Johnson and his advisers, in struggling to bring in a non-inflationary budget, decided to have their cake and eat it, too." Having added $13 billion on the expenditure side, the Johnson budgeteers in the Institutionalized Presidency found it necessary to exercise considerable ingenuity in projecting revenues for the coming year. They managed to boost estimated tax revenues by about $10 billion without raising income tax rates.

The Johnson budget for Fiscal 1967 assumed that economic growth would generate an additional $7–8 billion of revenues. In addition, the budget-makers changed reporting procedures so that the paying of corporate income taxes was speeded up. This was to bring in another $3 billion. Cuts in the telephone and automobile excise taxes which had just gone into effect were to be rescinded, thus producing an additional $1 billion of revenue. Finally, procedures for reporting the withholding of personal income taxes were altered so as to produce an estimated additional $300 million in the next fiscal year. But there was to be no increase in income tax rates. All of this was supposed to bring about the smallest deficit in years. And well it might have, if the costs of Vietnam had not escalated beyond anything mentioned in the budget presentation. The revenue estimates proved substantially accurate. What the budgeteers failed to gauge accurately were the additional expenditures directly caused by Vietnam. Of course, the significant increase in the level of expenditure helped validate the revenue estimates.

The Johnson administration's utter lack of candor in presenting the budget to the Congress and to the nation helped feed a growing crisis in Presidential credibility. The January 1966 budget presentation estimated total expenditures of $112.8 billion with $58.3 billion going to Defense. Within eleven months, the cat was out of the bag. Edwin Dale, Jr., reported early in December 1966 that Federal expenditures were running at a level of $125 billion (not 112.8) with the costs of the Americanized war in Vietnam skyrocketing out of control.[11]

Toward the end of January 1967, as the Johnson administration was placing the final touches on the presentation of still another war-inflated budget, Dale revealed that Defense expenditures were running $10 billion higher than the January 1966 estimate. Dale's figures indicated an annual Defense expenditure in the vicinity of $68 billion. Dale also reported that the Council of Economic Advisers had been kept in the dark for several months by national security advisers about the sharp rise in Vietnam costs.[12]

At this point—late in December 1966 and early in January 1967—the Johnson administration faced a budgetary crisis. The multibillion dollar increase (above estimates) in the level of Defense spending which resulted from our military escalation in Vietnam had almost certainly muddled United States economic policy. One assumes that the advice which the Council of Economic Advisers gave the President was distorted if it was based on erroneous data about Federal expenditures. If so, the budget submitted to Congress in January 1967 represented a reasonably straightforward attempt to present expenditure projections which recognized the deepened involvement in Vietnam. By January 1967 the budgetary impact of Vietnam was too large to be denied or obscured. Hence, expenditures were projected to run at a level of $135 billion in Fiscal 1968 with Defense eating up $75 billion. After three years in office, the Johnson administration presented a budget in which its principal priority (and, in a sense, its obsession) was quite clear. By this time, the costs of Vietnam approximated $25 billion a year.

A ONE HUNDRED BILLION DOLLAR WAR

In January 1968, only a short time before he startled the nation by announcing his intention of retiring from office at the end of his term of office, President Johnson presented his final budget. Expenditures were projected at $147 billion. This time Defense outlays were projected with impressive precision at $79.789 billion, of which an estimated $25.7 billion was to be charged to Vietnam. Furthermore, in this final submission, the Johnson administration carefully estimated expenditures for special support of Vietnam operations in the five full fiscal years of the Johnson era. The figures are:

TABLE B

Special Vietnam Expenditures

Fiscal Year	Defense	Economic Assistance	Total
	(in millions of dollars)		
1965	103		103
1966	5,812	282	6,094
1967	20,133	424	20,557
1968	24,531	458	24,989
1969	25,784	480	26,264

Assuming a comparable rate of expenditure in Fiscal 1970 and assuming further that Vietnam expenditures in Fiscal 1970 were largely the result of Johnsonian policy, it is fair to say that the initial decisions to escalate in 1965 which led to the

Americanization of the war involved ultimate costs of $100 billion in one-half decade. It is inconceivable that analogous decisions could have taken place in nondefense matters with so little regard for costs, economic effects, and budgetary implications. The decisions of 1965 to stay in Vietnam, to shore up the Saigon regime, and to make the prosecution of the war an American military responsibility, were evidently entered into on an unstated assumption that our staying in was vital to our interests *regardless of costs.* *

President Johnson was in office only a short time when he assumed responsibility for submitting an annual budget in which the ongoing expenditure level approximated $98 billion annually. His predecessor, as Mr. Johnson very well knew, had experienced considerable difficulty in holding Federal expenditures below the $100 billion line. If Mr. Johnson wished to be an innovator in domestic policy, he would necessarily be forced to raise the level of expenditure. He seemed perfectly willing to do so—he gladly launched his famous war on poverty in his first State of the Union address—but, for tactical reasons, he wished to have it appear that his actions were consistent with practicing "economy in government." And so he turned off the lights in the White House.

When reporters asked where the money was coming from to finance the initial $1 billion attack on poverty, President Johnson replied that the savings being effected by Secretary McNamara in Defense spending would finance the new domestic program. This may have been a sufficiently plausible first answer, but by the next year, Mr. Johnson was driving ahead with a domestic legislative program of vast proportions. At this point—let us say, January 1965—only a remarkably optimistic view of economic growth would have supported the Johnsonian drive to outpace FDR as a domestic reform President. When, at the same time, the Johnson administration decided to assume an open-ended, the-costs-are-irrelevant approach to Vietnam, it was only a matter of time until even the mighty

*I am willing to broaden the concept to include "psychic" as well as "economic" costs.

American economic machine proved unequal to the combined task.

Our analysis of the impact of Vietnam on the Johnson budgets, accurate though I believe it to be, tends to obscure the other fascinating aspect of the Johnson regime: namely, that Mr. Johnson, while preaching economy in government, brought about an expansion of education, health and welfare programs without precedent in the history of the Presidency. Federal aid-to-education expenditures which had reached an annual level of $1.5 billion when LBJ entered the White House had increased to nearly $4.7 billion when he left. Health, Labor and Welfare outlays totalled about $28 billion in the final Kennedy budget. The comparable figure for Mr. Johnson's last budget was just under $52 billion.

Lyndon Johnson has commonly been judged a failure as President by his contemporaries. The fact that he virtually abdicated his position perhaps indicates that he may have partially shared this assessment. Yet history, long on perspective and capable of making finer distinctions, may come to rank him among the strong presidents for his impressive record of legislative accomplishment. He confused the public and obscured his domestic legislative triumphs by preaching economy in government while significantly expanding national programs in the fields of education, medical research and human welfare. By 1967, his domestic program seemed almost obliterated from view by the obsession with Vietnam.

If President Johnson is to be judged a failure, it will not be on the basis of a weakness of Executive drive. Johnson was the victor in one of our rare Presidential landslides. He was given a Congressional majority strong enough to support a full legislative program. He had such a program, and he pushed it through the Congress with extraordinary skill and zeal. Yet he enjoyed neither the confidence nor the trust of the American people. Perhaps Mr. Johnson misread the victory of 1964 and overreached. Whatever the explanation, he often seemed to have no sure sense of the limits of his power or of American power, and he may have tended, occasionally, to confuse the two, as well. If Johnson had a theory of Presidential power, it was not grounded in notions about protecting his own power stakes, à la Neustadt. To the contrary, President Johnson seemed to squander power. His willingness to commit the Presidency to the cause of equality in June 1965 was impressive and magnificent. But he did not keep the commitment. He was busy at the same time making other vast commitments in Southeast Asia. Before it was over the American involvement in Vietnam preoccupied the President, drained the energies of the men he relied upon for advice and sorely divided the nation.

Why did President Johnson allow himself to make the Howard University address almost at the moment he was facing ever-accelerating military commitments in Vietnam? Did he think it was possible to honor both commitments at the same time? In the same budget? Why?

Part of the answer may lie hidden in the mystery of Lyndon Johnson's unique personality, a mystery which was not lessened by his post-Presidential television interviews. Did President Johnson believe that he could accomplish what most political leaders would hardly dare to dream: the gradual elimination of poverty at home, the approximation of equality for all Americans and the establishment of peace as enforced by the American technocratic empire? Was his vision authentically heroic?

Our analysis stops short of psychoanalysis. We have no way of knowing what Mr. Johnson's Presidential vision may have been, although some of us may be skeptical of his retrospective view that he did not feel up to the job. This analysis is interested in what the Johnson era can tell us about the nature of policy leadership. We do have some evidence, fragmentary though it may be, about Mr. Johnson as policy leader and about the nature of the advice he received from agencies in the Institutionalized Presidency. The performance record at this level seems far more human than heroic.

This analysis suggests that the President necessarily relied greatly on technical advice coming to him from such key White House staff agencies as the national security advisory group, the Council of Economic Advisers, and the Bureau of the Budget. The President's national security advisory team, a group of exceptionally competent and conscientious men, certainly encouraged him to take the steps which effectively Americanized the war in Vietnam. An alternative to this policy was not thought through and successfully pressed at the Presidential level until shortly after Mr. Clifford took office as Secretary of Defense in 1968. By then there were half a million American troops in Vietnam and annual costs were running close to $30 billion.* It is doubtful that the Johnson administration attempted a calculation of the probable costs of this hazardous and expensive undertaking when the fateful decisions to escalate the war were taken.

Budget Bureau professionals who ought to respect the integrity of the budgetary process, if anyone should, appear to have exercised unusual ingenuity in helping the President put together his "guns and butter" budget of January 1966 with its suspiciously small deficit. No doubt the President was pleased to have such clever technicians in his corner, but the Johnson administration's budget performance contributed more than has generally been recognized to the credibility gap which later led to the President's retirement.

The Council of Economic Advisers, devotees of pure scientism, generated an official optimism about future growth in the course of 1965 which did nothing to restrain the President's natural expansionist bias.

The national security establishment was less than zealous in getting the facts concerning the rising costs of Vietnam to the Council of Economic Advisers at a time when hard judgments about future taxation might have been made.

In short, Mr. Johnson's "failure" was not all personal any more than it was all failure. Utilizing his rich background of political experience and applying his special talents as a legislative leader, President Johnson, more than any other man, was

---

*I am aware that Mr. George Ball came to play the role of in-house skeptic, but the limits of this form of domesticated dissent have been shown by James Thomson—and by the fact that the dissent was ineffective. Further confirmation comes from some members of Johnson's team of advisers who repudiated the policy *after* they had left office.

responsible for the enactment of a backlog of domestic legislation which had been building up for two decades. His record of accomplishment in this area was one of phenomenal success, not failure. The failure of the Johnson administration is found largely in the area of foreign affairs. A case can be made that the decisions taken in 1965 to prevent the collapse of the Saigon regime were "rational" decisions within the context of the containment dogma. It was the failure of the national leadership (and the Congress and the attentive public) to question the dogma *as applied in Vietnam* which led to a disproportionate allocation of resources to the war. The war distorted national priorities as it blunted the drive toward social justice at home, and in doing so, it deeply divided the American people.

Our analysis of policy-making, as we have seen the process at work as reflected in the annual budgets, suggests that while the process moves incrementally, it is not impervious to policy leadership. President Johnson's difficulty was not that he could not move the process in the directions he wished to, but that he was moving in several directions at one time. The "process" did not fashion the war on poverty and then turn away from it. The "process" did not pledge the President to the cause of equality in June 1965 nor did the "process" Americanize the war in Vietnam. For all we know, the "process," in the absence of Presidential leadership, might have witnessed the collapse of the Saigon regime. Lindblom, the father of incrementalism, is dead right when he tells us that policy-making is what it is because the participants in the policy-making process behave as they do. Our task, which we find is not a simple one, is to discover, if we can, more about who the key participants are and why they behave as they do. *How* we make policy helps to determine *what* the policy is, as we suspected. And *how* we make policy is dependent in part upon *who* the policy-makers are (some of them are professionals and technicians) and *what they perceive their roles to be.*

CHAPTER SEVEN

THE MILITARY-CONGRESSIONAL
COMPLEX: IS THERE AN ALTERNATIVE?

*Congress can, if proper information is available
and the proper institutional framework created,
critically but responsibly examine and debate
all of the basic assumptions and concepts
which underlie the military budget.
And it can do so in the context of comparing priorities.*
CHARLES L. SCHULTZE, *June 3, 1969.*

No one is likely to insist that the decade of the sixties found
the solutions to the nation's most difficult and perplexing problems. Many Americans have been "turned off" to the political
process. A sense of alienation, anguish, even, in some cases,
despair marks the common mood among the idealistic and the
young—especially the young. But the decade did not start out
this way. No one—well, almost no one—insisted in 1961 that
our basic institutions could not be made to serve the higher
purposes of American society. The challenge of the Kennedy
Inaugural went directly to a new generation, asking what each
of us could do for his country rather than for himself.

It would be a serious error to assume that the nation accomplished nothing in the 1960s; it would be a greater mistake to
believe that we learned very little in the last decade. We
learned a great deal that we had not previously understood
about economic growth and about its limitations as a solution
to the ills which beset us. The fact that we finally found a way
to bring medical care to many of the elderly through the existing machinery of Social Security is not to be regarded as a

minor matter. For a few moments we found ourselves encouraged by a Chief Executive who felt bold enough to take on the hitherto unthinkable task of eliminating poverty in this rich and restless land. Let it also be noted that the same President seemed more willing than any of his predecessors to face up to responsibility of making available to all Americans, black as well as white, the opportunity of participating meaningfully in the abundance of this great technocratic empire. The point is made here briefly to serve as a reminder that the present mood, which despairs of effecting constructive change, did not obtain throughout the 1960s. It did not begin when Lyndon Johnson assumed the responsibilities of the Presidency. The mood did not set in until *after* the Americanization of the war in Vietnam.

The war in Vietnam touches so many nerve points. Vietnam or all of its horror has demonstrated military technology's limits in solving deeply-rooted social-economic-political-cultural problems. Vietnam also has driven finally into the popular consciousness an initial, tentative awareness that we have indeed let grow up in the center of American society a military-industrial establishment possessing an inertial force of its own. The military force may not be quite out of control, but if we are able to check it, it will have been none too soon. Given the ancient American instinctive bias against concentrated power, and recognizing the equally authentic American tendency to seize upon instantaneous "solutions" to the most complicated problems, there is now some danger that we may, in our haste, perceive only the most superficial aspects of the problem.

We do have a military-industrial complex of vast size and unprecedented power. Of this there no longer seems any real doubt, and Vietnam has done much of the convincing. Annual military expenditures which were being held close to $50 billion as recently as 1963 threatened to go above $80 billion as the 1960s ended, thanks again to Vietnam. We were shocked to learn that if our involvement in Vietnam were terminated or even lessened, the Pentagon has anticipated us and has devised a rationale for using more than $80 billions annually *without* a Vietnam. This message came through quite clearly after the new Nixon administration arrived in Washington.

As the debate over the military-industrial complex becomes an increasingly popular issue, the common tendency is to equate Pentagon power with men in uniform. Popular discussion of complex matters invariably inclines to the use of slogans, symbols, and "shorthand." In this fashion, the military-industrial complex tends to be spoken of simply as "The Pentagon," which is, after all, only a building. "The Pentagon" in turn is easily transformed into "The Military." Reality, of course, is far more complicated than this. The military chieftains, generals, and admirals, are key participants in the group decision-making processes of the military-industrial complex, and so also are the men who manage and control the vast industrial organizations, so-called "private" corporations which build the military hardware. The newer of these giant corporations actually serve no real purpose other than this. Even the most simplified and popularized analysis of the military establishment will not fail to note the presence of the military chieftains and the new corporate managers. What the popular discussion seems most likely to overlook happens, unfortunately, to be of central importance. Professor Galbraith[1] describes the problem as "one of uncontrolled bureaucratic power, which in the manner of all bureaucracies, governs in its own interest and in accordance with its own parochial view not only of that interest, but of the world."

Once again, we are about to encounter a group of key participants in policy-making who are influenced in the way they perform by a special view of the world. Professor Galbraith finds this view "parochial." Who are the men who staff the military bureaucracy and wield this bureaucratic power?

THE CIVILIAN MILITANTS

What we are in danger of missing as the popular debate in the halls of Congress and in the mass media swirls around the specifics of the ABM controversy or the MIRV is that it has not been the uniformed military chieftains *alone* who have sponsored the new militarism. There is a new breed of civilian militants, creatures in part of the cold war and of the new technology, who figure prominently in national-security decision-making. We should be clear in thinking about this. The civilian militants in the Department of Defense, in the Institutionalized Presidency, and as we shall note later in this chapter, in the Congress, played a vital role in taking us down the road to the computerized, body-count tactics of Vietnam and to the crisis point where military demands outweigh other national priorities. Earlier, we traced briefly the process by which Secretary McNamara, assisted by Charles Hitch, Alain Enthoven, et al., used the techniques of systems analysis, and in doing so, strengthened the centralization of weapons-systems decision-making in the Executive branch. The McNamara managerial revolution in the Pentagon represented the triumph, at least temporarily, of the civilian leadership over the uniformed leadership in the huge Defense establishment.[2] There is no evidence that McNamara's victory represented a diminution of the power and glory of the military-industrial complex. The total McNamara experience, in fact, included a sizeable expansion of the Defense establishment.

It would be wrong to place all of the responsibility at Robert McNamara's door. The civilian militants played a dominant role in national-security decisions before McNamara became Secretary of Defense, as Professor Samuel Huntington has shown us. McNamara looms large in this picture because his apologists gave him at least as much credit as he deserved, and no one should doubt that his personal contribution to a more effective central management of the Defense establishment was extraordinary. The reason McNamara's role is stressed as much as it is in the analysis in this book stems from a wholly different point. The usual assumption has been that McNamara's managerial accomplishment was not only large but also benign in its impact. Since McNamara was a "good" man, the results were assumed also to have been "good." This commonly held view, which is eminently fair to McNamara the man, misses the essential point that, in reorganizing the permanent warfare machine, Secretary McNamara made it a *more effective* war machine than it had been. The McNamara managerial reforms presumably had an effect in encouraging the President to think that it was possible to engage the nation militarily in Southeast Asia at the same time we continued expending vast sums on nuclear deterrence. Both tasks may have seemed feasible in part because a brilliant manager happened to be in "control" of the Pentagon. Isn't this what McNamara's theory of flexible response was all about?

A DIFFERENT GROUP

After McNamara had left the Pentagon, and as the cumulative costs of the war in Vietnam approached $100 billion, a new spirit of critical inquiry appeared in the Congress among men not identified with the conservative Coalition. Senator Proxmire, one of this new breed and one of the few with sufficient seniority to head a committee, undertook an inquiry which revealed, among other things, the terribly important fact that the huge Defense budget, $80 billion worth, was not subject to the kind of critical review by the Bureau of Budget which has long been considered normal and appropriate for agencies and departments dealing with domestic programs. In the case of Defense spending as we noted earlier, the customary budgetary procedures were reversed, thus weakening the independent review. In the Federal agencies having responsibility for health, education, manpower and welfare programs, budget examiners from the Bureau of the Budget review critically and independently all Departmental budget requests. This reviewing process culminates in the office of the Director of BOB, a Presidential appointee; hence, the Bureau of the Budget makes the ultimate recommendation to the President concerning each domestic agency's budget for the coming year. The Cabinet officer on the domestic side of Government who finds himself at odds with the Budget Bureau's recommendations also finds that the burden of proof is upon him in any appeal he may wish to make to the President, the final budget authority.

Senator Proxmire's inquiry uncovered a totally different relationship between the Department of Defense and the Budget Bureau. BOB examiners worked alongside the budget officers in the Defense Department. They were not free to make the customary independent reviews of departmental estimates. The Defense budget went directly from the Secretary of Defense to the President. The Director of the Bureau of the Budget, rather than making the budget recommendations for Defense spending to the President, found himself in the position of appealing to the President against Secretary McNamara's recommendations if he wished to effect any changes in the budget as formulated in the Department of Defense.

Philip S. Hughes,[3] the deputy director of the Budget Bureau and a senior career employee of this elite Presidential staff agency, offered the following explanation to Senator Proxmire's subcommittee:

> The most relevant consideration is, in blunt terms, sheer power —where the muscle is—and this is a very power-conscious town, and the Secretary of Defense, and the defense establishment are a different group to deal with, whether the Congress is dealing with them or whether the Budget Bureau is dealing with them.

Mr. Hughes had been an influential technocrat within the Institutionalized Presidency long enough to realize that his "real political" views of Washington as a power-conscious town would be understood by the members of the subcommittee. In his own deft way Hughes seemed to be reminding the Proxmire committee that the Congress also employs a different standard when it deals with the Defense establishment. Unfortunately, it is precisely the Congressional role in the military-industrial complex which is most likely to be overlooked in the popular discussion. If Congress had not long since abdicated its responsibility as evaluator of defense policy-making, we might not be facing the specter of a military state.

THE COALITION AND DEFENSE

Thus our analysis returns to a familiar phenomenon, the conservative Congressional Coalition, this time as it relates to Defense policy. The Congressional Coalition apparently considers Defense important to its interests since it has gone to some trouble to dominate the committees responsible for Defense matters. The four committees which oversee military programs are the Armed Services and the Appropriations Committees of both Houses of Congress. Most Congressmen consider membership on either Appropriations or Armed Services a choice assignment. Such an assignment is thought to bring prestige within the Congress. No small point. Seymour Hersh[4], a critical observer of the Pentagon, notes also that membership on these committees is commonly assumed to be an important factor in influencing the location of defense facilities. In any event, Hersh reported in April 1969 that the six ranking Democrats on the House Armed Services Committee had forty-three military bases and plants in their districts.* It is a tired joke in Washington, hopefully repeated here for the last time, that if one more defense facility is located in Georgia, Senator Richard Russell's home, the entire state faces the imminent danger of sinking into the Atlantic ocean.

President Johnson, no newcomer to the reality of this aspect of Congressional power, traveled to Marietta, Georgia, in 1968 for the unveiling of the since rather infamously expensive C-5A Galaxy cargo plane. The ceremony took place at a Lockheed plant located in the city. The President spoke knowingly of the social benefits of this kind of Federal expenditure which evidently does not shock Southern conservative sensitivities. "I would like to have you good folks of Georgia know that there are a lot of Marietta, Georgias scattered throughout our fifty states," the President told the crowd. "All of them would like to have the pride that comes from this production. But all of them don't have the Georgia delegation."[5]

Indeed, they do not. And none of them, except Georgia, has Senator Richard Brevard Russell of Winder, the man principally responsible for making Lyndon Johnson the Majority Leader of the Senate. Senator Russell served for many years as the chairman of the Senate Armed Services Committee before succeeding Carl Hayden as chairman of the Senate Appropria-

*Rep. Mendel Rivers of South Carolina, Chairman of the House Committee, has an especially diverse and generous assortment of Defense facilities located in his home district, as Hersh has shown.

What Do You Expect for a Lousy Ten or Twelve Billion Bucks?'

Copyright 1970 *by Herblock in The Washington Post*

LARGEST MILITARY CONTRACTORS GAIN FROM 2% TO 96% OF TOTAL BUSINESS FROM DEFENSE CONTRACTS

The following table lists the 38 U.S. companies that were awarded prime military contracts totaling in excess of $1 billion during the fiscal years 1961–1967. In the column at far right, the cumulative totals for the seven-year period are expressed as percentages of the companies' total business. Amounts are in millions of dollars.

	Fiscal Year	1961	1962	1963	1964	1965	1966	1967	7-Year Total	Percent of Total Sales
1.	Lockheed Aircraft	$1,175	$1,419	$1,517	$1,455	$1,715	$1,531	$1,807	$10,619	88%
2.	General Dynamics	1,460	1,197	1,033	987	1,179	1,136	1,832	8,824	67
3.	McDonnell Douglas	527	779	863	1,360	1,026	1,001	2,125	7,681	75
4.	Boeing Co.	920	1,133	1,356	1,365	583	914	912	7,183	54
5.	General Electric	875	976	1,021	893	824	1,187	1,290	7,066	19
6.	North American-Rockwell	1,197	1,032	1,062	1,019	746	520	689	6,265	57
7.	United Aircraft	625	663	530	625	632	1,139	1,097	5,311	57
8.	American Tel. & Tel.	551	468	579	636	588	672	673	4,167	9
9.	Martin-Marietta	692	803	767	476	316	338	290	3,682	62
10.	Sperry-Rand	408	466	466	374	318	427	484	2,923	35
11.	General Motors	282	449	444	256	254	508	625	2,818	2
12.	Grumman Aircraft	238	304	390	396	353	323	488	2,492	67
13.	General Tire	290	366	425	364	302	327	273	2,347	37
14.	Raytheon	305	407	295	253	293	368	403	2,324	55
15.	AVCO	251	323	253	279	234	506	449	2,295	75
16.	Hughes	331	234	312	289	278	337	419	2,200	u

17. Westinghouse Electric	308	246	323	237	261	349	453	2,177	13
18. Ford (Philco)	200	269	228	211	312	440	404	2,064	3
19. RCA	392	340	329	234	214	242	268	2,019	16
20. Bendix	269	286	290	257	235	282	296	1,915	42
21. Textron	66	117	151	216	196	555	497	1,798	36
22. Ling-Temco-Vought	47	133	206	247	265	311	535	1,744	70
23. Internat. Tel. & Tel.	202	244	266	256	207	220	255	1,650	19
24. I.B.M.	330	155	203	332	186	182	195	1,583	7
25. Raymond International*	46	61	84	196	71	548	462	1,568	u
26. Newport News Shipbuilding	290	185	221	400	185	51	188	1,520	90+
27. Northrop	156	152	223	165	256	276	306	1,434	61
28. Thiokol	210	178	239	254	136	111	173	1,301	96
29. Standard Oil of N.J.	168	180	155	161	164	214	235	1,277	2
30. Kaiser Industries	–	87	49	152	219	441	306	1,255	45
31. Honeywell	86	127	170	107	82	251	306	1,129	24
32. General Tel.	61	116	162	229	232	196	138	1,124	25
33. Collins Radio	94	150	144	129	141	245	202	1,105	65
34. Chrysler	158	181	186	170	81	150	165	1,091	4
35. Litton	–	88	198	210	190	219	180	1,085	25
36. Pan. Am. World Air.	127	147	155	164	158	170	115	1,046	44
37. F.M.C.	88	160	199	141	124	163	170	1,045	21
38. Hercules	117	182	183	137	101	120	195	1,035	31

u-unavailable
*Includes Morrison-Knudsen, Brown & Root, and J.A. Jones Construction Co.

SOURCE: Dr. Ralph E. Lapp, *The Weapons Culture* (W. W. Norton, 1968). p. 186-187

tions committee. When Senator Russell switched from one key committee to the other, the way was open for John Stennis of Mississippi to advance the final rung on the seniority ladder to the chairmanship of the Armed Services Committee.*

Senators Russell of Georgia and Stennis of Mississippi are joined by Representatives L. Mendel Rivers of South Carolina and George H. Mahon of Texas in chairing Armed Services and Appropriations. The four Coalition leaders score higher, as a group, in opposing liberal domestic legislation than do most Republicans in Congress.** In brief, the failure of Congress to come to grips with the accelerating growth of the new militarism is primarily a function of the Congressional seniority system and its insidious connection with those areas where political competition has been virtually nonexistent.

It is a notorious fact among close students of Defense policy that the four basic Congressional committees holding the power to subject military plans, programs, and budgets to critical analysis and review do no such thing. Lewis Anthony Dexter,[6] to whom we are indebted for a number of penetrating insights into the mysteries of Congressional political behavior, undertook an intensive study of the Armed Services committees in the 1955–57 period. Mr. Dexter found the committee members almost completely uninterested in military *policy* as such. In the words of an influential committee member, as reported by Dexter: "We mostly reflect what the military people recommend; military policy is made by DOD." One notes that this view predates the arrival of Robert McNamara on the Washington scene.***

---

*Litton Industries, one of the "hot properties" in the expanding military-industrial complex, is building an ultra-modern $130 million shipyard financed and owned by the state of Mississippi but leased to the company. Obviously, only Federal Government contracts or subsidies can sustain this yard. This is "economic growth," Southern variety, not as taught at Harvard but as practiced with skill by the Senate oligarchs. Litton seems to have sensed that Senator Stennis is part of the complex.
**The Democratic Study Group published a study in 1969 which made this point clear.
***The point is sometimes made that Congress has failed to come to grips with the accelerated growth of the new militarism because it lacks the capacity to get the information necessary to mount the challenge. I do not for a moment

Senator Edward Kennedy provoked a major debate in the Senate after the Defense Department had decided to place ABM missile sites near cities (a decision subsequently modified by the Nixon administration, which found sites in Montana and North Dakota less provocative than those in suburbia). While urging his colleagues to sharpen their critique of military policy, Senator Kennedy observed that "national defense programs have somehow been above the battle; it has always been implicit in many of our debates that it is perhaps unpatriotic to question the recommendations of the Department of Defense."[7]

A REAL ESTATE COMMITTEE

Actually, as Dexter discovered, the problem goes deeper than the patriotic reflexes of the Congressmen. The basic difficulty arises from a Congressional role perception. The Coalitionists who dominate the Armed Services committees have defined their role, and they define it as a *non-policy-oriented* role. The limitation on Congress as critic of the military is self-imposed. Little wonder we have experienced a weak Congressional check on the military bureaucracy. It is not that Congress lacks the power to check the military. The Congressional power of the purse has an enormous potential for control. Congress may investigate anything it wishes to investigate. But Congress has been dominated for three decades by a Coalition leadership group with little interest in undertaking a critical analysis of national security policies. A member of one of the Armed Services committees summarized the prevailing attitude for Dexter when he said: "Our committee is a real estate committee."[8]

doubt that there is an information gap between Congress and the Defense Department. But this gap is as serious as it is because the appropriate committees are dominated by men who are not greatly concerned to close the gap. Actually, Richard Russell would experience no difficulty in getting any information he wanted from the Pentagon. He has "access" if anyone does. The Armed Services committees, unfortunately, are locked into the Defense Department, and are not much inclined to be critical. It is, in any case, vitally important that Congress prepare itself technically to engage the Pentagon in serious intellectual combat.

Consider the role of Senator Richard Russell as a shaper of military policy. Senator Russell is an able legislator and a man of great personal integrity who has been in public service all of his adult life. It is almost literally true that he has no other life. He has been a senator for more than thirty years and a leading figure in the Senate since the end of the Second World War. Some observers rate Richard Russell as the single most influential man in the Senate. His special field of interest and competence in a body which respects specialization has long been military affairs. Senator Russell is, in short, an able, powerful, widely respected legislator in an unusually strong position to influence the making of national defense policy. Furthermore, he has, on more than one occasion, publicly stated his belief that the Americanization of the war in Vietnam was a classic mistake. Yet as chairman of the Armed Services Committee Russell used his committee not once to enlighten the American public by a thorough questioning of the basis for our involvement in Vietnam. The real questioning, when it came—and it came none too soon—emanated from Senator Fulbright and his colleagues on the Foreign Relations Committee.

There is not the slightest chance that Senator Russell will use his strategic position in the Senate as a means of exercising an effective control on the military-industrial complex. And for a very good reason. Senator Russell has become as much a part of the military-industrial complex as the Chairman of the Joint Chiefs of Staff or the Chairman of the Board of General Dynamics. The Senator has had a special vantage point, shared by no other American, from which to observe the nightmare of Vietnam, a war which he thinks is senseless but has not seen a way to use his power to stop. Senator Russell and his friend and colleague, Senator Stennis, believe, at least as emphatically as the admirals and the generals, that only a preponderance of American military power can save the world. Their problem is as much intellectual as anything else.* After all, it was Senator

*This is not to suggest that the problem is simply that Senators such as Senator Russell and Stennis have an intellectual commitment to cold-war militancy. We should not forget the enormous political and economic advantages of military bases or of having the plant which is to build the giant C-5A cargo

Russell, not a fire-eating Air Force general, who looked across the abyss toward the unthinkable horror of a nuclear Armageddon and observed; "If we have to start over again with another Adam and Eve, then I want them to be Americans and not Russians, and I want them on this continent and not in Europe."[9] These are hardly the views of a man who is likely to be preparing a critique of American defense policy.

This *is* a problem. If the Bureau of the Budget, elite Presidential staff agency, finds itself incapable of taking on the power of the Defense establishment, and if the appropriate Congressional committees, headed by some of the most experienced and powerful men in Washington, do not see this as part of their responsibility, where in the structure of the national government is a countervailing force to be located? Is it *possible* for Congress to exert effective control over the military technocrats?

While no one can be certain that there is a way of controlling our war machine, Vietnam has alerted us to some of the more serious proportions of the problem. For the first time since cold-war attitudes hardened in the late 1940s and early 1950s, thoughtful people in government, as well as diverse critics on the outside, realize that a serious crisis in national priorities exists, and that it will continue to exist until the new militarism is brought under control. By all odds, one of the most interesting, and curious, developments is a new Congressional mood, suddenly critical of the military. Is there anything substantial which underlies the mood? It seems advisable that we look more closely at certain transformations which are well under way within the Congress itself.

THE DEMOCRATIC STUDY GROUP

The largest, best organized and most promising reform group within the Congress has been gaining strength slowly for a decade and a half. The group first came together in a rather

---

plane located in one's state. It is the interaction and the reenforcement of the intellectual and the self-interest factors which make these men staunch non-critics of the military.

tentative way in 1956 under the equally tentative leadership of a now famous non-organization man, Eugene McCarthy, then an unknown young liberal representative from Minnesota. It was a bright, hopeful group of newly-arrived young Democrats, many of them ardent Stevensonians. As a group, they suffered one major handicap: they lacked seniority in the Congressional power system. Since they were also Stevensonian liberals interested in supporting a program of domestic reform legislation, the senior men who led the conservative Coalition were not likely to offer encouragement.[10]

The odd and interesting fact is that Speaker Sam Rayburn of Texas, always considerably less conservative than the other Coalition leaders, did not go out of his way to discourage the newcomers. Instead, he asked Rep. Richard Bolling, a special Rayburn protégé, to keep in close touch with the young liberals. Eugene McCarthy, perhaps seeing no future in the House, ran successfully for a seat in the Senate in 1958. The leadership of the group, which had been referred to occasionally as "McCarthy's Mavericks," was assumed by Frank Thompson of New Jersey and Lee Metcalf of Montana. At the beginning of the next Congressional session in 1959 the young liberals, now joined by two veteran Congressmen, Rep. Chet Holifield of California and Rep. John Blatnik of Minnesota, felt strong enough (or frustrated enough) to go to Speaker Rayburn urging that action be taken to reform the Rules Committee, center of Coalition strategy-making under the wily generalship of "Judge" Howard Smith of Virginia.[11] The Speaker agreed to do what he could, but what he could do turned out to be very little, indeed. The conservative Coalition, not the Speaker, controlled the Rules Committee, using a variety of procedural devices to weaken or kill the substantive legislative proposals which the liberal representatives supported. Judge Smith and his committee colleagues had spent years perfecting the devices which were used to stalemate the liberal programs. The first session of the Eighty-sixth Congress (1959) did nothing to lessen the sense of frustration which was increasingly felt by the House liberals.[12]

Their frustration was the greater because the November

1958 election had added significantly to the numbers of the House Democrats. There were now 283 Democrats in the House and only 154 Republicans. Still the southern Democrats and midwestern Republicans managed to dominate House legislative inaction. If anything, the Coalition seemed slightly tougher in 1959 than before because the Republican caucus dethroned the aging Joseph W. Martin, Jr. of Massachusetts, a gentle conservative who was close to Speaker Rayburn personally, and replaced him with Charles A. Halleck of Indiana, a partisan with a well-deserved reputation as a "gut fighter."

Toward the end of the first session of the Eighty-eighth Congress the liberal group solidified as an organization. The Democratic Study Group was formally launched on September 12, 1959 with Rep. Lee Metcalf as chairman. When Metcalf moved to the Senate following the 1960 election, Chet Holifiield of California, an experienced legislator who had been in the House since his first election in 1942, took over the chairmanship of DSG. William G. Phillips, an experienced Capitol Hill technician, became staff director of DSG, a post he held from 1959 until 1965. He was succeeded by Richard Conlon, former press aide to Senator Walter Mondale of Minnesota.

1960–61: CRUCIAL YEARS

The years 1960–61 proved to be crucial for the new organization. The election of President Kennedy in November was accompanied by the loss of twenty Democratic seats, as casualties ran high among the liberals who arrived so hopefully in 1958. But the DSG, which has never published a membership list, claimed to have a hundred members "affiliated" with it. At least as important, it also had a respected veteran member of the House as Chairman for the first time. DSG decided to approach Speaker Rayburn once again. This time it sought an expansion of the Rules Committee, hoping to alter the political balance within the Committee so that Judge Smith and his senior Coalitionists might be outvoted. All of this in order to get liberal legislation to the floor for a vote! The Speaker agreed to make expansion an issue. A floor fight ensued. The Speaker himself made a rare personal appeal on the floor of the

House, and by a vote of 217–212 the membership of the Rules Committee was expanded in a way which gave the liberals a tenuous 8–7 split on the Committee. A small revolution promised to transform the Rules Committee from obstacle to instrument.[13]

In the 1960 and 1962 Congressional elections, the DSG staff headed by Phillips supplied campaign materials to liberal Democratic candidates. For the new Congressional hopefuls, running alone in what must surely be one of the loneliest political experiences our system offers, the material on the issues as prepared by the DSG staff often proved more helpful than the "boiler plate" ground out by the Democratic Congressional Campaign committee.[14]

In the spring of 1963, Rep. John Blatnik, a ring-wise veteran who had arrived in the House in 1947, was elected to the DSG chairmanship, succeeding Holifield. The liberal legislative program was bogged down despite the enlargement of the Rules committee and despite the presence for more than two years of a modern Democratic activist President who was in sympathy with the program objectives of the House liberals. The DSG may have had a hundred "affiliated" Representatives, but the liberal group lacked sufficient votes to control the House Democratic caucus, and the liberal bloc was not strong enough to enact very much of the Kennedy domestic program.

1964: A BUMPER CROP

The stage was set for the 1964 election. The Johnson landslide victory over Senator Goldwater carried with it the largest Democratic House majority since 1938. By this time, Richard Bolling, who had originally been advised by the late Speaker Rayburn, his mentor, to keep his eye on McCarthy's Mavericks, had become an active leader of the DSG. Bolling headed up DSG's campaign committee in 1964. For the first time, the new organization had a little money at its disposal in addition to its rather considerable campaign knowhow. Thirty-eight of the thirty-nine incumbent Representatives who received DSG campaign assistance were returned, perhaps not surprising in an age of the incumbent. More important, the election brought to the House forty freshmen who had received help from DSG. For the first time DSG had the voting power to control the Democratic caucus in the House: a majority of House Democrats were DSGers. The DSG leaders wisely decided to use this new strength to alter certain basic procedures since it was the procedural labyrinth which the Coalition leaders had used to block so much liberal legislation since 1938. The new Speaker, Rep. John McCormack of Massachusetts, had no alternative but to negotiate with the DSG leaders. When the DSG met on the morning of January 2, 1965, prior to the scheduled Democratic caucus, 150 Congressmen were present.

At the caucus later the same day, a secret ballot yielded a 157–115 vote in favor of stripping Rep. Albert W. Watson of South Carolina and Rep. John Bell Williams of Mississippi of their seniority rights, both gentlemen having supported Senator Goldwater during the fall campaign. The gesture seemed to have little meaning in the case of Watson who had little seniority, but an important precedent may have been established in Williams' case since he was an eighteen-year House veteran with only one rung of the seniority ladder separating him from the chairmanship of the Commerce Committee. Next the Democratic caucus agreed to submit two basic rules changes to the House for a vote. The first proposal called for the enactment of a modified twenty-one day rule to unbottle the Rules committee, and the second called for a rule permitting the Speaker to recognize the chairman of a substantive committee to offer a privileged motion to send to conference by majority vote a bill passed by both houses. In both cases, the rules changes being proposed were aimed at undoing the obstructive powers of Judge Smith and his conservative cohorts on Rules.*

When the issue came to the floor of the House, the DSG liberals won their greatest single victory as the rules changes carried by a margin of 224–201, despite an all-out effort by Judge Smith and his Republican counterpart, the late Clarence

---

*Previously it had been necessary to get the Rules Committee's approval in order to send a bill to conference. The twenty-one day rule, as a practical matter, placed a twenty-one day limit on the Rules Committee's delaying tactics.

Brown of Ohio. Obviously, the victory was made possible, in large part, by the additional forty liberal representatives who entered the House on Presidential coattails in 1964. But, the vote also made clear that DSG had arrived as an organization with a tactical plan and with skilled, experienced leadership. It was a force to be reckoned with.

The DSG leaders won other important concessions in quiet, behind-the-scenes negotiations with the Speaker. The Ways and Means and the Appropriations Committees were to havè new party ratios more accurately reflecting the changed party balance in the House; and liberal representatives, according to a tacit understanding, would have easier access to positions on these committees in the future. A few weeks later, another DSG demand was met when the leadership created a new Democratic steering committee to be chaired by Rep. Ray Madden of Indiana, an original DSG member who was now near the top of the ladder on Rules. Madden, of course, was far less conservative than Smith and Colmer. Late in January, Speaker McCormack called a special Democratic caucus (this was the second caucus) to approve committee assignments as they had been proposed by the Committee on Committees. The Democrats traditionally use the Democratic members of Ways and Means as their "committee on committees." DSG leaders elected not to challenge any of the committee assignments as recommended by Ways and Means Chairman Mills and his colleagues. The feeling apparently was that the mere precedent of having the second caucus to review the work of Mills and company provided sufficient leverage for the time being.

Nineteen sixty-five was a momentous year for House liberals. The DSG had achieved a major victory against the entrenched power of the Coalition by combining caucus reform with reform of the procedural rules. But the question persisted: how lasting would the reforms be? After all, the Eighty-ninth Congress contained a swollen Democratic majority, a majority which could realistically be expected to shrink in a non-Presidential election. And so it did.

KEEPING THE PRESSURE ON

Nineteen sixty-six was a disappointing year for the House liberals as the Republicans gained forty-seven seats, most of them from DSG sympathizers, restoring the balance in favor of the conservative Coalition. But the results were not all bad from the DSG standpoint, since Judge Howard Smith went down to defeat in his primary election. The House conservative Coalition regained some troops while losing its ablest "general." Meanwhile, the DSG leadership kept the pressure on Speaker McCormack by challenging the right of Rep. Colmer of Mississippi to assume the chairmanship of the House Rules Committee. Colmer had the seniority, heaven knows. He had been in the Congress since 1933 with a voting record which showed consistent opposition to the Democratic national administration's domestic program. Another quiet, behind-the-scenes agreement was worked out whereby Colmer was advanced to the chairmanship with a tacit understanding that the majority of the Rules Committee would be able to work its will. Considering the DSG's loss in voting power as a result of the 1966 election, its leadership appears to have done well in continuing the drive to curb the Rules Committee's obstructionism.[15]

Although the election of the Ninety-first Congress added little to the numerical strength of the House liberal bloc, DSG members nevertheless displayed a new activism on a variety of issues ranging from tax reform to the ABM controversy. They were encouraged no doubt by the presence in the White House of a Republican figure who was very familiar to, and warmly distrusted by, the men who provided most of the original leadership of DSG. The evolution of the DSG from McCarthy's Mavericks to an organized and effective liberal force in the House is the more remarkable because the clientele upon which the group must draw has a disproportionate share of marginal political men. The best prospects for DSG affiliation are found among the men from the most competitive and least secure (the marginal) political districts. These representatives are more exposed than is usual to the ebb and flow of Presidential politics.

The DSG also is likely to attract to its banner those young, aspiring legislators who perhaps feel the frustrations of House membership most acutely and who will occasionally be attracted to the greener pastures of the Senate. One thinks immediately of Eugene McCarthy, Lee Metcalf and George McGovern, all first-generation DSGers. Another serious early loss was Frank M. Coffin of Maine, now a Federal judge. Coffin, also a DSG charter member, had the intellectual and the organizing skills so necessary in building any new group; he had something else DSG needed during its formative years, the respect and confidence of Speaker Rayburn. Coffin's decision not to seek reelection to the House in 1960 after two terms illustrates a general problem DSG has faced. A long career in the House may not always seem attractive to men who actively seek progressive change.

On the other hand, DSG has had a few advantages. Although it was put together originally by the young liberals who entered Congress in the mid-1950s, it also attracted a few durable, veteran legislators—men like Holifield, Blatnik and Madden. Typically, the conservative Coalition leaders are tired old men, their average age well over seventy. The DSG leaders, those who came in during the mid-1950s, have considerable seniority but they are far this side of senility. Some of the ablest men in the House today are DSG veterans: Reuss and Kastenmeir of Wisconsin, Hechler of West Virginia, Thompson of New Jersey, Bolling of Missouri, O'Hara of Michigan and Brademas of Indiana.

NEW LIBERALS

But the force which gives DSG its potential to remake the House of Representatives in fundamental ways has been the steady influx of able younger liberals during the 1960s. Donald Fraser of Minnesota, DSG chairman in the Ninety-first Congress, first entered the House in 1962. William D. Hathaway of Maine, DSG program chairman in the Ninety-first, won his House seat in 1964. Fraser and Hathaway offer interesting parallels. They were born one day apart (Fraser on February 20, 1924; Hathaway on February 21 the same year). Fraser served in the Pacific theater in World War II; Hathaway with the Air Force in Europe. Fraser unseated Walter Judd, veteran GOP convention keynote orator and China-lobby spokesman. Hathaway replaced Clifford McIntire, a conservative farm spokesman from Maine's northern potato country who had served in the House for more than a decade. Men like Fraser and Hathaway represent a new breed among Congressmen. They do not intend to serve a House apprenticeship extending over five or six terms before having a voice in the discussion of the serious issues which beset the nation. They insist upon "a piece of the action" now. They are very unhappy to find a conservative Coalition in charge of the House. They do not find the country all that conservative, and they resent an oligarchic Congressional control system, which, as they see it, has deprived the nation of the choice of those policy alternatives which a national legislature, with any pride in its own role, ought to be shaping in a free, open and sorely troubled society. And an interesting side point: combat veterans of World War II, they seriously question the new militarism.[16]

American politics was in a state of transition as the decade ended and so was the DSG. For the first time since the days of McCarthy's Mavericks, DSG faced a Republican president. But now DSG was an experienced and established force. Despite substantial losses in the 1966 and 1968 elections, it had a solid base of 120 dues-paying members in the Ninety-first Congress. At least another twenty Representatives were considered generally sympathetic to the DSG position. The programs which had traditionally drawn strong DSG voting support in the House had been enacted into law—Medicare, civil rights legislation, aid to education. Hence, DSG entered the 1970s in search of a new program, or if this overstates it, actively seeking new issues. And the growth of the new militarism loomed as a prime target.

Perhaps the most significant development in terms of its potential for affecting the work of Congress was the growing interest shown by DSG as a group, and by individual Congressmen of DSG persuasion, in drawing upon the knowledge of technical experts. During the Ninety-first Congress nationally prominent experts in a variety of professional fields were brought to Washington to address DSG seminars. In addition, the DSG research staff published impressive fact books on the Fiscal 1970 Defense budget and on the ABM controversy as well as an analysis of tax reform proposals. DSG established substantive task forces in a dozen subject-matter areas extending from food and agriculture to international affairs and defense policy.

If the conservative Coalition seemed unconcerned about the technical information gap between Congress and the Executive branch, there were clear signs that DSG had taken the initial steps to close the gap. At the same time, a smaller group within DSG was pressing for a stronger stand on basic issues. There was a general restiveness among DSG members in the Ninety-first Congress about the quality of the House Democratic leadership under Speaker John McCormack. DSG expected to play a very strong hand in the choice of a new Speaker when the opportunity presented itself, assuming the Democrats maintained their House majority.

THE SENATE'S NEW BREED

The Senate of the United States, often considered—and with good reason—the most secure bastion of entrenched, institutionalized conservatism, may very well offer the most hope for effecting the fundamental changes in the policy-making process which the nation urgently needs. This does not mean, as we saw in Chapter Three, that the conservative Coalition lacks power in the Senate, far from it; nor is it at all clear that the struggle between the Coalition and the newer forces, representing a far different view of the national interest, will be decided before time runs out on such explosive issues as those related to the urban crisis. But the Senate appears to be changing more than any of the other political branches of the national government. This may help explain the absence of a DSG or its equivalent in the Senate. It may be that the new breed which has been entering the Senate steadily since the mid-1950s does not feel quite the same sense of frustration which so affects a new member of the House.

By the end of the 1960s the Senate contained a "moderate-to-liberal" quasi-majority on most of the key issues of domestic policy. The following list of Senators showing the year each arrived in the Senate offers a simple way of revealing how this "moderate-to-liberal" coalition has been taking shape since the mid-1950s.

Senator	State	Year of Arrival
Anderson	N. Mex.	1949
Pastore	R.I.	1950
Gore	Tenn.	1951
Jackson	Wash.	1953
Mansfield	Montana	1953
Symington	Missouri	1953
CASE*	N.J.	1955
COOPER	Kentucky	1956
Church	Idaho	1957
JAVITS	N.Y.	1957
Yarborough	Texas	1957
Proxmire	Wisc.	1957
Randolph	W. Va	1958
Hart	Mich.	1959
Hartke	Ind.	1959
McCarthy	Minn.	1959
McGee	Wyo.	1959
Moss	Utah	1959
Muskie	Maine	1959
SCOTT	Pa.	1959
H. Williams	N.J.	1959
S. Young	Ohio	1959
Burdick	N. Dakota	1960
Metcalf	Mont.	1961
Pell	R.I.	1961
Kennedy	Mass.	1962
McIntyre	N.H.	1962
Bayh	Ind.	1962

*(Republicans are indicated in capital letters)

Senator	*State*	*Year of Arrival*
PEARSON	Kansas	1962
Inouye	Hawaii	1963
McGovern	So.Dakota	1963
Ribicoff	Conn.	1963
Nelson	Wisc.	1963
Harris	Okla.	1964
Montoya	N.Mex.	1964
Mondale	Minn.	1964
Tydings	Md.	1965
GRIFFIN	Mich.	1966
BROOKE	Mass.	1967
PERCY	Ill.	1967
HATFIELD	Ore.	1967
GOODELL	N. Y.	1968
Eagleton	Missouri	1968
COOK	Kentucky	1969
Cranston	Calif.	1969
Hughes	Iowa	1969
MATHIAS	Md.	1969
SAXBE	Ohio	1969
SCHWEIKER	Pa.	1969

Grand Total   49

Of the forty-nine Senators on this list, only fourteen are Republicans and nine of them have joined the Senate since 1966. The growth of this small but strategically significant group of moderately liberal Republicans, combined with the larger and more experienced Democratic contingent, makes it possible to think in terms of a moderate-to-liberal Senate majority in the 1970s. While forty-nine is obviously not quite a Senate majority, a block of forty-nine votes becomes a potent force when mobilized. This is especially true because there are always some few Senators who are on the line, for one reason or another.

The moderate-to-liberal group is sometimes joined on spe-

160

cific issues by Margaret Chase Smith of Maine, George Aiken of Vermont or Warren Magnuson of Washington. Some observers would include these Senators in a moderate-to-liberal grouping. Smith and Aiken seem to me best thought of as plain, old-fashioned, Yankee independents. Magnuson is not an illiberal man, by any means, but his long years of Senate service perhaps account for a slight tendency to adjust to the conservative Coalition's domination of the process. On some domestic issues, where race is either not present or is hidden, an occasional southern Senator, such as Sparkman of Alabama or Long of Louisiana, will be found voting with the moderate-to-liberal group. There are others one can think of. Senator Dodd of Connecticut, for all of his dogmatic anticommunism and despite his discredited personal position, casts his vote with this group more often than not on items of domestic legislation.

The list,* in other words, is not perfect, nor are the Senators. Senator Jackson, to take just one example, may appear quite "illiberal" occasionally on specific issues relating to the military-industrial complex; no doubt this is due in part to the imposing presence of Boeing in his home state. He was, after all, considered as a possible candidate for Secretary of Defense in the Nixon cabinet. On the other hand, Jackson chairs a subcommittee which has done an admirably perceptive and scholarly study of our national security decision-making machinery, and this interest goes back ten years before the subject enjoyed any degree of political popularity. It was Jackson's subcommittee which recently undertook a searching inquiry into the PPBS revolution. The study, while cutting through much of the PPBS mysticism, maintained the subcommittee's customary high standard of objectivity.[17] Furthermore, Senator Jackson is a long-time supporter of those programs which would raise the quality of education, health, welfare and manpower services. He is, also, along with Senator Muskie of Maine, a leading Senate voice for strengthening the nation's

*It is simply one man's list based on a study of Congress which he has conducted for more than twenty years.

antipollution and environmental-control efforts. (On this issue, the two Senators were ahead of the youthful critics—and the Nixon administration—by several years.)

The listing of the forty-nine Senators provides a way of showing how close the Senate is to a moderately liberal majority; and it also makes it easy to see how wide the geographic distribution of moderate liberalism has become. One expects to find New York, New Jersey, Pennsylvania, Massachusetts, Connecticut and Rhode Island represented by men who are likely to differ with the conservative Coalition on many issues. But the list includes major figures from Maine, South Dakota and Oklahoma. Texas has produced Senator Yarborough, a hard-core Stevensonian liberal, who has survived long enough to win an important chairmanship. Frank Church of Idaho, whose youthful appearance when he first arrived in 1957—so the legend has it—caused him to be mistaken for a page, has been elected to a third Senate term. Church was one of the first to open the Vietnam question to public debate. Ohio, the solid WASPish land of Bricker and Taft, is represented on the list by two outspoken liberals, one a Democrat, the other a Republican. Indiana, which often seems solidly midwestern and conservative in eastern eyes, has produced Hartke and Bayh. Maryland, a primitive political subculture when it comes to gubernatorial politics, has elected Joseph Tydings, Democrat, and Charles Mathias, Republican, to the Senate since 1964. Both men have the capacity to become influential figures in a new liberal coalition.

By 1970 the moderate-to-liberal group showed signs of an awareness that it was in a position to assert itself against the entrenched power of the conservative Coalition. The election of Senator Kennedy to the Majority whip position at the opening of the first session of the Ninety-first Congress symbolized the growing strength of the new group as well as an increasing awareness of the need to occupy positions of authority in the Congressional hierarchy. The choice of Hugh Scott to succeed the late Senator Dirksen as Senate Minority leader likewise indicated that Senate Republicans were beginning to respond to the pressures of their recently expanded liberal contingent.

The handiwork of the moderate liberals was to be seen in a number of specific instances in the Ninety-first Congress: in the rejection of the nominations of Judge Haynsworth and Judge Carswell to the Supreme Court; in the tax reform struggle; in challenging the Nixon administration by increasing appropriations for health, education, manpower and welfare; in supporting Senator Mansfield's drive to reduce American troop commitments in Europe, among others. The probability was that an essentially moderate-to-liberal majority would be firmly established in the Senate during the early 1970s. This seemed more in line with long-range political developments than the popular assumption that Mr. Nixon's (or Mr. Agnew's) silent majority was about to fill the national legislature with a sizeable force of neo-fascists. Indeed, if President Nixon were to hope to achieve any of the qualitative changes in American society set forth in his 1970 State of the Union address, he would have to rely principally on the interest and support of the moderate liberals in Congress.

Popular notions about the sudden demise of Democratic Presidential expectations in the immediate aftermath of Chappaquidick also seemed somewhat exaggerated. Mr. Nixon's victory in 1968 was not exactly of landslide proportions. He and his campaign managers, in fact, just barely managed to eke out an extremely narrow victory under most unusual circumstances. The Democrats are almost certain to nominate an experienced liberal candidate in 1972, probably a member of the Senate group. Assuming Edward Kennedy were to remain "not available" in 1972, the Senate includes such obvious Presidential possibilities as Muskie, McGovern, Hughes, Harris and, although this seems less likely, McCarthy. No doubt a Democratic ticket headed by a candidate from this group would be hard-pressed to defeat an incumbent President who had disengaged from Vietnam, managed the economy successfully, and refrained from emasculating recent social programs. But even an unsuccessful Democratic challenge under these hypothetical circumstances might be expected to assist in the election of a sufficient number (only a few more are needed) of basically

163

liberal new Senators from both parties to give the Senate a reasonably solid moderate-to-liberal majority.

It is also part of the profound change underway that the Senate of the United States has quietly replaced the gubernatorial office as the place where the leading Presidential aspirants serve their apprenticeship. Only a few short years ago conventional wisdom held that *no* United States Senator could make it as Presidential candidate. Perhaps Harry Truman's amazing victory in 1948 and his subsequent conduct of the office should have told us something about former Senators as Presidential material. In our day, at any rate, *only* Senators now seem to have a chance for the biggest prize the system awards. Kennedy, Johnson, Goldwater, Humphrey and even Nixon, if his eight years as presiding officer of the Senate count, were Senate products. And so are Edward Kennedy, Edmund Muskie, George McGovern, Fred Harris, Harold Hughes and Eugene McCarthy.

Those original Stevensonians among us who felt so badly when the Governor did not win the highest office perhaps failed to understand that Adlai Stevenson may have been the last of the Governors. One thinks of the others who have since fallen by the wayside: Rockefeller, Wallace, Romney and Reagan, among them, and asks whether Richard M. Nixon would now be in the White House if he had been elected Governor of California. In any event, it is the Stevensonian generation, the men who admired Stevenson and who ran with him in the 1950s and won, who now form the leadership corps in an emerging liberal coalition in the Senate.

Consider the current roles of Senators Randolph, Proxmire, Hart, McCarthy and Muskie in Senate activity. The fact that Jennings Randolph chairs Public Works with Edmund Muskie next to him on the seniority ladder means that the liberal coalition controls—and has defense in depth on—the most important "pork barrel" committee.* Senator Proxmire, who has a touch of LaFollette in his approach, steadily climbs the sen-

---

*Southern Conservatives love "pork" and ought to be made to pay the price —i.e., if you want to "get" a Post Office, vote "right."

iority ladder on the powerful Appropriations Committee. The Conservative Southerners ahead of him have also built their defenses in depth, but Proxmire may conceivably be the most determined man in the Senate today. He is never to be dealt with lightly. Proxmire also currently is the leading Senator on the Joint Economic Committee. His subcommittee's investigations of Pentagon procurement abuses in the Ninety-first Congress point the way to a direct assault on the military side of the military-industrial complex. Proxmire does not share the conservative Coalition's monumental lack of interest in the way the Pentagon uses and misuses the tax dollar.

Senator Hart, comparatively unknown outside the Senate, would be one of the most likely to provide the steady leadership which a liberal coalitional majority would have to have. A man of intelligence, integrity, and legislative-strategic skill, Hart has the basic qualities to become the liberal's Richard Russell—that is to say, the informal and highly respected strategist for a bipartisan bloc. McCarthy has already made a unique contribution outside the Senate. Muskie possesses essentially the same balance of qualities we have noted in Hart. Muskie, of course, is much better known to the general public following his role in the 1968 Presidential campaign. If national political developments do not take him out of the Senate, he is likely to remain the leading liberal candidate to succeed Senator Mansfield as Majority leader. Indeed, the Senator from Maine has the capacity and the insight to lead the Senate to a position of increasing relevance and effectiveness in responding to the educational, environmental, racial, and urban crises.[18]

The struggle between the old conservative Coalition trying to hang on to power and the emerging liberal Coalition seeking to assert itself with greater authority in the making of public policy, and in the remaking of institutions, promises to be a momentous struggle—a little like putting the gladiators in the arena, so far as potential for excitement goes. The conservative Coalition will not give up power easily. Its leaders have seniority on their side, and they know how to use it. But seniority proves to be a double-edged sword. Senior men grow older.

Richard Russell, the leading Coalition strategist, was both old and sick as the decade ended. Herman Talmadge, his junior colleague from Georgia, was one of the few "younger" Southerners who might have the capacity to become an effective "general." However, Talmadge lacked much of Russell's presence, and politics in Georgia was subject to change with 300,-000 of its black citizens registered to vote.

The hardest part will come when the new liberal Coalition challenges the Congressional wing of the military-industrial complex, for here the stakes could scarcely be higher. And defenses in depth have been years in the building. The top rungs of the Democratic seniority ladder on the two Senate committees with the largest potential for exerting an effective control on the new militarism were occupied as follows in the Ninety-first Congress:

Appropriations	*Armed Services*
Russell, Georgia	Stennis, Mississippi
Ellender, Louisiana	Russell, Georgia
McClellan, Arkansas	

The average age of these senior figures in the conservative Coalition exceeded seventy years in 1969. Senator Stennis, the youngest of the four, was the only one who was born in the twentieth century. He was born in Kemper County, Mississippi on August 3, 1901.

It is time for a change. Both Houses of Congress failed in their important function of providing an independent review of Executive policies in the 1960s. Congress failed most conspicuously to develop a responsible critique of the nation's military programs. Congress did not evaluate critically the assumptions and concepts of our national security programs largely because the senior men who dominated the Armed Services and Appropriations Committees in both Houses did not see the need to do so. Armed with the power of the purse and the power of investigation, Congress, more than any other national legislature of which I am aware, has the inherent power to provide the independent critique of Executive policies which we must have. What is lacking, thus far, is a political force in the Congress which *perceives* this as a vital Congressional function and which is strong enough to undertake the task. In the meantime, the moderate-to-liberal quasi-majority in the Senate and the DSG in the House must be stronger than their numbers, if the military-industrial complex is to be contained.

CHAPTER EIGHT

THE CHANGING POLITY

We have met the enemy and they are us.
POGO

ALTHOUGH PUBLIC POLICY tends to change slowly in America, everything else is subject to continual and, often, rapid change. Ironically, the first generation of young people to witness man's leap beyond earth half-believes that most of our institutions are incapable of change. Yet the inexorable process of change has produced a number of things they criticize most: the close ties between military-industrial power and the universities, the squalor of the cities, the shallow and tasteless materialism of suburbia, the dehumanization of man's work. The truth is that Americans have more change right now than we know what to do with. Several of the most critical problems facing us in the 1970s stem directly from profound institutional changes which occurred during the previous decade. The family, the school, the church, the military, the business corporation, all are changing, and some of them are changing at a pace which challenges the ability of ordinary mortals to comprehend.

Without being too facetious, one is tempted to suggest that what we lack is a better label for the new era. We have often been told that we are now entering the post-industrial society. A nation so restless and so technically gifted that it finds a way to land men on the moon deserves a better billing. No wonder our young people are dissatisfied. What gifted, spirited young person would want to spend his days in a post-industrial era?

The industrial period was dreary enough, full of lives of quiet desperation. This may even account for some of the noisiness of today's youth. They at least are not going to be *quietly* desperate. There is the real danger that our students, bewildered and disenchanted, may miss the rather important point that they themselves are almost the best example of the apparently limitless capacity for change within the American experience. College and university enrollment in the United States had approached seven million before the 1960s ended and was expected to exceed nine million by the middle of the 1970s. The figure is almost too large to grasp, but a subculture of nine million college students would doubtless appear to some leaders in a number of the smaller new nations as constituting a sizeable *over*-developed nation. In any event, our university enrollment figure will soon overshadow the number of Americans living in the rural countryside. This is likely to happen at some point about midway through the 1970s since there were only ten million Americans in the rural population at the end of the 1960s.

Richard Hofstadter[1] opened one of his brilliant interpretations of our past with the observation: "The United States was born in the country, and has moved to the city." This needs amendment. The United States was born in the country, moved to the city, and is now going to college. Is it any wonder that the provincialism of the old-time Congressman finds itself at odds with so many aspects of the changing American scene? The men who dominate the conservative Congressional Coalition, men who grew up in rural small towns six and even seven decades ago, have experienced some difficulty understanding urban America as it has taken form since the end of the Second World War. They are hopelessly remote from the needs, aspirations, and values of the university-spawned meritocracy now on the ascendant.

At the very moment the astronauts set foot on the moon, the census clock in the lobby of the United States Department of Commerce building showed a population of 203,377,182 Americans—24 million more than there were when President Kennedy originally announced the moon goal.[2] Even the incredible American productive machine must hit on all cylinders if its momentum is to keep pace with this kind of population growth. By adding 24 million people in the 1960s, the United States increased by a number almost as large as the total British labor force. And the British labor force grows scarcely at all. The decline of British economic power is blamed on many things, including the balance of payments. Actually, it is the balance of people which runs heavily to the disadvantage of the British as they try to compete industrially with the USA, the USSR, and Japan. One also hears a great deal about the brain drain and the technological gap as they weaken the British position. What are the British supposed to do? There are more students enrolled in the various colleges and universities which happen to be located in the state of Ohio than there are in all of the British universities.

Yes, the United States will continue to change, powered as it is by the steady growth of a restless population increasingly trained to serve the technological revolution. Change is the essence of the American experience. It is less certain that we shall be able to detect the patterns of change or that we shall be able to discern the direction of change; it is not even clear that anyone will be able to control change. Our recent experience with certain population changes is not very encouraging on this score. The changes we are about to examine took place beginning in the 1950s and recurred in the 1960s. Only now are we beginning to perceive their significance with some clarity and depth of understanding.

THE BLACK MIGRATION

The history of this country may be told largely in terms of population movements: the landings of the early settlers, the westward movement, the tides of European immigration bringing more than 35 million individuals to this new land between the age of Jackson and the Wilson era. Another great American population movement has recently taken place. In the process the black American has become the most urban of all Americans. He has been "ghettoized" to an extent which makes it exceedingly difficult for the poor black family to find a way out of the tangle of urban pathology. Few Americans, even now when this latest population shift is almost over, realize how complete the transformation has been. Of the 22.3 million Negroes estimated to have been living in the United States in July 1968, little more than a million—about five percent—were on farms. As recently as 1950, more than 2.5 million Negroes lived on farms, most of them in the South. The patterns of the migration off the farms are interesting and significant. Although the movement from farm to city is a national phenomenon, the big migrant streams have come from the South. In the peak years during the 1950s and 1960s, migration from the South made up approximately one-half to nearly two-thirds of the country's total population shift from farm to city. The Negro farmers of the southeast and their families, most of them poor tenant farmers, headed for the cities in the northeast—principally Washington, Baltimore, Newark, New York, and Philadelphia, but also to Rochester, Syracuse, Boston, Providence, Waterbury, New Haven, Hartford, and Bridgeport. One of the most primitive rural subcultures in the nation fed its poor tenants into one of the most highly industrialized, sophisticated, cosmopolitan urban-suburban areas in the world.[3]

Poor blacks from Mississippi Delta country headed chiefly for Mayor Daley's Chicago, increasing the size of the nation's (and the world's) largest dark ghetto. Farm families from Louisiana and Texas headed west, to Los Angeles, for example, later the scene of the Watts rebellion. Those from the middle South and Tennessee followed a more diverse pattern; their favorite destinations were Chicago, Detroit, and Cleveland. The demographers insist that this momentous mass movement is about over. It is to be hoped that scholars will write about its significance, its impact upon our society and its politics and values, much as Frederick Jackson Turner and his followers did for the White western Frontier. It is hard to imagine a research project with a greater potential for adding substantively to black studies.

THE DEMISE OF THE URBAN MACHINE

The point has occasionally been made that this movement of poor black Americans northward and to the west was not planned; hence, so much human misery. But the movement of hordes of European peasants to America throughout the nineteenth century also was unplanned, and human misery was encountered along the way. A principal difference between the two experiences seems to have been the political and social contexts within which each took place. For one thing, during the earlier nineteenth-century movements of peoples to our cities, there were political machines in virtually every east-coast city prepared to assume some responsibility for the task of assimilation. This is not a minor matter. The old-time urban machine went in search of votes, to be sure, but it also provided certain basic services, a measure of human warmth, and, not infrequently, menial jobs for the newcomers from Europe. The poor blacks who have moved recently from the small southern rural towns to the teeming squalor of the big city ghettos might often have wished that there was a man on every block to whom a poor black might have turned for help, and Martin Lomasney would have understood.[4]

The movement of poor blacks to the cities is evidently about over, if only because so few blacks are left on the land. But the problems created by the black migration pose as sharp a challenge as we have known. The movement of millions of people, most of them dirt poor, from the small, simple, agricultural villages to the vast impersonality of the modern metropolis has taken place at a time when jobs requiring no skill are drying up and during a period when public services have been increasingly bureaucratized. Worse still, no one bureaucracy has had the responsibility of easing the adjustment for these unlettered, untrained, and unsophisticated people. The assimilation process which took place in American cities throughout the 1950s and 1960s was worse than unplanned; it was ignored. It would be difficult to devise a "system" so well calculated to engender widespread alienation from the larger purposes of the society.

The Progressive Reformers, good white middle-class Protestants with their notoriously strong bias against political party organizations, had at least this much success: they assisted mightily in the destruction of the very organizations which had eased the political assimilation of millions of humble European immigrants. When the demise of the urban machine was accompanied by the welfare-social-security innovations of the New Deal, the fate of any latter-day migrants was left in the hands of local bureaucracies staffed by well-trained, middle-class professionals, the products of Progressive reform. The movement of poor blacks to the slums of the inner city and the movement of the affluent whites to the split-level comforts of suburbia have isolated the blacks in conditions of misery and degradation. The city, in the meantime, finds itself enmeshed in the resulting tangle of pathology.

THE PLIGHT OF BLACK YOUTH

The plight of black youth trapped in the ghetto is most acute. He cannot get out, and yet, if he stays in, he cannot join the ranks of the growing meritocracy. After eight years of continuous economic expansion during the Kennedy-Johnson era, and after four years, 1966–69, in which it was commonly believed that the nation had achieved full employment, the official figures, hedged on the conservative side, showed almost one in every three black youth out of work. This is the posture in which we entered the 1970s. Official projections were not reassuring. The number of nonwhite youth in the 14-to-24-year-old bracket will increase at a rate nearly twice that of white youth in the period 1965–80. Many more young blacks will be entering the labor force which already contains tens of thousands of unemployed black youth.[5] (Idealistic young whites who seek meaningful challenges outside the established institutions may find special meaning in this problem which thus far defies solution. It is not a problem which is likely to be solved by shouting obscenities in the street.)

This much we know. The majority of young poor blacks are supported at one time or another by public welfare programs, and every week brings new evidence that the existing welfare system is about to collapse under the sheer weight of the numbers. The American public welfare system, product of an earlier era and a jerry-built structure at best, was clearly not designed to support a tidal wave of human migration from the rural south to the larger cities of the north and west. But the welfare system, especially that portion which supplies Aid to Families with Dependent Children, is there. It exists. AFDC in particular tends to fit a critical part of the current problem—the poor, fatherless family—and so the program grows and grows and grows. And those who "fit" the program survive. By the end of the 1960s the welfare programs in New York City alone bore an annual price tag well in excess of a billion dollars, approximately half of the annual expenditure of all Economic Opportunity Act programs for the whole nation. By the end of the decade New York City was expending more to support its expanding welfare clientele than it was for public education. Under these circumstances the possibility of finding a better alternative generated an appeal that transcended the usual partisan barriers.[6]

The Nixon Administration had been in office only a few months when the President proposed a drastic reform in the approach to Federal welfare assistance. In directing a special message to Congress on August 11, 1969, President Nixon[7] declared; "A measure of the greatness of a powerful nation is the character of the life it creates for those who are powerless to make ends meet." He then recommended the most important changes in the welfare system since the Social Security Act of 1935, including this central point: "I propose that the Federal government pay a basic income to the American families who cannot care for themselves in whichever State they live." Thus, the first White House proposal for a form of income maintenance came from a Republican president, a man not noted in his earlier political career as an ardent advocate of social reform, and it came at a time when his administration was applying a policy of fiscal restraint. The Nixon administration, presumed to be the defender of States' rights against an interventionist Federal government, advocated a change in Federal welfare programs which, by its own reckoning, would increase the number of welfare recipients, estimated to be 10 million individuals in March 1969, to 22.4 million in one year. If Congress were to enact the Nixon reforms, the Federal costs of welfare programs estimated at 4.2 billion dollars in Fiscal 1970 were expected to rise in the first year to 8.2 billion dollars, just shy of a 100% increase.[8]

For the time being this will serve as a reasonably adequate example illustrating the extent to which the contemporary Institutionalized Presidency finds it necessary to respond directly to the social pressures and the human needs of urban America.

DEFENSE COMES FIRST

But no one was sure that this reform of public welfare, or any similar welfare reform, would be accomplished in time because the decade of the sixties which saw the culmination of the black migration also produced a drastic transformation in national security decision-making. The connection between the two, we are beginning to realize, is real. In changing the decision-making procedures, we altered the priorities; altered them so much, in fact, as to effect a crisis in priorities. The analysis in this book shows that national security questions were handled quite differently than were domestic matters by both the Kennedy and the Johnson administrations. We first discovered that Defense budgets were put together in a manner which minimized the ability of the Budget Bureau to put the figures to an independent review. More significantly, Secretary Robert McNamara instituted a decision-making process in the Pentagon which tended to centralize the larger issues of defense strategy in his office as Secretary. In the process, military need was to be viewed on a long-range basis while domestic needs were not; in this fashion, long-range military needs subtly moved to a position of highest priority.

CRISIS IN PRIORITIES

Six months after the Johnson administration left office, Stewart Udall, who served as Secretary of the Interior throughout the entire Kennedy-Johnson period, told a Congressional committee examining the relationship between the military budget and national priorities that neither the Kennedy nor the Johnson administrations had "any institutionalized way whereby there was a forum where you could intelligently argue domestic priorities versus military priorities." Speaking of the budgetary process, the former Cabinet officer observed: "We were under the magnifying glass and the military was not being scrutinized nearly in the way the domestic side was." Joseph A. Califano, a top White House assistant during the final years of the Johnson administration, told the same committee that both Congress and the Executive lack the mechanisms to make "informed and intelligent" choices between competing priorities, such as missiles and job training. Califano felt that at best the President had the tools to make only "rough trade-offs" between domestic programs. "The military situation," he asserted, "was quite different." "We have never hesitated to provide the resources or make the sacrifices that were considered necessary to protect our national security from foreign dangers," Califano continued. "Time after time we have failed to provide the resources and make the sacrifices necessary for all Americans to live at some minimal level of human dignity and spiritual tranquility."[9]

The crisis in priorities which Udall and Califano identified has been created in part by a basic change which took place between the 1950s and the 1960s. During the Truman-Eisenhower years, the amounts allocated for defense purposes were arrived at by what Professor Samuel Huntington[10] has described as the "remainder method." The two Presidents, assisted of course by the Budget Bureau, decided what they thought ought to be spent for domestic matters, and the remainder was assigned to Defense.* Eisenhower with his five stars was in a commanding position to enforce his judgments as against those of the Joint Chiefs of Staff. His defense budgets were modest in contrast with what was to follow.** What followed was a reversal of the way in which the essential

---

*This was not the case during the Korean war, obviously.
**Some would say that the Eisenhower budgets were modest—period.

budget calculations were made. In the 1960s the remainder method was applied to the domestic programs which Kennedy and especially Johnson inaugurated. Defense came first. Next one encountered the uncontrollable items: veterans payments, interest on the debt, farm subsidies, and so forth. Finally came the "remainder" to be divided among manpower training, anti-poverty efforts, model cities, etc. When we recall that as late as 1965 Federal budgets were constructed with $100 billion as an arbitrary ceiling, with Defense taking more than $50 billion, it is obvious that any expansion of military spending was to place several of the newer domestic programs in a tight fiscal squeeze.

The nation changed during the sixties in ways which threatened to tear apart the social fabric. One set of social changes made the ghetto with its tangle of pathology a national phenomenon; the other changes, managerial and technological in nature, helped effect a centralization of defense decision-making which distorted national priorities by pushing explosive domestic issues into budgetary limbo. The managerial revolution was directed at the prestigious problems of national security while the mundane problems at home were left to be dealt with within more traditional limits. It is important to remember that it was the Americanization of the war in Vietnam which converted Lyndon Johnson to budgetary magic.

TWO PRESIDENCIES

In reviewing recent American experience one is struck by the contrast between the way in which governmental decision-making processes responded when the need was military and the manner in which critical domestic issues were dealt with. It is not obvious why the nation as a whole, so recently converted from isolationism, should have accepted the dichotomous relationship. Aaron Wildavsky[11], one of the most perceptive analysts of the national policy-making process, has suggested that we have evolved two Presidencies, one for defense and foreign policies and one for domestic affairs, with foreign affairs having all the better of it.

177

Since World War II, Presidents have had much greater success in controlling the nation's defense and foreign policies than in dominating its domestic policies. Even Lyndon Johnson has seen his early record of victories in domestic legislation diminish as his concern with foreign affairs grows.

How are we to account for the difference? A President, as we have seen, will encounter great difficulty in getting Congressional support for the domestic programs he prefers, especially those with a potential for reform. In foreign affairs, by way of contrast, as Wildavsky[12] suggests, "he can almost always get support for policies that he believes will protect the nation— but his problem is to find a viable policy." We noted previously that President Johnson found it necessary to perform feats of great dexterity in order to gain sufficient support in Congress for his antipoverty program in 1964. Yet, the same President received almost unanimous Congressional support for his Tonkin Gulf resolution after only a few days of perfunctory debate in the legislative chambers.

Wildavsky argues that in the realm of foreign policy there has not been a single major issue on which Presidents, when they were serious and determined, have failed. Serious setbacks to the President in controlling foreign policy are extraordinary. Actually, if one were to go back to the 1930s, a strong case can be made that President Roosevelt's foreign policy initiative was substantially limited by isolationist sentiment in Congress from 1933 at least through 1939.[13] But even if the discussion is limited to the postwar period, the noteworthy fact, it seems to me, is that American Presidents have received solid bipartisan support for policies which have been consistently cold war in nature. Every American President from Truman through Johnson has been careful to keep his foreign policy activities well within the framework of the containment doctrine. In short, Presidents in the period since World War II have been "successful" in their foreign policy and defense policy leadership at least in part because that leadership has been remarkably cautious and uncreative most of the time. Kennedy's Nuclear Test Ban treaty represents the rare example of a postwar President maneuvering successfully outside the conventional limits of cold-war orthodoxy as it has been formulated by the military-congressional complex.

One of the reasons a President enjoys less success as policy-leader in domestic affairs is that there are pressures at work within the society which force Presidential leadership on issues of race, education, health, poverty and human welfare in ways which rapidly bring the Chief Executive into conflict with the Congressional Coalition. Postwar Presidents have felt remarkably little public pressure to take on the Congressional chieftains, the military brass and the civilian militants who have designed and perpetuated the official national security dogma. Writing in 1966, at the very moment when Vietnam commitments and expenditures were skyrocketing out of control, Wildavsky[14] called attention to Huntington's thesis that

> major military leaders were seduced in the Truman and Eisenhower years into believing that they should bow to judgment of civilians that the economy could not stand much larger military expenditures. Once the size of the military pie was accepted as a fixed constraint, the military services were compelled to put their major energies into quarreling with one another over who should get the larger share. Given the natural rivalries of the military and the traditional acceptance of civilian rule, the President and his advisers—who could claim responsibility for the broader picture of reconciling defense and domestic policies— had the upper hand.

The seduction of the military innocents sounds a trifle odd today, but the notion that the military services came off second-best in the struggle for the budgetary dollar may have some validity as a description of the situation before Robert McNamara became Defense Secretary in 1961. Wildavsky is relying on Professor Huntington's major study of Defense policy-making in the period *before* the McNamara managerial revolution. But Wildavsky's essay appeared in December 1966, and hence his views become seriously inaccurate and even misleading when applied to 1966, as the analysis of the budgetary picture in Chapter Six makes clear.

Wildavsky's view of the two Presidencies misses a key point: that men below the Presidential level have great influence in establishing and maintaining policy. Civilian militants in the Pentagon, already in a strong position vis-à-vis the uniformed military during the Eisenhower years, as Huntington has shown, found their position enhanced by McNamara's centralizing system. The natural rivalries of the armed services which are so relied upon in the Wildavsky-Huntington interpretation as a check on overall military expansion were considerably weakened by the change in the Pentagon's managerial system after 1961. Civilian control of defense policy reenforces a traditional American value, but it does not necessarily diminish the power or the threat of the new technocratic militarism. It may, in fact, increase that threat and that power by making it more efficient.

This much seems clear: the escalation and Americanization of the war in Vietnam in 1965-66 appears to have been a largely civilian-dominated group decision, concurred in—participated in—by virtually every one of the President's top civilian national security advisers. Coincident with the Americanization of the war in Vietnam, Secretary McNamara and a team of talented technicians installed a new decisional system which affected the structure of national priorities. The success of the Kennedy administration in changing basic national strategic plans to make room for "flexible response" also made it seem technically feasible to escalate the war in Southeast Asia. The achievement of our objectives in Southeast Asia, however ambiguous they may have been, were to be pursued regardless of cost. The search for solutions to the stark and deep dilemmas within the domestic society were to be sharply limited by the imbalance of a budget whose military costs were soon veering out of control, thanks to Vietnam.

POLITICS AND POLICY-MAKING

The relationship between our failures at home and our increased military role in Southeast Asia is a direct and intimate one. Wildavsky's suggestion that we have two Presidencies is helpful in this analysis up to a point, but it misses the vital political fact that the foreign affairs Presidency "gets along" with the cold-war orthodoxy of the dominant Congressional Coalition while the domestic Presidency is forced to take the initiative in matters relating to race, urban crisis, poverty, and ignorance, and in doing so stimulates a resistance on the part of the Congressional barons.

Two serious analytical defects mar Wildavsky's otherwise suggestive essay. As noted above, Presidential policy-leadership is reliant on the policy base largely created and maintained by career professionals. Wildavsky in looking back to an earlier experience in defense decision-making fails to note the subtle shift in priorities which accompanied McNamara's managerial revolution. President Johnson looked forward to a reduction in the level of defense spending to be effected by the application of cost-benefit analysis thus providing additional resources for the support of expanded domestic programs. This hope was not sustained. Whether it might have been or not, if Vietnam had not existed, seems impossible to judge. Vietnam was there, and the national security decision-making team thought there was a technical (military-technological) solution to a terribly complex foreign-affairs problem. And so the war in Vietnam was Americanized in incremental stages.*

Wildavsky, a keen critic of PPBS as a means of supplanting political choices, appears to have been attracted by the notion that somehow national security matters are technical in nature and, therefore, stand outside politics. It seems best to let Wildavsky[15] speak for himself on this vital point:

> In foreign affairs we may be approaching the stage where knowledge is power. There is tremendous receptivity to good ideas in Washington. Most anyone who can present a convincing ra-

---

*It is perhaps not unusual for our military planners to make remarkably optimistic assumptions about the effectiveness of military operations when they seek to apply their technical knowledge to complicated political problems, such as Korea in an earlier period or Vietnam in the 1960s. Civilian political leaders, by the same token, ought to appreciate the limits of military advice in such a context and apply all the skepticism that the situation requires. The intellectual defects in our official political view of Asia encouraged us to escalate and finally to Americanize the Vietnam war.

tionale for dealing with a hard world finds a ready audience. The best way to convince Presidents to follow a desired policy is to show that it might work. A man like McNamara thrives because he performs. He comes up with answers he can defend.

In this fashion Professor Wildavsky concluded his essay in December 1966.

The analysis in this book maintains the opposite position. In 1965 and 1966 there was receptivity in the Institutionalized Presidency to ideas in the national security field which proved to be politically disastrous. These ideas depended upon the assumptions of an official doctrine of containment which had long since outlived any usefulness it once may have had. In any event, the doctrine was not designed with Asian problems in mind and it had never been reformulated to take into account the changing facts of international life. Nevertheless, policies based on containment orthodoxy persisted through decades and through several changes of national administrations. These policies won easy, uncritical assent in a Congress dominated most of the time by a conservative bipartisan Coalition. The prudent test of a wise policy is not necessarily to convince a President that it *might work*. Evidently, the Americanization of the war met that simple test. The suggestion that Secretary McNamara thrived because he "performed" well leaves unexamined the basic questions about what it was he was performing. One normally expects a Cabinet officer to come up with answers he can defend. Secretary Dulles doubtless had a defensible answer to those who might have asked (evidently no one did) what we were doing in taking over the bankrupt French position in Indochina in 1954. But having an answer which the Secretary could defend did not make this a wise policy. Secretary McNamara performed well before Congressional committees, part of whose business is the asking of questions. He defended his decision to build the F-111 with consummate skill and great assurance against unfriendly critics.[16] The decision, nevertheless, appears to have been dubious at best. The fact that we have the technical capacity to build an F-111 or to take over the fighting in Vietnam or to build an ABM system or to tip our missiles with the MIRV does not mean that we *ought* to. In making a judgment of any of these questions it is also important that it be made in a context which considers how the same resources might be applied to meet nonmilitary needs.

Something more is involved in national decision-making than the technical capacity to show that a proposed policy might work. What are the implications if the proposed policy does not work? Is there an alternative policy which might work better? What *purposes* are to be served if the policy does work? Wildavsky[17] notes how difficult it is to devise

> good policies or to predict their consequences accurately. Nor is it easy to convince others that a given policy is superior to other alternatives. But it is the way to influence Presidents. If they are convinced that the current policy is best, the likelihood of gaining sufficient force to compel a change is quite small. The man who can build better foreign policies will find Presidents beating a path to his door.

POSING THE ALTERNATIVES

The most difficult problem in the whole American political system—in the decision-making processes of the national government—is to sharpen the posing of alternative policies. The shaping of public policy alternatives ought to be the guts of politics. Our political problems have proved far more intractable than our technical problems. Let us pray that landing on the moon will teach us at least this much. We landed but our earthly problems remained, including how we were to finance more moon landings. It is hard to change policy, not because the President thinks current policy is "best" (Richard Nixon knows that our welfare policy is a mess), but because it is hard to change policy, even a disastrously wrong policy. It is never easy to gain sufficient force to compel a significant policy change, because the resistances to change in a complex organization (or system) which tends to decide incrementally are steady and persistent. One doubts that there was any intellectual obstacle in the way of conceptualizing a "better" American policy in Asia than the one we have followed for the past two decades or more, but effecting basic policy changes in a system which features the military-congressional complex committed to the dogmas of containment has proved extraordinarily difficult.[18]

We need to face the fact that an American President experiences as much difficulty as he does in asserting policy leadership because his leadership is compromised at the outset by a political tradition, paradoxically enough, which tends to deny the legitimacy of politics. E. E. Schattschneider,[19] a wise student of American politics, has described our system as "a non-political, anti-majoritarian democracy." As a result, the political involvement of the vast majority of Americans is slight. Forty million adult Americans manage to avoid the simple act of voting even in our highly publicized, mass-media-glamorized, expensively and elaborately organized Presidential contests.* In the Nixon-Humphrey struggle of 1968 an estimated fifteen million Americans *who were registered to vote* managed to avoid the voting booth completely on election day. Some of them may even have been protesting the absence of alternatives.

In an earlier chapter we noted briefly the apparent tendency in Congressional politics for the triumph of incumbency. Once elected to the House or Senate the chances are excellent that the incumbent will be returned again. Party organization, as such, which has been on the decline at the local and state levels since the days of the Progressives, now approaches an all-time low. Candidates for major offices—Congress, Senate, Governor, President—characteristically build their own organizations. The Kennedys built a great personal organization for the 1960 campaign. Nixon, the victim that year, took a leaf from their organizational book in 1968. In American politics, at all levels, it is increasingly a matter of every man for himself.[20]

One of the fundamental reasons formal party organization de-

*The President who would lead the nation may attract the attention of some of the nonparticipants momentarily, but he cannot reasonably expect that he or his public policy program will gain the support of the millions who are profoundly committed by deeply ingrained habit and ancient life styles to attitudes of complete political apathy.

clines, while candidates find it expedient to run on their own, is that many of them experience great difficulty in convincing the public that politics is relevant to their lives. The methodologically elegant studies of voting behavior which have graced—and enriched—American political science these past twenty years all show huge masses of American voters lacking any very specific knowledge of substantive issues, especially issues as they are shaped in the national legislative arena.[21] Is it any wonder? How is anyone, even the specialist in the legislative process, to know who is responsible for what? A liberal Democratic President faces a majority of his own party in both houses of Congress, but legislative policy is influentially shaped by conservative Congressional barons whose views and legislative activities are almost invisible to the average citizen.

The nation has been through more vital changes in the last thirty-five years—depression, war, cold war, vast technological expansion, the neo-Keynesian policy revolution, the rise of the military technocracy, the growth of the welfare state, the suburban sprawl, the black migration, the deepening urban crisis, the stridency of student protest, the threat of political assassination, the growth of the knowledge industry—than it went through in the previous two hundred years. But national legislative politics seems to have changed hardly at all, at least so far as its visibility to the general public is involved. Social scientists probing the mysteries of voting behavior have frequently noted that many Americans, even the vast majority who hold a traditional, habitual attachment to Party, have trouble connecting the party of their choice to specific national issues. Which party position are they supposed to perceive with clarity? The President's, their Congressman's (assuming they know who he is), the barons of the Congressional Coalition (assuming they know that they exist) or the local party boss (assuming they can find one who has not been mummified and installed in the nearest museum)?

It is not surprising that most Americans are nonpolitical. Most citizens everywhere may be presumed to be nonpolitical most of the time. But we have devised a system which makes it extraordinarily difficult for the most intelligent and sophisticated among us to maintain an active, alert interest in public affairs. The search for relevance can begin right here.

THE SEARCH FOR RELEVANCE

Even the dimwitted must begin to sense how much the polity is changing. Politics has taken to the streets. This alone should alert us. The black migration has taken place. All American problems are nationalized, sooner or later, and black poverty is no exception. We have landed on the moon. This provides another sea to sail on, and we are the most expansionist nation among the current great powers. Entrenched technocratic militarism is now part of the American society with *civilians* proving to be better militarists than the career soldiers. Nearly five million American children are living on public welfare. Seven million other Americans, most of them young, are studying in our colleges and universities. What some of the young people seem to be trying to say to us, sometimes in rather strange ways, is that politics ought to be made relevant to the changing society. And, they insist, let's get our priorities straightened out.

This is not a bad charge for the 1970s. The President who would lead the way to relevant politics has great technical resources at his command, but he will soon discover that his technicians will have policy preferences of their own which they would love to make "presidential." They often have control of, or access to, esoteric data which promises to be helpful in solving some of technocratic society's perplexing problems, but experience teaches that technicians also have dogmas which they exalt. The more highly placed among them may have bureaucratic interests of their own to protect. The President who would lead also faces a Congress with a mind and will of its own—or, more probably in the 1970s, a Congress which contains conflicting wills. Congress historically has demonstrated an institutional interest in resisting a popular President who would lead in any direction, and especially in the direction of social reform. A Congress which is dominated by the conservative Coalition will have its own additional reason for resisting Presidential leadership which is aimed at basic reform.

If one finds no reason to be sanguine about the possibilities, there may be less reason for despair. A tiny band of college students followed a middle-aged poet-politician into the cold hills of New Hampshire and promptly provoked the abdication of one of the proudest and most powerful political men ever to enter the White House. Student protesters have stimulated reforms in university structure and administration. Groups within the Congress responding to new pressures on the outside have forced full-scale debate of the ABM issue. Reform of national taxation suddenly becomes a national imperative. A Republican President proposes a program of income maintenance and urges a multibillion-dollar drive to improve the quality of our environment. The military-congressional complex finds itself on the defensive, the subject of critical examination. Poor blacks in nearly every city of any size are now organized to put pressure on City Hall and the Board of Education, much as middle-class whites have always done. Major cities have eleted black mayors. Young blacks in significant numbers are studying in every important university in the country. And their numbers will increase steadily.

The process of political change was well underway as the nation entered a new decade. Whether the nation was entering a new era depended on the shape of the new politics.

CHAPTER NINE

IDEOLOGY AND POLITICAL CHANGE

> *"When I use a word,"* Humpty Dumpty said,
> *in rather a scornful tone, "it means just what*
> *I choose it to mean—neither more nor less."*
> *"The question is,"* said Alice,
> *"whether you* can *make words*
> *mean so many different things."*
> *"The question is,"* said Humpty Dumpty,
> *"which is to be master,—that's all."*
> LEWIS CARROLL, *Through the Looking Glass*

IF WE are to have a new politics in this country, we may be sure that it will be based upon a new ideological cleavage. There were some signs as we entered the seventies that a new ideology was in the making. Traditional liberalism, pragmatic liberalism, label it as you will, appeared to be in a state of steady decline, although many liberals hoped it was not too late for a fundamental transformation. We noted earlier in this book the appearance of an academic study in 1969 which carried a scathing indictment of what it termed "interest-group liberalism."* At times it appeared that there was scarcely anyone left in the country who seriously thought it possible for pragmatic liberalism as practiced in recent years to survive, except possibly those politicians who, having been brought up on the rhetoric, repeated the words, not knowing a better alternative. At the same time, the more prescient liberal politicians have often been among the first to sense the need to rationalize what is typically called "an approach" to a new politics. If they

*See Chapter One

cannot see the substance of the new ideology (and who can?), they can at least affect a change of style. John F. Kennedy, Robert Kennedy and Eugene McCarthy, each in his own way, are examples of this trend.

Underlying the groping of the politicians for a new rationale, and the writing of serious social criticism, is the failure in practice of liberalism—with its immediate antecedents in the issues of the Great Depression—to generate enthusiasm today among the idealistic youth, the restless blacks, and the poor. The new forces seeking basic changes in American society find much of traditional political rhetoric meaningless. Sit before the television set with an intelligent eighteen-year-old today observing one of the better contemporary political speakers, and note the mixture of slight amusement and even greater bafflement with which his words are received. What in hell is he talking about, the eighteen-year-old is most likely to ask. It is not an unfair question.

I wish to make it perfectly clear that I am questioning at this point the relevance of a political tradition whose values I share. The Preface to this book states my bias. So there will be no doubt about this bias in the context of the problem we are now discussing: I share the political position of the men in the House of Representatives who have made the DSG an important liberal legislative force. If I had won a Congressional election in 1960, I would have immediately joined the DSG. If I were in the House today, I should wish to be an active member of the DSG. During a period of active participation, 1954–65, I was closely associated with liberal politicians. One of them is a major national political figure today. From 1962–65 I was an assistant to a member of the Kennedy-Johnson cabinets who for me represents the very best in Stevensonian liberalism. I am not prepared to disown contemporary political liberalism because I find it impossible to believe that the liberal politicians I have mentioned by name in Chapter Seven do not have an enormous contribution to make to American public life and public policy in the 1970s. I should hate to think of facing our current grave issues without them.

It is not that the political liberals in Congress do not have the capacity to deal with the problems of race, poverty, urban chaos, and the new militarism, *at least as well as any political grouping we can presently identify,* but that they may very well not have sufficient political force to mobilize an effective national will before time runs out. While thoughtful liberals are concerned about liberalism's—and the nation's—failure to find the solution to the poverty of millions of black Americans, they have every reason to ask where there is a political force in America prepared to effect the remedy. As I read the New Left, there is as yet nothing from that quarter coherent enough to appeal to more than a tiny percentage of the attentive public, to say nothing of the nonparticipants, the poor, the alienated, and all of the others for whom the New Left presumes to speak.

In saying this, I do not believe that liberalsim will survive, nor would it deserve to, unless in the years immediately before us, the nation finds the means (and the will) to provide for black Americans the same opportunities which most white Americans now take for granted. And meaningful work is a first priority. Nor do I wish to minimize the very great difficulties liberal politicians face in trying to gain the interest and support of the new political generation which is beginning to feel its oats. The gap may not be bridgeable.

There is a further possibility, far more troublesome and far more difficult to assess. We may now be living in a society whose very "success" (the achievement of eccnomic growth, for example) defeats our best efforts to build a Good Society. It is possible that we have reached the point where the sum total of our successes has produced a cumulative reality which was *unintended.* I feel certain that my own generation looks out upon a world we did not envisage as recently as ten years ago. Many of us, and this includes large numbers of so-called "successful" people, find ourselves profoundly dissatisfied before this new society (the post-industrial society). Yet we are shocked, as Professor Everett Ladd, Jr.,[1] recently suggested, when we discover how difficult it is to chart a course from these dissatisfactions to acceptable or feasible public solutions. It may be, as Ladd has also suggested, that we are at one of those rare points of massive transformation from one political agenda to another. And public men, at the beginning of a new decade, experience great difficulty in solving the crisis of public authority because they have not been able to articulate the causes of the dissatisfactions nor have they been able to propose solutions.

Not the least fascinating aspect of all this is the possibility that a new ideological division may already be forming in the attitudes of many Americans towards public issues; the attitudes, as one gets glimpses of them, do not easily translate into the traditional political categories. The terms "liberal" and "conservative" as they have been used in normal political discourse in recent years may not be satisfactory labels for the emerging views of society. They may not fit. At this stage, one is hard put to find the appropriate labels for the new attitudes. But the reality appears to be that Americans in their community relationships are currently displaying attitudes which may be thought of as either "parochial" or "cosmopolitan." This reality, rooted in attitudinal changes, is reenforced by elements in the American governmental system. The Congressional Coalition displays a natural bias toward the parochial position while the contemporary Presidency speaks for a more cosmopolitan constituency.

The rapid processes of technological change are forcing an ever-expanding range of interactions, essentially cosmopolitan in nature, among social and even national groups of people. Technological advances, especially in communications and transportation, have made next-door neighbors of peoples who are widely scattered geographically. We should expect to find, therefore, among the new scientific and technocratic elite, a gradually growing impatience with the narrower views of more parochially minded individuals, especially those who have power to influence the making of policies which relate to the expansion of technology's frontiers. This basic conflict between the cosmopolitanism of the scientific elite and the more limited perspective of political parochialism might be expected to increase in intensity in the nation which leads in the technological revolution.

THE POLICY MAKERS

Professor Everett Ladd, Jr., on the basis of extensive interviewing at the local community level, finds a "distinctly new pattern of ideological conflict" emerging which goes beyond the mere toning down of the older economic conflict. Problems which were not seen very clearly in the studies of academic social science of an earlier period have moved center stage. Ladd[2] poses some of the troublesome questions as they now appear:

> What do we do about the growth of Negro population in the city ghetto? How do we lower the unemployment rate of Negro Americans, a rate two and one-half times that of whites? How can the income of Negro families, little better than half that of white families, be brought to parity?

THE SCIENTIFIC CULTURE

In a sense these are old problems, not new, as Ladd acknowledges. But with the experience of the 1960s behind us, and as gross discriminations have been largely overcome (or so, at any rate, we like to think), we are better able to see the complexities beneath. Social problems of such technical complexity are increasingly being dealt with by those who "know," and "knowing" means sharing in the assumptions, methods and findings of the "scientific culture," to use Ladd's terminology. The boundaries of the scientific culture are broad; they inevitably include an essentially cosmopolitan view of the world. Ladd, following the earlier work of David Apter, believes that henceforth attention will have to be paid by political analysis to the fundamental division between those who comprehend the approach of science to these complex problems and those who do not. Apter[3] puts it this way:

> Any political conflict quickly becomes a problem of evaluating evidence. . . . Modern society then is composed of a small but powerful group of intellectually participant citizens, trained, educated, and sophisticated, while all others are reduced in stature if they are scientifically illiterate. . . . The new "ideology" is increasingly rooted in a professional cadre of highly trained men.

Many urgent urban problems relating to race and poverty require asking the key question which, for Ladd, often is not "Is the leader liberally or conservatively inclined?" but rather, "Is he conversant with a body of expert knowledge dealing with these problems?" Furthermore, as class politics of the New Deal period give way to status politics of the post-industrial order, the division widens between those who "really understand" the needs and directions of the modern technocratic society and those who necessarily cannot. These views, it should be stressed, are not simply an abstract construction by Professor Ladd; they are based on his extensive soundings in communities where these attitudes have been found to exist. Community leaders, in Ladd's findings, no longer act and react in ways which fit neatly the liberal-versus-conservative dichotomy. The white working-class union spokesman who votes Democratic may insist that Negroes in the community "stay where they belong" while the upper middle-class corporation official or professional who lives in suburbia where Negroes are few in number may see the need for carrying on measures of social reform in the ghetto. A group of community influentials, the upper professionals, sharing in the assumptions of the scientific culture, their status assured, will be most likely to invoke the spirit of expertise in meeting contemporary social problems. The positions of such people, fusing together, are generating an ideology to which Ladd attaches the label Cosmopolitanism.

The Parochial, on the other hand, as Ladd has found him, sees politics from close up, as it were. He lives where many of these problems are. His perspective tends toward a narrow bias. The cult of science holds little meaning or interest for the parochial person. Poverty, to take an excellent example, he views in rather old fashioned ways.

If conservatively inclined, he opposes "schemes" to take money away from those who have worked hard for it and give it to the lazy; if he is liberal, he urges the redistribution of wealth. Cosmopolitans see poverty not as a problem of redistribution, but rather as one of effective management of national resources and of equipping the poor, psychologically as well as technically, to compete in contemporary America.[4]

Professor Ladd's pioneering study reveals how far the nation has been shifting away from the simpler cleavages of thirty years ago. The attempt to discern the patterns of incipient ideological conflct merits respect. But difficulties remain. The "scientific culture" is not an unambiguous concept. Is there a scientific answer to the problem of black poverty? Does every complex economic, social, and political question have a clear and obviously correct technical solution? Why are we endlessly nibbling away at some of the most basic issues a modern technological society faces each day?

When David Apter finds the new ideology rooted in an elite cadre of trained, highly professional men and suggests that theirs is the advantage of scientific literacy, he has given us an important insight into modern decision-making. At the same time, one recalls that President Johnson's decisions to Americanize the war in Vietnam were supported by the continuing advice of a group of highly trained upper professionals, attuned to the scientific culture, all apparently cosmopolitan in outlook. On the domestic side, another group of competent professionals saw to it that the Presidential antipoverty program included a socially militant version of Community Action. In both cases, professional men offered technical advice containing an extraordinary potential for political upheaval of the kind which can shake a great nation to its foundations.

THE PRESIDENCY: A COSMOPOLITAN OFFICE

We have noted previously that a fundamentally parochial view of public questions may expect to receive a respectful hearing in the centers of Congressional power. The Presidency is, of course, the logical place to reenforce cosmopolitan interests. The Presidency is the one truly great national office in the whole system, and the Presidency, likewise, has long been the most reliable political institution for the expression of the nation's international responsibilities. The experience to date tends to suggest that, in elevating the professionals, the institutionalization of Presidential decision-making adds to the difficulties a President experiences in maintaining his position of policy-leadership. He needs their experience but they may unwittingly help to weaken his power base. Presidents will continue to surround themselves with professionals, managers, technicians, administrators, special assistants, economic advisors, science advisors, urban affairs specialists, ad infinitum. As President Nixon has demonstrated, even in a period of withdrawal and deflation the number of Presidential technicians steadily increases.

In other ways, too, recent experience indicates that the presence of growing numbers of highly regarded professionals in the center of presidential decision-making is not exactly an unmixed blessing for the President. Modern social science has not reached the stage of exactitude where it can offer clear-cut policy alternatives to the political leader who is seeking tolerable solutions to explosive social issues. The formulation of the Johnson antipoverty program has been cited as one of the best examples we have of "the professionalization of reform." Yet from the very beginning of the program, the professionals and technicians disagreed among themselves about the causes of poverty and about the most advantageous ways of attacking it. After the program had lost its glamor, the charge was made that the government did not know what it was doing in launching the attack on poverty in 1964. The political leadership was wrong in labeling it a "war on poverty," unless an all-out attack was to follow. But professionals in the Executive office of the President should bear most of the responsibility for not *knowing,* since their expertise was relied upon in formulating the program.[5] One doubts that the new administration had any real choice about launching the new program, the planning of which had been underway for several months, especially in view of the cries for action coming from the civil-rights leaders as President Johnson entered the White House. How much longer should the Johnson administration have waited for the professionals and the social-science advisors to offer a "sounder and better" program?

A second major point about decision-making in the national

government should be emphasized: when a momentous and complicated new program such as that proposed in the Economic Opportunity Act is put together, there is not likely often to be a self-conscious searching for the social-scientifically "correct" approach. If anything, the case of the antipoverty program is an unusual one in the receptivity which was shown to fresh approaches.[6] New programs tend to be put together from what is known in government about the problems with which the proposal wishes to deal. New programs combine elements from existing programs and from program concepts having bureaucratic sponsors. The Community Action program is a case in point. The Ohlin-Cloward views, which have since been questioned, had been adopted by technicians working directly and closely under Attorney General Robert Kennedy at least a year before the assassination of President Kennedy.[7] It was these professionals and technicians who put together the Community Action program for other professionals in the Bureau of the Budget. The Ohlin-Cloward views were not merely social-scientific and technical in nature; they had a political and bureaucratic history, and an incalculable political potential. It would be interesting to know whether this key political fact was called to President Johnson's attention by the high-level professionals who figured so prominently in the formulation of the new Presidential program.

The cosmopolitanism of the professional may be assumed. His influence on the making of public policy may be expected to increase in the immediate future. No one should imagine that it is possible for a modern technocratic society to be governed except by making full use of those who are technically expert. What should be questioned is the quality of the technician's *judgment* on the great issues of the times. He is often a special pleader for his own views and even for his own techniques. His technical competence, even when it is exceptional, offers no guarantee that he possesses political wisdom or virtue. All human experience warns that wise and human judgments are not the product of expertise. There is no assurance that men of cosmopolitan instincts and large talents will not succumb at times to the most stereotyped views of the world.

Witness the tendency on the part of a number of sophisticated men in the Kennedy-Johnson administrations to adopt uncritically the containment dogma inherited from the past.

This preliminary review of the cosmopolitan-parochial dichotomy is indebted to the creative work of scholars such as Apter and Ladd who are breaking new ground in the search for an ideology-in-the-making. At the same time, the expectations tentatively identified as "cosmopolitan," though they may be real enough in attitudes which are present in the community, may also prove unrealistic in relation to the results which are likely to be achieved by the application of a more rational or scientific approach to policy issues. The capacity of social science to provide a satisfactory answer to any of the really tough questions currently on the American agenda is open to some doubt. The best social scientists may be limited by their own ideological preconceptions. Some of the most eminent social scientists have occasionally failed to apply their analytical skills to data which is readily available. Social science is created by highly trained professionals who are finite, fallible and all-too-human. In this important respect, they resemble the political men who find they must make hard judgments on partial "facts" under the pressure of imminent crises.

The analysis in this book has shown that important public policy decisions, foreign and domestic, are increasingly group decisions in which politicians and technicians work together in seeking solutions to problems of enormous complexity. These group decisions, furthermore, tend to be made incrementally, bit by bit, a step at a time, as part of an ongoing process in which policy leadership at the top of the structure experiences considerable difficulty in asserting its affirmative will. In part, this difficulty appears to be inherent in the nature of large-scale modern organizations. It has been complicated in the Executive branch of the American national government by the increasing reliance upon the professional expert at a time when traditional political ideologies appear to be in a state of decline. If political differences were found to be insubstantial, or if they proved to be of only marginal importance, then perhaps executive leadership in a modern technocratic state would find no greater purpose than to react in a technically adroit way to the changing tides of human affairs. The prudent President seeking a viable role in the vast expanse of the executive establishment might be well advised to lead the technocracy by cooperating with those elements and agencies in the ongoing process which have the largest interest in doing what they have been doing. And well advised to leave social reform to the knowledgeable professionals, some would doubtless argue.

WHICH VOTERS?

The political leader presumably is mindful that there is a voting public whose views and interests must be considered. In the American polity today it is not necessarily a simple matter to know what those views and interests are. There are, in fact, quite diverse groups of voters, and a national leader may see them in all their variety and still be uncertain where *his* majority is to be located.

The elaborate studies of voting behavior, so much admired by contemporary social science, show a large mass of voters, approximately two of every three participants in national elections, who are devoid of ideological passion and whose perceptions of national issues are hazy at best. The American political system, we are told, relies heavily for its continuity and stability on the habitual attachment which this great voting mass has for one or the other of the two major parties.

The voting studies also confirm what every perceptive political analyst already knows—that most American boys and girls are "born alive" Republicans and Democrats. The typical American child adopts party preference uncritically early in life in much the same way he accepts other traditional attitudes, as, for example, religious attitudes. The tendency of voting studies devotees has been to place a positive assessment on this habitual, uncritical, "standing decision" which most voters have made for either the Republican or Democratic party. This unthinking attachment of the great mass gives the system a sense of concord.[8] Presumably, the large mass which coalesces towards the center of the system would be very little perturbed by the sort of analysis contained in this book. Many of these citizens are perhaps ready to accept the legitimacy of the efficiently run technocratic society, especially one that is affluent, and will rest content, leaving social reform in the reliable hands of the professionals until something goes drastically wrong!

But the voting studies have called attention to two other categories which are quite relevant to this analysis: the interested voter and the nonvoter, who between them may constitute a potential majority. The early Michigan Survey Research Center findings reported a large third of the national electorate showing a rather considerable interest in politics. This finding has stood up fairly consistently in subsequent studies. And a group of twenty to twenty-five million reasonably alert voters is not to be lightly put aside. This is not to suggest, however, that the lot of the issue-oriented voter is an easy one. If the interested voter opposes Senator Goldwater as a fire-eating cold warrior, what is he to think when Mr. Johnson succeeds in Americanizing the war in Vietnam while interest rates rise higher than even the late George Humphrey would have dared to suggest? Or, to take a more ordinary perplexity, how is the voter who perceives issues with a fair degree of accuracy supposed to relate his perception to Party performance in government, given the reality of the Congressional Coalition?

The nonvoter poses other problems for us. He is out of it. In a certain sense, one could argue, he is not really relevant to this analysis since the policy-maker can so easily ignore his interests. On the other hand, the nonvoter is out of it because he chooses to be. He is unable to see that politics affects him. In this way, he ignores the policy-maker. This might be a minor matter were it not for the fact that there are probably almost as many nonparticipants in national elections as there are voters who show an orientation towards issues. All studies show a powerful correlation between nonparticipation and low income and lowly status. One is hence a little suspicious of those facile assumptions of the behaviorists (surely they are political innocents, at heart) which value the nonvoters for the positive contribution they make to the cause of social stability. The unstated assumption seems to have been that if the lower classes understood social reality better they would be likely to blow the lid off. They might at that. In any event, the question poses itself: how would policy leadership be transformed if somehow it were possible to stimulate large numbers of the apathetic to participate in elections? The question may be shaped a little more perversely: what would happen to the American political system, and to political leadership, if the previously apathetic were stimulated to participate at a time when policy leadership was unable to prevail against superior forces of resistance?

THE RESTLESS VOTER

There is another category whose behavior has been little studied by the behaviorists: the citizen who shares with the first category both knowledge and interest but who also feels an increasing disenchantment with traditional politics. The student rebels of the New Left have tended to monopolize the attention of the mass media. Yet something more than youthful rebellion was reflected in the Vietnam moratoria which took place in the final hours of the fateful decade. The McCarthy and Kennedy campaigns of 1968 aborted because the leaders were not there towards the end—one having been murdered and the other preferring poetry to power—and not because their supporters were attracted back to the clichés of traditional politics. Then there was the special appeal of Senator Muskie, running in the normally least advantageous position in national politics, the second spot on a ticket destined to lose. McCarthy, Kennedy, Muskie, each so different from the other in personal style, but each revealed the presence of a potential basis of popular support among voters seeking a fresh approach to American politics. Evidently, not all Americans, including some over thirty, had acquiesced and given themselves over to the unstated goal of technocratic efficiency. One sensed a probing rather to discover an authentic—or even a plausible—spokesman for all of those inchoate forces which were drawing some Americans away from the shibboleths of an era all but dead.

The phenomenon is not an American monopoly. The London *Observer*,[9] commenting on British politics, noted that "a large number of voters are disorientated and find it increasingly difficult to make sense of the parties as they have evolved during the past years. The old signals and slogans, to which they were trained to react like Pavlov's dogs, are no longer being given."

There is now a minority of voters, a group with a highly volatile political potential, which does not respond to the old signals and slogans. There is a tendency in the circles of respectable discourse to assume that the disenchantment with the old political struggles is limited to those who seek an idealized polity. We tend to forget that the largest current protest in American politics comes from the Right. A reactionary demagogue polled ten million votes in the 1968 Presidential election. It is true that his most reliable support came as expected in the Deep South, the most primitive political subculture in the nation; but the Wallace campaign was a vital factor in defeating the Humphrey-Muskie ticket in a number of industrial states in the North. Wallace's appeal showed no signs of diminishing after the election. Another ominous sign was the increasing tendency of a small group of young Left dissidents to take the struggle to the streets, not by way of peaceful demonstration but with clubs and chains, provoking bloody clashing with police.

It has been fashionable in our country to place most of the responsibility for these stirrings of discontent on Vietnam. Our overcommitment of resources to the fighting of the war in Southeast Asia represents a distortion of public priorities which took place during the 1960s. It has been part of our purpose to discover *how* and *why* a great nation was thrown off the track so far. We are facing something more than minor social dislocations, after all. By the end of the decade our largest cities often seemed almost ungovernable, especially to those who were trying to govern them. Despite several years of virtually unprecedented economic growth, the affluent society faced at home an underclass of ignorant and impoverished people the majority of whom appeared hopelessly trapped in new forms of self-perpetuating poverty. What does our experience in the sixties tell us about political leadership as it responds to these recent challenges?

CHANGE OF GENERATIONS

The United States entered the decade of the sixties with a change of administration. It was more than a change of administration, at least symbolically, because the leadership of the new administration, filled with a spirit of generous enthusiasm, self-confidently presented itself as representative of a new generation. President John F. Kennedy, himself a glamorous and battle-tested representative of the new political generation, displayed a personal style which at times held forth the promise of establishing a new relationship with the idealistic youth, the poor and the dispossessed, on the one hand, and with the rapidly expanding academic and scientific estate, on the other. The Kennedy administration diligently sought out some of the nation's ablest managers and technicians, men of the new meritocracy, Robert McNamara being only the most notable example. At the same time, President Kennedy personally recruited several leading academic intellectuals, Professors Galbraith, Schlesinger and Bundy, among them, for his inner circle of Presidential advisors. There were no noisy student protests and no satiric counterceremonies on Inauguration Day, 1961.

And yet, John F. Kennedy, a remarkably sophisticated politician, was the product of what we have been referring to as traditional politics. At no point in his career did he ever break with the political "regulars" in his own party, any more than Franklin Roosevelt did. Kennedy dealt unselfconsciously with John Bailey and, yes, Richard Daley in his ascent to power. In addition to his easy acceptance of the obviously practical side of Presidential nomination politics, Kennedy was apparently by nature a somewhat cautious and reserved politician. "There is no sense," Schlesinger[10] quotes Kennedy as saying, "in raising hell, and then not being successful. There is no sense in putting the office of the Presidency on the line on an issue, and then being defeated." Kennedy accepted Jefferson's view: "Great innovations should not be forced on slender majorities." Kennedy's Congressional majority was slender, indeed. There may be reason to speculate that had a kinder fate matched Kennedy against Senator Goldwater in 1964, the young President might finally have been given a Congressional majority large enough to support his legislative program. One can go further perhaps in speculating on the success Kennedy might have enjoyed in breaking through to a new kind of politics, but there is relatively little in his actual record which offers substantial assurance on this score.

Ironically, it was Lyndon B. Johnson, one-time Populist, leader of orthodox Congressional-Coalition politics, original New Dealer grown accustomed to the ways of power and the sins of pride, Washington influential writ large, Texas style, who was destined to head the Kennedy team of technocrats, managers, intellectuals and the new-generation politicians during the decade's worst hours of crisis. It was Johnson of Texas who had the responsibility for policy leadership when the nation's stickiest foreign and domestic policy problems converged into one grand dilemma. Johnson was not a cautious politician as he led the Congress in 1964 and 1965, and he was in office only a year when he was given the largest Congressional majority any activist President had enjoyed since 1936. Thirty years of inside-Washington political experience and an intimate knowledge of the labrynthine processes of Congress had left Johnson with an extraordinarily acute appreciation of the special time-cycle which is built into the Presidential-Congressional relationship. Johnson knew that great legislative innovations had better be innovated fast or not at all. Johnson understood better than most Presidents that the nature of the Executive-Congressional relationship forces the hasty making of great policies. Hence, Johnson was unwilling to wait for the arrival of a large Congressional majority before seizing the legislative initiative. He became an aggressive Chief Legislator within hours of taking over the White House following the assassination of John F. Kennedy. The results could scarcely have been more impressive. The Johnson record of legislative achievement deserves to be ranked alongside the monumental accomplishments of his twentieth-century activist predecessors, Franklin D. Roosevelt and Woodrow Wilson.

There was nothing of the "new politics" in either the style or the conception of Johnson's politics. In a sense, Lyndon Johnson was closer to the William McKinley-Mark Hanna conception of national political leadership (although not, of course, on matters of program substance) as he pursued a course of consensus politics by weaving together with apparently inexhaustible energy an all-group combination in which there was room for big business as well as for the traditional elements in the post-New Deal Democratic coalition; labor, ethnic groups, Negroes, urban machines and intellectuals. The implicit assumption underlying Johnson's legislative strategy seemed to be that there were no conflicting interests in the Great Society, at least for the purpose of getting on with the enactment of the President's broad legislative program.*

Kennedy had not been a consensus politician in this sense. While Kennedy worked for a time trying to gain the support of Big Business for his trade and tax proposals, he also fought Big Steel bitterly, recalling at the time his father's experienced warning about the dubious paternity of American businessmen. Kennedy's presidential rhetoric minimized the role of conflict in society as he shifted gradually to the view that the nation's fundamental problems were increasingly technical and administrative in nature more than they were political.

The central issue, as Kennedy came to view it in 1962, with the assistance of Walter Heller, another talented academician recruited to the New Frontier, was the management of the complex American industrial economy using the esoteric insights of the new economics. Kennedy, after all, had inherited a great industrial economy whose sluggish growth rate during the 1950s had left unemployment at an intolerably high level. The manipulation of fical policy required the judgment of the economically expert far more than it called for the special talents of Kennedy's exceptionally well-turned political organization.

THE END OF IDEOLOGY

Kennedy came to power at a time when it seemed that none of the nation's most difficult problems would be solved unless

*Johnson in 1964–65 showed that "interest group liberalism" was capable of accomplishing rather impressive legislative results.

a way were found to stimulate the massive American industrial machine to operate at its fullest potential. In our retrospective view of the past decade it is important that this point not be neglected: public policy was formulated to promote a high level of economic growth, and it worked. Unfortunately, our success in meeting this goal left the problems of black poverty, urban blight, pollution of the environment, and control of the new militarism virtually untouched and at the point of supreme crisis. Kennedy also came to power at a time when academic intellectuals popularized the notion that political ideology was dead. The efficient managing of a technocratic industrial empire did not involve questions of an ideological nature. Barrington Moore, Jr., a Harvard sociologist, was one of the first American social scientists to wonder whether the gradual reduction of economic inequalities did not also carry with it the elimination of these sources of discontent that historically have produced genuine political alternatives. Writing towards the end of the Eisenhower period, Moore asked whether a society based on liberty did not perhaps require the presence of an oppressed group in order to grow in quality. Moore[11] speculated further that this might be

> the tragedy as well as the glory of liberty. Once the deal has been achieved, or is even close to realization, the driving force of discontent disappears, and a society settles down for a time to stolid acceptance of things as they are. Something of the sort seems to have happened to the United States.

If the Eisenhower era marked a settling down to a stolid acceptance of things as they were, it should be noted that some of the nation's leading social scientists were also apparently affected by the prevailing mood. Seymour Martin Lipset published a book in 1960 called *Political Man* which was widely acclaimed as a major contribution to the expanding literature of political sociology. The author ended by adding a personal postscript entitled "The End of Ideology?" (And it is to be noted that Lipset put the proposition in the form of a question). At the close of an unusually ambitious social-science live in conditions of unspeakable degradation. Entering the 1970s, thousands of black Americans were denied what Lipset treatise surveying a vast range of monograph materials, Lipset[12] was willing to say unequivocally that the fundamental problems of the industrial revolution had been solved. He wrote:

> the workers have achieved industrial and political citizenship; the conservatives have accepted the welfare state; and the democratic left has recognized that an increase in over-all state power carries with it more dangers to freedom than solutions for economic problems. This very triumph of the democratic social revolution in the West ends domestic politics for those intellectuals who must have ideologies or utopias to motivate them to political action.

That same year the question mark was removed as Daniel Bell, well-known sociologist, then of Columbia University, published a book, *The End of Ideology*.[13] Twice during the year of 1962, President Kennedy gave important addresses in which "the end of ideology" theme shone through clearly.

FAULTY ANALYSIS

Is it possible that we face a different problem from the one which intrigued a number of leading social scientists a decade earlier? Ideology may not be dead, only seriously ill, an illness which has been complicated by faulty diagnosis. Lipset was prepared to say as early as 1960 that the fundamental problems of the industrial order had been solved and the workers had achieved industrial and political citizenship. Yet even today millions of Americans who are poor are also employed. They work for wages which fall far below the level necessary to maintain a decent standard of life. This basic problem has not been solved. Organized labor, with a few exceptions, no longer organizes. Even its best friends sense hardening of the arteries. Three million adult black citizens were not even allowed the right to vote at the time Lipset was writing his book. A sizeable portion of the total black community continues even now to

206

calls "industrial citizenship." They did not even have jobs. A significant group of trade unions tacitly practices racial discrimination.

Lipset felt that the "triumph" of the democratic social revolution had ended domestic politics for many intellectuals. This seems a pity. Why withdraw so early? Intellectuals who need visions of Utopia to spur them on to political and social action are a special case. But how is one to explain those gifted with superior analytical skills who failed to illuminate the triumphant social revolution so that thirty million fellow citizens might better understand why the revolution stopped before they were included in its benefits?

It may be argued that social scientists like Moore, Lipset, and Bell were writing primarily for an audience of social scientists and that their theories did not affect popular conceptions. This may be so. If one is to look further for a book which was a popular success and which also illustrates both the strengths and weaknesses of liberalism, there is, of course, the book which gave us the phrase, *The Affluent Society.* When the book appeared in 1958, only a few short months after Sputnik, it was immediately recognized that Professor John Kenneth Galbraith, Harvard's peripatetic social critic, had launched a devastating attack on those public policies which were starving the public services. It was hard to imagine a book more likely to irritate the more conventional, to say nothing of the less literate, social scientists. Galbraith's book not only ridiculed the dogmas of modern economics but did so in a style which brought handsome sales in the marketplace whose wisdom it questioned.[14]

Today Galbraith's view has won wide acceptance. We have experienced a decade in which the glorification of Gross National Product has produced social results which are often, in fact, rather gross. Galbraith was right, and brilliantly eloquent, in warning that the affluent society was failing to meet urgent social needs in the headlong rush to achieve greater growth rates. The plea for a more generous material investment in human beings is almost emotional, a rare posture for Galbraith. Yet how familiar and meliorist it all sounds today. "Education, no less than national defense or foreign assistance, is in the public domain," Galbraith[15] insists toward the end of his book, and young readers will wonder that the point had to be made. "It is subject to the impediments of resource allocation between private and public use. So, once again, our hopes for survival, security and contentment return us to the problem of guiding resources to the most urgent needs." By insisting that public policy be directed to meet these urgent needs, Galbraith, a good Stevensonian, served liberalism well. Unfortunately, his analysis of poverty also reveals how deficient liberalism was in perceiving the full nature of poverty in affluent America.

Although his book runs to approximately a hundred thousand words, Galbraith devotes one slim chapter, about three thousand words in all, to the analysis of poverty in rich America. Perhaps not surprisingly, poverty appears to have been transformed into a largely technical problem. The affluent society has reduced poverty from majority to minority status. It can no longer be presented as "a universal or massive affliction." "It is more nearly an afterthought." Poverty appears not as a general but as a special case. "People are poverty stricken," in Galbraith's definition, "when their income, even if adequate for survival, falls markedly behind that of the community."[16]

Modern poverty is portrayed as falling into two broad categories: case poverty and insular poverty. "Case poverty is commonly and properly related to some characteristics of the individuals so afflicted. Nearly everyone else has mastered his environment; this proves that it is not intractable." Insular poverty is found in those areas or communities where "everyone or nearly everyone is poor." The causes of insular poverty are said to be complex, but Galbraith does not see fit to explore them in detail. He apparently has *rural* islands of poverty principally in mind. Thus, he observes: "The modern locus of poverty is even more the rural than the urban slum."

There is virtually no analysis of urban poverty in the 1958 version of *The Affluent Society.* The black ghetto is not mentioned. There is exactly one sentence on the relationship between race and poverty: "Especially in the urban slum, race or poverty may confine individuals to an area of intrinsically limited opportunity." Professor Galbraith, a leading figure in the liberal intellectual community, an eminent and richly rewarded writer on economic affairs, studied poverty in the 1950s, yet failed to note the deterioration of the black employment situation then taking place during a period of sluggish growth. Nonwhite unemployment in 1953 stood at an annual rate of 4.1%. Five years later as The *Affluent Society* rose on the best seller lists, unemployment among black Americans soared to 12.6%, a sickening figure. This, one must insist, was an empirical fact of central importance to any analysis of poverty in the midst of affluence.

Galbraith was also largely unprepared for the possibility that poor people might leave the rural islands of poverty. For some reason, he seemed convinced that something he repeatedly referred to as "the homing instinct" would keep the insular poor down on the farm. He put it this way:

> Insular poverty has something to do with the desire of a comparatively large number of people to spend their lives at or near the place of their birth. This homing instinct causes them to bar the solution, always open as an individual remedy in a country without barriers to emigration, to escape the island of poverty in which they were born.

And escape they did. Not a few individuals but, first, thousands, and finally, millions of them. The homing instinct proved not so strong after all as a human tidal wave of poor blacks moved away from the southern islands during the 1950s and the 1960s. They found their way to a new environment, the dark ghettos in the urban slums of the northern cities. They left one island for another, if you wish. As a result, case poverty, if we are limited to Galbraith's second concept (we are talking about the same people, in any event), became one of the fastest growing enterprises in the country in the ten years which followed the appearance of *The Affluent Society.* There were somewhat fewer than three million people supported (after a fashion) by the AFDC program at the beginning of the 1960s. By 1969 the number had swollen to six and a half million.

When Professor Galbraith[17] issued a revised second edition of his book in 1969, his chapter on poverty was altered to make room for these profound changes. His original error, a "considerable" one as he viewed it, was in "understatement." He was consoled by this thought: "If, ten years ago, one had foreseen and described the disaster that lay ahead for our urban communities, he would have been dismissed as a silly alarmist." Perhaps so. But one would today feel somewhat more confident in assessing the ability of contemporary liberalism to provide a solution to the problems which beset the nation.

The failure of the nation to find the way to a solution of the ominous issues of race, poverty and urban chaos during the past decade was a failure of intellectual analysis as well as of national will.

CHAPTER TEN

EPILOGUE—
WHERE DO WE GO FROM HERE?

*The crisis of our times spares no group;
not even the social sciences. The pressures
to utilize all our resources in critically evaluating
goals as well as in providing effective means
are too great to be denied. For increasing numbers
of us, it is no longer practical or morally
tolerable to stand on the political sidelines
when our expertise alerts us to disaster.*
DAVID EASTON, *at the annual meeting
of the American Political Science Association,
September 6, 1969.*

THE DILEMMA PERSISTS

The most pressing immediate American objective is to disengage from the Vietnam war. When that has been accomplished, we will know that the nation has finally taken the first step toward controlling the new militarism; at the same time, the nation will be forced to return to its greatest internal dilemma: the making of a full life for all its citizens, black and white. That dilemma, brilliantly illuminated by Gunnar Myrdal[1] more than a quarter of a century ago, persists as everyone knows, but the terms have been altered drastically and irretrievably. The black American insists upon being treated as a man, and this demand will not easily be turned aside so long as the American society retains any interest in honoring its creed, the creed which Myrdal found to be its vital force.

Is the nation prepared to honor this vision? Only a fool would discount the current mood of cynicism and despair. But the current mood may prove to be more reliable as a guide to the future than similar moods have been in the past. Political leadership which charted the American course in 1932 and 1933 on the basis of the dominant mood would have misserved the nation. How many now recall the prevailing mood in the western nations, including the United States, in June 1940? The demand of the black American that his manhood be respected—and this is what it comes down to—surely does not exceed the capacity of the nation to respond nor is it unreasonable in terms of the national creed. Black leaders were the first to note that a nation which has put men on the moon can do anything it puts its mind to. Putting black Americans to work in jobs of dignity and worth seems well within our technical capacity. The fact is that we have failed in meeting the challenge because we have not accepted the commitment to do so nor have we yet fashioned the tools.

We have excuses, of course, for our failures. The nation is sick at heart, deeply troubled and sorely divided by our hapless involvement in a neocolonial war which teaches how easily the sense of rational purpose may be obliterated by the misapplication of technology. This is not a minor lesson, and it comes at an exorbitant price. And yet it is not surprising that the people in the most advanced technocratic society should find themselves beguiled by technology which seems to be able to solve every problem except the ones which are tearing us apart. What precedents are we supposed to follow? How do Americans go about gaining control of the processes of technological change so as to direct them toward the objectives of social reform? If we have tossed and nearly foundered, who offered to navigate the uncharted seas? Where does one find the model society offering liberty and equality to all of its people?

Americans are supposed to know instinctively how inexorable the processes of change are. This is an important part of what being an American implies, so it is said. We have very little feeling that our society next year should look as it did last year. In this we are surely quite different from our British cousins, for example. We are by nature, by conditioning, and, perhaps, by preference, a restless, striving people. Although it is the neurotic potential which fascinates our critics, the quality of restlessness and unfulfillment also holds the promise that we may be able to deal with our dilemma by exploiting this capacity for change. It is easy to overlook the fact that the dilemma is ours only so long as the vision is honored. Americans are also remorselessly self-critical. If all the world is aware of the imperfections of the American reality, who has been shouting loudest from the housetops?

All American problems are nationalized sooner or later, and the problem of black equality is no exception. This is not to say that several million poor black citizens will achieve equality tomorrow morning, nor will their poor white neighbors. Nationalizing the problem does not mean that it will be easily solved, but it does elevate the black problem to the level where it becomes part of the continuous struggle of national politics. The plight of the poor black, desperate as it may be, gains in hopefulness when it is assessed in terms of the national standard rather than the norms which prevail in, let us say, Alabama or Mississippi.

The struggles of national politics are real despite the modish tendency to wish them away by "technocratizing" them. This book has pointed to certain institutional and political barriers which impede reform and which, curiously, have occasionally avoided the attention of intellectual critics. There is political opposition to change including change which would vitally improve the lot of poor Americans. But we also are highly uncertain as to *how* we should go about channeling the forces of change in ways which will rejuvenate the society, improve the quality of the common life, and restore a sense of civility and high purpose to the mundane daily struggles in which we are inevitably engaged.

A society groping for its soul, or the authenticity of its vision, needs prophets. Our prophets have been few and far between—Roger Williams, Thoreau, and who else? It has been said of the idealistic youth who went south to integrate lunch counters and who returned to question the foundations of the social order that theirs is a prophetic vision.[2] This may be. The courage and idealism of these young Americans is not in question. Their vision seems less clear. But this much is certain: the

protests of American youth have forced us to examine the
nature of the national malaise. This invaluable service could
never have been performed by the new mandarins, the managers and manipulators of technology. The mandarins, who are
marvelously trained for their work within the technocratic society *as it is,* perhaps should not be expected to initiate dissent
within the *civilisation technicienne* which rewards them so
well. It is a rare animal that will bite the machine which feeds
it.

A NEW CLASS STRUGGLE

There is the matter of this basic difference between the professional and the protestor which has to be reckoned with. One
is product and purveyor of the scientific culture while the other
carries his anti-intellectual banners proudly. Viewed another
way, the meritocracy manages the technocratic revolution
from positions securely based in the huge organizations of
modern society. The social protest comes from those who see
themselves in the existential revolt against the impersonality
and the dehumanizing force of the same huge organizations.
The underlying conflict between Establishment professional
and anti-Establishment rebel has many of the characteristics of
a class struggle, based as it is upon wholly different life-styles,
manners of speech and dress, and contrasting values. The differences between the two add a new dimension to the national
political struggle. It is no longer a struggle between the Haves
and the Have-Nots, as Marx insisted, or even between the
What-Have-Yous, as Madison suggested. The struggle transcends economics. It has to do with the nature of the society,
its pattern of organization and the possibilities for individual
fulfillment in a technocratic society. The national politician
who hopes to play a leadership role in shaping the policies of
the future will ignore the new basic conflict at the risk of his
own relevance.

Actually, the perceptive national politician of cosmopolitan
instincts recognizes, at least vaguely, how troublesome his position is fast becoming.[3] Even when he thinks in customary
terms of traditional pluralist doctrine, in which this group in-

terest is pitted against that, he may tend to view the profes-
sional-technician category as representing a group interest. If
so, the youthful protestors constitute a quite different "special
interest". Assuming that the young rebels are partially to be
identified with broader constituencies of students, artists, and
intellectuals, imagine what would happen to the calculus of
American politics if charismatic leaders effected their alliance
with the poor and the disadvantaged. These are emergent
group interests, if you please, which the ambitious cosmopolitan politician will seek to accommodate, if only he can find a
way.

The national politician who has this perspective will understand how technically complex the social issues of post-industrial society have become. As a cosmopolitan, in Ladd's sense,
his own judgment and his well-cultivated political instinct will
tell him to seek the advice of those who are technically expert
whenever he can. There is no important American politician
with pretensions to leadership who does not already do this as
a matter of course. At the same time, the politician with cosmopolitan values is likely to be sensitive to the demands of
social protest since he is prepared to accept the legitimacy of
protest. It is not at all difficult for the parochial-conservative
politician to ignore the protest, if he chooses to. The unflinch-
ing parochial may sincerely feel that he has no mandate to deal
with issues raised in the protest. But, more typically, the con-
servative-parochial in politics will find that his immediate interests are readily served by joining the demand that the
protest be put down in the name of "law and order."

Then there are the organizational politicians in the major
parties who experience no great difficulty in avoiding the serious implications of social protest. As political men whose habit
it is to swim along the surface of events where only the tip of
the iceberg shows, organizational politicians are the first to
note what a small minority the active protesters are. It would
never occur to them that organizational politicians are also a
small minority. In any case, organizational politicians function
in the arena of "practical politics" where conventional wisdom
has categorized the majority of voters as unpoor, unblack, and

unyoung. So why be concerned that grave political issues are being taken to the streets?

The men of the emergent moderate-to-liberal bloc whom we met in Chapter Seven, the new cosmopolitans, are being forced by changing circumstances to take a broader view. Having conducted themselves for years well within the confines of traditional politics (this is where they have won or lost), they have a natural interest in making the system work. They are part of it. But they also recognize the validity of much that is included in the critique the protestors have presented. They are perhaps more likely to recognize the legitimacy of the protest than most of the protestors are to accept *their* legitimacy. The cosmopolitan politician will find meaning in a significant portion of the protestors' agenda: the overweening influence of the military-industrial complex, the mechanization of the multiversity, the tangle of pathology in the urban slum, the shoddy materialism of affluence, the pollution of the environment. In part, this relative openness to the substance of protest is based on a consuming self-interest, the trademark of political men. As politicians who have fought and won within the system while standing to the left of center, they are naturally sensitive to the challenge of a new force arising on their left. Like the mythical general, any number of liberal politicians today are hastening to catch up with the troops who are out in front, even, occasionally, with troops carrying unrecognizable banners.

Political self-interest, important though it obviously is, may not be the whole explanation for the visible reactions of national politicians to the young protestors. Men like Senators Muskie and McGovern, whose local constituencies are not thought to be notably cosmopolitan in outlook, are responsive to the protest, one feels certain, because they realize that failure of the "system" to respond may leave protest with nowhere to go except to street militancy and more violence. Such national political leaders also know, however, that the social protest movement, whatever virtues may be ascribed to it, lacks a program of social reform. The movement, if it is a movement, exudes passion and a healthy sense of moral outrage. This may be its most significant contribution to a society which seemed for a time to have lost the capacity for outrage in the face of evil. The protest has pointed at weaknesses in basic structures. It has shown the tendency for mindless incrementalism to creep into the policies of huge organizations. But it does not have a detailed program of reform.

The men of moderately liberal persuasion who are just coming to positions of power and influence within the system of traditional politics, and this is especially the case in the Congress, are precisely the politicians who are most likely to place a reliance on the application of reason and science to social problems. Yet these same men who sense the rare opportunity of leading a far less conservative Congressional majority also must face a growing impatience, especially among the young, with traditional procedures. The anti-intellectualism of the young rebels includes an almost total neglect of history. Hence, the responsibility for the inadequacy of social reform measures in recent decades is placed squarely on the "liberals." The critics of the New Left simply ignore the basic fact that the men standing to the left of center in Congress often have been able to exert only marginal influence on policy because the conservative Coalition dominated the legislative process.

The problematic position of the cosmopolitan politician who is functioning within the structure of the existing system, often without a sustained progressive political force supporting his efforts, criticized for the inadequacies of his program by a new group of dissenters who are obsessed with their own moral purity but lack a program of reform of their own, hardly needs embellishment. Nor will the cosmopolitan politician appreciate being told of additional complications. Yet they are there. Until recently, only slight attention has been given to the application of social intelligence to the future needs of the nation. No systematic process exists by which the findings of modern social science are assessed against urgent public needs. We plan socially in America by stealth and indirection. To be sure, the Council of Economic Advisers has become an agency with some influence within the Institutionalized Presidency especially on questions of fiscal policy having to do with demand management. But there is no office of social-science adviser analogous to that which exists to represent the views of natural science at the White House level. Mr. Nixon is the first President to establish a special office for advice on urban problems. Mr. Moynihan is the first person trained as a social scientist, other than an economist, selected to occupy a special White House office with a small staff who has been asked to offer advice to the President on a range of problems which are susceptible to the techniques of modern social science, broadly viewed.

The picture in Congress is bleaker. Congress as an institution has sedulously avoided systematic exposure to modern social science. With the exception of the Joint Economic Committee, it is scarcely an exaggeration to say that Congress manages to avoid anything more than sporadic exposure to the findings of modern economic analysis. This is especially true in the committees dealing with taxation, finance, and public expenditures.

SOCIAL SCIENCE IN POLITICS

Despite these patterns of institutional rigidity and resistance, one senses a tendency for the techniques of social science to find their way into policy-making. Bertram M. Gross—who played a major part as a Capitol Hill staff technician in drafting the Employment Act of 1946, who was a principal architect of the Council of Economic Advisers, and who pioneered in bringing economic advice to bear on Presidential decision-making—foresees the emergence of a politics which will be based, in part, on modern social science. Gross and Springer[4] have written:

> Economic and sociological jargon is rapidly supplanting "the flag," "patriotism" and "God" in the public announcements of many political figures. More importantly, solid social analysis has been introduced into Congressional debates, White House staff meetings and occasionally crops up in city halls and state houses.

Gross and Springer are doubtless correct in sensing a greater receptivity to the findings of social analysis. One would expect this among the member of the DSG, for example. Intelligent politicians, and not simply those who are members of the moderate-to-liberal group, wish to find solutions to our common problems, after all. Most politicians are flexible when it comes to affecting what is now often referred to as a "political style," quite apart from the seriousness with which they view the issues or the stand they may take upon them. So, one listens respectfully when Gross and Springer speculate about the style of new politics. It will, they believe, eschew rhetoric and traditional ideology. And further: "It rests upon a basic commitment to confront our social ills and is buttressed with candor, flexibility and empiricism. The new politics demands public leaders who will admit their confusion, uncertainty and mistakes."[5]

This may very well be. It seems a little premature, however, to put upon those courageous enough to practice the new politics the additional burden of openly professing their uncertainty and confusion. Gross and Springer reach solider ground as they discuss the characteristics which will distinguish the new approach to politics. They see three principal features:

(a) an open and experimental approach to the formulation of public policy and the rejection of any *Weltanschauung* which would link social goals with particular administrative mechanisms;

(b) an emphasis upon probabilities rather than possibilities; grandiose dreams will be replaced by a calculation of incremental improvements in existing conditions;

(c) well-ordered information and careful analysis as the chief instruments of persuasion with an appeal which is explicitly cerebral rather than visceral.

The style of the new politics, as perceived by Gross and Springer, seems well designed to mesh with the interests, the values, and the jargon of the technocratic elite. It almost certainly will hold little attraction for those who are in dissent. Gross and Springer refer to a politics marked by a "general lack of passion" whose practitioners feel "a strong sense of mission" while their "deeper feelings are held carefully in check." The general approach, we recall, is cerebral, experimental, incremental and empirical, and it avoids "grandiose dreams." The men who are attracted to the new political approach are described as being "liberal, secure and well-disciplined," and we are further advised that they are "often unable to strike the emotional chord that elicits widely-based and enthusiastic public support."[6]

The difficulties this poses in an era when people of passionate concern are seeking new methods of achieving a broader participation in politics and decision-making are obvious. A politics divorced from passion will seem as sterile to those people as a politics which denigrates reason will appear reckless to others. On one extreme, the coolly rational technician may not show complete appreciation for the views of those who are passionately committed to the thwarting of his objectives. On the other side of the issue are all of those citizens who have come to believe that the Americanization of the war in Vietnam was brought about by secure, well-disciplined men who managed to hold their deeper feelings in check.

Politics in a democratic society should be led by men who share the deeply-felt needs of ordinary people. Such a society proceeds on the assumption that politicians who are subject to the controls exerted by the electorate should prevail in policy leadership. Democracy has been defined by Schattschneider[7] as "a competitive political system in which competing leaders and organizations define the alternatives of public policy in such a way that the public can participate in the decision-making process." Our analysis supports the thesis that in the future the advice of the technical expert, including the trained social scientist, will increasingly be sought after by public officials. The technicians's expertise permeates the decision-making processes of the modern state. Since this is the case, how much more hopeful we would be if social science were to walk the corridors of power with a sharpened awareness of the need to become involved in the terrible issues which have given rise to the social protest. If modern social science were in a position to assist political leaders in finding ways of controlling the power of the giant organizations which are such a characteristic feature of modern technocratic society, one might be a little less apprehensive about a future in which technocrats are destined to proliferate and flourish.

We assume that our system contains effective checks on concentrated power. We assume, further, that the decision-making processes of our complex governmental apparatus do not run unchecked. We should be horrified if it were suggested that possibly no one is in charge of the great American technocracy. Yet we have been told by both Sorensen and Schlesinger that President Kennedy did not authorize the Bay of Pigs operation, *as it was carried out.* But neither was he able to stop it, according to Sorensen. A less friendly observer might suggest that there is not a great deal of evidence that he wished to stop it. Either way, bureaucratic drift was apparently a large element in bringing on the Bay of Pigs fiasco. President Kennedy, we are told, then overhauled the national-security decision-making process. Nevertheless, bureaucratic momentum appears to have been a considerable factor in the escalation of American military force in Vietnam during the Johnson years. Bureaucratic do-gooding was instrumental in elevating Community Action to a prominent place in what was billed as a Presidential war on poverty.

American politics faces momentous challenges in the 1970s. Policy leadership must prevail in the complex organizations of the technocratic society during an era of unprecedented turmoil and change. If it is to do so, we shall have to find a way of sharpening policy alternatives.

SUGGESTIONS FOR FURTHER RESEARCH

As A PARTIAL, and not necessarily minor, contribution to the task of institutional reform, political scientists may wish to consider the priorities which might govern further study and research in three broad areas touched upon in the preliminary examination contained in this book: decision-making in the Institutionalized Presidency; the nature of Congressional leadership in an era of rapid social change; and the political behavior of those who reject the system. My suggestions follow below.

THE PRESIDENCY

We ought to know more than we do about the actual influence exerted by the various agencies within the Institutionalized Presidency in the making of public policy. In recent years attention has tended to focus upon the Council of Economic Advisers and the part it plays in domestic policy. A cynic might suggest that the explanation lies in the unwillingness of the professional economist to hide his light under a bushel. Modern economic analysis has come into its own as a force in public policy-making everywhere in the industrialized world since the end of World War II. In the United States the most notable recent example came during the Kennedy-Johnson years during the Council chairmanship of Walter Heller, a highly competent professional who combined political sagacity with an exceptional talent for publicity. Heller not only utilized his position within the White House staff agency to convince a rather skeptical President of the usefulness of modern economic analysis but he also popularized the doctrine of the new economics in the busy marketplace of ideas.

The Bureau of the Budget ought to hold the same degree of interest for the policy-oriented political scientist that the Council of Economic Advisers has for the professionally trained economist. It is a remarkable insight into the state of American political science that only one major political scientist has ever served in the highest echelon of the Budget Bureau; and no major political scientist has yet examined this elite Presidential agency's policy-making role in the way that Professor Fenno,[1] for example, has painstakingly revealed the functioning of the Congressional Appropriations Committees. Professor Neustadt[2] opened the door to the Bureau when he published his essay on the growth of central clearance of legislation within the Institutionalized Presidency. His article appeared in 1954. A decade and a half later it may be said that we know a little more about the Bureau of the Budget as the molder of policy, but only a little more. Aaron Wildavsky's[3] brief study of the politics of the budgetary process is admirably suggestive but far from definitive in outlining the political role of the Budget Bureau.

As we enter the 1970s, the political analyst who wishes to assess the forces at work within the Institionalized Presidency soon discovers that he is working with bits and pieces garnered from this case study and that. The door which Neustadt set ajar in 1954 has recently been opened wider by Moynihan and Blumenthal, as we have seen. And, as might have been expected, the Budget Bureau is found playing an influential policy role. What surprises is the manner in which Budget Bureau professionals assumed the initiative in shaping explicitly political, socially explosive and highly controversial portions of the antipoverty program. If this seems unusual, there is the recent report of James Sundquist, who knows the Budget Bureau well from years of intimate association, in which he ascribes a significant part in the writing of national manpower legislation to a conscientious technician who was not even at the Assistant Director's level in the Bureau's hierarchy.

THE POLICY MAKERS

We have seen enough to convince us that the political process includes professionals and technicians in the Budget Bureau who have their own views of the public interest. What happens when these technicians disagree among themselves or when they find themselves in conflict with departmental views or, indeed, with the views of other Presidential staff agencies? How is the Budget Bureau's view of the public interest arrived at? These and similar questions would soon take us beyond the examination of the techniques used to clear departmental bills, important though that power has been in establishing Budget Bureau ascendancy over at least some of the departments. In short, a contemporary political science which wishes to learn more about who exerts influence in national policy-making will have to devote more time, energy and ingenuity in getting inside the agencies of the modern Presidency. One assumes that the silly myth about the President heroically making all the fateful decisions in lonely contemplation has long since been placed on the shelf where it belongs. Presidential policy-making is a group process, and there undoubtedly are conflicts within the Institutionalized Presidency which may be reflected in policy. We have learned that shortly after President Johnson appointed his own Secretary of Defense he began receiving a view on Vietnam which contrasted sharply with that which his national security advising team had been offering for months.[4] In the first year of the Nixon administration a fierce struggle evidently took place between two White House special offices headed by Messrs. Burns and Moynihan over the question of welfare reform. The Secretary of Labor was called in to arbitrate the differences before a Presidential proposal was brought forth. Presumably, the Nixon plan for overhauling the public welfare programs of the nation reflected the outcome of a policy struggle within the Institutionalized Presidency.[5]

No doubt the examples will multiply, and our understanding will gain in sophistication, as we learn more about the making of policy within the contemporary Presidency.

THE CONGRESS

The Congress of the United States, so little understood by the public at large, continues to hold the interest of political scientists, as it has since Woodrow Wilson published his classic study late in the nineteenth century. Unlike the Institutionalized Presidency, the modern Congress has not suffered from neglect on the part of academic political scientists. A number of recent studies rank among the best in a body of literature which is vast in scope and volume. At the present time, a series of Congressional studies sponsored by the American Political Science Association is well underway.

This interest in Congress happily extends to the younger members of the political science fraternity. One hopes that the more gifted of these younger scholars, riding a wave of renewed interest in the Congress, will resist the temptation to succumb totally to the seductive wiles of the new bitch-goddess, Methodological Elegance. We need more, and better, studies which examine the nature of Congressional power and the role of Congressional leadership in the broader system. It is a matter of deep regret that an empirical-behavioral revolution in political science has taken place but has thus far left the legislative careers and the influence of men like Richard Russell and the late Everett Dirksen virtually unexamined. These powerful shapers of public policy throughout the postwar period have been left to the all-too-tender mercies of the freelance journalist and the cliché-laden profiles of the Sunday supplements. How little we know about the role of Congressional leadership in the broader system in which it takes place! And it is not that we lack models for such studies. Professor Huitt showed the way in his pioneering studies of Senate leadership and the Senate Maverick. Professor Manley's recent essay analyzing the manner in which Wilbur Mills functions as chairman of the powerful Ways and Means Committee provides a superb model.[6]

Congressional leadership groups and patterns of leadership are bound to change in the current decade, perhaps in significant ways. It is entirely possible that Congress will change more than any other major political institution during this decade. In any event, it is a virtual certainty that the essential control of Congress will shift to new hands as the leaders of the old conservative Coalition pass from the scene, one by one.

Serious political analysis must be prepared to keep pace with the political and institutional transformations taking place within the national legislature. One simple example may suffice to illustrate the point. Since it is believed that Rep. Wilbur Mills has ambitions for the Speakership of the House, it seems fair to assume that his role as Chairman of the Ways and Means Committee may be subtly affected by a need to reassure the Democratic Study Group members that a Mills speakership would not be inconsistent with the objectives of a more liberal House majority. If this were to happen, Mills would respond to views more cosmopolitan in nature than those which prevail in his home state.*

Fortunately, there probably has never been a time when so many able political scientists were concentrating their attention on the Congress. In addition to the work of Professors Huitt and Manley alluded to above, one thinks immediately of Richard Fenno's magnificent study of the appropriations process, James Robinson's explorations of Congressional decision-making and the House Rules committee, Lewis Anthony Dexter's bold initiatives across the customary boundaries and especially his study of the role of the Congressman, and Roger Davidson's recent detailed analysis of the Congressional role.[7] Each of these studies is an impressive example of empirical political science at work, and yet each study tends to differ from the others in methodology, scope, and aim. One does not carp about the diversity, especially when it is so productive. But the time draws near when the effort will be made to construct a theoretical framework broad enough to place the powers and functions of the Congress in the larger political "system."

POLITICAL BEHAVIOR

The behavioral revolution in political science thus far has been largely a study of *voting* behavior. A major part of the empirical-behavioral revolution in American political science was initiated when Paul Lazarsfeld,[8] who is not a political scientist

*Mills' handling of the Nixon welfare reform proposal is a case in point.

and whose original interest was the psychology of choice, undertook an examination of the impact of the mass media (radio and press) on voting behavior during the Roosevelt-Wilkie 1940 Presidential contest. The rest is ancient history, at least so far as American political science is concerned.

It is time to note the limits of this particular phase in the development of contemporary political science. We know a great deal about political behavior within the system *as it relates to voting,* but we are unable to say, with any degreee of assurance, what it is that the young Americans we are supposed to know best, our students, are likely to do next by way of their political behavior. We do know that many of them (this is not unusual among the young) have a great disinterest in *voting.* We may even know, or think we know, why some of them are protesting and what they are protesting about, or what they think they are protesting about. But we cannot say, with any degree of certainty, where the youthful protest will lead next. It is a safe bet that the way in which the young people carried Senator McCarthy to victory in the New Hampshire primary came to the political scientists as it did to the politicians and the public at large—a complete surprise. It would appear, likewise, that no university president has yet found it desirable to call in the political science department to help chart the course through the maelstrom. One major university president who began his academic career as a political scientist and whose principal aide was a highly respected student of the political process sadly misgauged the nature of the student protest. The university's response was such that eventually both gentlemen resigned from their positions in the university. No doubt these examples from the recent past prove very little except to suggest the limits which currently surround the field we refer to, rather facilely, as *political* behavior.

American political science is far more knowledgeable than it was twenty years ago about the behavior patterns of those who vote within the confines of traditional party politics. There was a time, not so long ago, when we were forced to rely on the accumulated folk wisdom of the practitioners. We now realize

227

that it was often surprisingly accurate. It was not really necessary, after all, for James Michael Curley, to select an eminently nonacademic authority, to wait for the soundings and samplings of the behaviorists in order to appreciate that income, religion, place of residence, social status, the family and peer group relationships profoundly influence the way Americans vote. Indeed, the remarkable fact is that it took political science as long as it did to get around to testing the assumptions drawn from folk wisdom by using the techniques of modern social science.

Modern political science has not probed very deeply into the behavior of the nonparticipants in traditional politics, although the nonparticipants were almost as numerous in 1968 as those who chose to vote either as Democrats or Republicans. We know still less about the newer manifestations of political behavior as devised by those engaged in social protest. It is a cliché by this time that idealistic young people, except perhaps the very tiny minority who have become ideologues, are sincerely trying to tell the rest of us something important about this society as it appears to them. Surely their perceptions are as interesting, and they may prove to be as important, as those of the Congressman or the suburban housewife. And without the benefit of anything like the massive research effort which has gone into the study of voting behavior, it is reasonable hypothesis that the youthful protest stems, at least in part, from the reaction to experiences with unthinking, unresponsive, mindless bureaucratic structures. The experience of the young has sometimes been with the multiversity, and their experience, in some cases, also includes the armed services and local governments, including police and the courts. In short, the youthful protest is at least partially based upon experiences with institutions which fall squarely within the domain of political science.

The young people who are rebelling have occasionally been accused of overreacting to petty tryannies. But it is noteworthy that in a significant number of cases the organization which is the object of their protest is found on closer examination to have been misserving its essential purpose or may actually have lost sight of a sense of purpose. There is no a priori reason I can think of for *not* bringing into close examination the purpose and functions of every major institution which has developed an entrenched bureaucratic structure, and what institution worthy of our concern has not? This is not to suggest that the modern technocratic society is about to be "debureaucratized." The young protestors may be naive in assuming that modern bureaucracy can readily be decentralized or that vast numbers of their fellow-citizens are aching to participate in organizational decision-making. But they are not wrong in thinking that a scheme of politics which accepts uncritically the legitimacy of the concentrated power of huge organizations cannot forever carry on the pretense of being "democratic."

Notes

Chapter One

1. Louis Hartz, *The Liberal Tradition in America* (New York: Harcourt Brace, 1955).
2. See Perry Miller, "The New England Conscience," *The American Scholar,* Winter 1958–59, Vol. 28, No. 1. Miller quotes two marvelously succinct New Englandisms. John Quincy Adams said: "New England was the colony of conscience." Henry David Thoreau summarized the issue this way: "The man of principle gets never a holiday."
3. Richard Goodwin, "Sources of the Public Unhappiness," *New Yorker,* Jan. 4, 1969, Vol. XLIV, No. 49, p. 53.
4. *Ibid.*
5. Samuel P. Huntington, *The Common Defense* (New York: Columbia University Press, 1961).
6. See report by William Beecher, New York *Times,* Nov. 29, 1969.
7. New York *Times,* March 11, 1969. See also "Military Programs and Policies Under Attack," *Congressional Quarterly,* March 28, 1969, pp. 451–453. Cf. the statement by Herbert York, Director of Defense Research during the Eisenhower period, who has called on the Congress to halt the growth of U. S. militarism before it becomes "a Frankenstein monster that could destroy us." New York *Times,* March 29, 1969.
8. There are many editions of the *Federalist* papers. I prefer the Doubleday Anchor version edited by Roy P. Fairfield whose introductory essay is one of the best brief statements of the enduring significance of these remarkable essays. The reference to Arthur T. Bentley is perhaps partly traditional at this point. His book, *The Process of Government* (Chicago: University of Chicago Press, 1908), has greatly influenced American political science for half a century. I return to this subject in Chapter Nine.
9. David G. Smith, *The Convention and the Constitution* (New York: St. Martins, 1965).
10. See John K. Galbraith, *American Capitalism* (Boston: Houghton Mifflin, 1956). For an interpretation of Madisonian theory which differs significantly from mine, see Robert A. Dahl, *A Preface to Democratic Theory* (Chicago: University of Chicago Press, 1956).
11. See E. E. Schattschneider, *The Semi-Sovereign˙ People* (New York:

Holt, Rinehart and Winston, 1960), especially Chapter II, "The Scope and Bias of the Pressure System"; and also Peter Bachrach and Morton S. Baratz, "Two Faces of Power," *American Political Science Review,* December 1962, pp. 947–952.

12. Theodore Lowi, "The Public Philosophy: Interest-Group Liberalism," in *The Bias of Pluralism,* William E. Connolly, ed. (New York: Atherton Press, 1969), p. 95. Professor Lowi's more complete thesis appears in his book *The End of Liberalism,* (New York: W. W. Norton, 1969). Professor Connolly's volume is highly recommended for those who wish to sample the literature which has developed in criticism of the pluralist model as laid down, for example, in David B. Truman, *The Governmental Process* (New York: Alfred A. Knopf, 1951). The Connolly collection of essays includes the Bachrach and Baratz article cited in the note above as well as the editor's own introductory essay, "The Challenge to Pluralist Theory" which serves as a handy bibliographical reference. For a lively dissent from Lowi's thesis see the review of his book by Richard E. Morgan in *The New Leader,* September 1, 1969, pp. 19–20.

13. Theodore Sorensen, *Kennedy* (New York: Harper and Row, 1965), pp. 301–302. One should read Chapter 11 of Mr. Sorenson's book for a view, sobering, to say the least, of Presidential policy-making during the Bay of Pigs period. See also Arthur W. Schlesinger, Jr.'s, *A Thousand Days* (Boston: Houghton Mifflin, 1965).

14. Daniel P. Moynihan, *Maximum Feasible Misunderstanding* (New York: Free Press, 1969). Mr. Moynihan's writings on the subject are rather extensive. Attention is called especially to his articles, "The Professionalization of Reform," *Public Interest,* No. 1, Fall, 1965, pp. 6–16, and "What is Community Action?" *Public Interest,* No. 5, Fall, 1966, pp. 3–8.

Chapter Two

1. Thomas E. Cronin and Sanford D. Greenberg, *The Presidential Advisory System* (New York: Harper and Row, 1960).

2. See David Truman's analysis of "the ordeal of the Executive" in *The Governmental Process* (New York: Knopf, 1951). Richard Neustadt's *Presidential Power* has been extremely influential among political scientists, if not among Presidents. Neustadt advised President Kennedy on matters having to do with the transition following the Eisenhower administration. President Kennedy is said to have read Neustadt's book, but the Bay of Pigs episode suggests that Neustadt's thesis did not make as deep an impression as it might have. It seems unlikely that President Johnson read books written by professors on the nature of Presidential power. President Nixon's team of advisers does not include Neustadt.

3. *Report of President's Committee on Administrative Management,* U. S. Government Printing Office, 1937, p. iv.

4. Neustadt, Richard E., "Approaches to Staffing the Presidency," *Ameri-*

can Political Science Review, Vol. LVII, no. 4, December 1963, p. 855.

5. Daniel Bell, *The End of Ideology* (New York: The Free Press, 1960. New York: Collier Books, 1962), p. 71.

6. Arthur M. Schlesinger, Jr., *A Thousand Days,* p. 681.

7. Kenneth O'Donnell made a conscientious effort to remain publicly anonymous during his period of service in the White House. He later tried unsuccessfully to obtain the Democratic gubernatorial nomination in Massachusetts. Theodore Sorensen, while never so removed from general public view as O'Donnell, managed nevertheless to remain well in the background so long as President Kennedy was alive. Since recovering from the shock of the assassination, Sorensen shows clear signs of intending to become a political personality in his own right.

8. Schlesinger, *A Thousand Days,* p. 681.

9. For more detail on this point, see my analysis in *The Politics of Poverty* (New York: Pegasus, 1967), and compare Schlesinger in *A Thousand Days,* pp. 708–9.

10. Daniel P. Moynihan writes in "The President and the Negro: The Moment Lost," in *Commentary,* Vol. 43, (February 1967): "Within weeks of the speech (Howard University, June 4, 1965) the President was caught up in a series of decisions that led to the large-scale introduction of ground forces into Viet Nam later that summer. The address at Howard was in a sense his last peacetime speech. Thereafter, one would assume, his mind was increasingly preoccupied with the war in Asia." Moynihan goes on to say that "this did not entail any backtracking on the commitment" to the blacks contained in the Howard University speech. Chapter Six of this book records my basic disagreement with Moynihan on this essential point.

11. Eugene Eidenberg has shown that the advice the President received from his national security advisers in 1965 was virtually unanimous in favoring military escalation. See his essay, "The Presidency: Americanizing the War in Viet Nam," in *American Political Institutions and Public Policy,* Allan P. Sindler, ed. (Boston: Little, Brown, 1969).

12. See Moynihan, *Maximum Feasible Misunderstanding* (New York: Free Press, 1969); James L. Sundquist, *Politics and Policy* (Washington, D. C.: Brookings Institution, 1968); Sar Levitan, *Great Society's Poor Law* (Baltimore: Johns Hopkins, 1969); and Richard Blumenthal, "Community Action: The Origins of a Government Program," (Honors Thesis, Harvard College, 1967). In a number of instances Blumenthal's study, although it was done as an undergraduate research project, is the most revealing in terms of who the key actors were in the writing of Community Action "theory." Blumenthal interviewed nearly every important technician who had worked on Title Two of the Economic Opportunity Act, and many of them shared their official files with him. In one or two cases the files shared by the technicians included the letters, memos, etc., of "principals" (i.e. Cabinet officers, the Director of the Bureau of the

Budget, the Chairman of the CEA). It is not clear how men who have left government service retain "official files" as part of their personal files to share with curious undergraduates, but in this case Blumenthal's findings are helpful in showing how strong a policy hand was played by the Bureau of the Budget technicians in shaping Community Action as part of the Presidential war on poverty.

13. Moynihan, *Maximum Feasible Misunderstanding* p. 143.
14. See both Moynihan and Blumenthal on this point.
15. Moynihan, *Maximum Feasible Misunderstanding* p. 80.
16. *Ibid.* p. 79.
17. Daniel P. Moynihan, "What is Community Action?" *Public Interest,* No. 5, Fall 1966, p. 7.
18. *Ibid.,* p. 6.
19. The report is entitled: "Review of Economic Opportunity Act Program, B-130515, Report to the Congress by the Comptroller General of the United States, March 18, 1969." The contents of the report were summarized and appeared in the public press in the spring of 1969.
20. Rowland Evans and Robert Novak, *Lyndon B. Johnson: The Exercise of Power* (New York: New American Library, 1966).
21. See Donovan, *Politics of Poverty* pp. 127–130.

Chapter Three

1. See Chapter Six, entitled "National Politics: Presidential and Congressional Parties," in Fred I. Greenstein, *The American Party System and the American People,* (Englewood Cliffs, N. J.: Prentice-Hall, 1963) for a brief, clear discussion of the two constituencies.
2. Andrew Hacker, "Are There Too Many Lawyers in Congress?" New York *Times* Magazine, Jan. 5, 1964.
3. It has become a ritualistic feature in current studies of the Congress for the author to indicate the number of Congressmen he has interviewed and to explain when he served his apprenticeship as a Congressional fellow as so many of the younger generation of political scientists have. The line of interpretation appearing in this chapter and which also appears in certain aspects of the analysis in Chapter Seven is based upon my interest in Congress which now goes back, I am a little shocked to realize, more than twenty years. The experience began, innocently enough, with the writing of a Harvard doctoral dissertation (1949) entitled, "Congress and the Making of Neutrality Legislation, 1933–1939." This study was ably summarized, I am happy to say, by James A. Robinson as part of his *Congress and Foreign Policy.* (Homewood, Ill.: The Dorsey Press, 1967). Hence it is no longer necessary to read the 439-page original. During the 1950s while teaching at Bates College, I joined a small group of people, led principally by Edmund S. Muskie and Frank M. Coffin, who decided to take on the task of rebuilding and modernizing the Maine Democratic Party, a task which one of my favorite Har-

vard professors thought to be a "futile undertaking." We were trying to develop a political alternative to the entrenched oligarchic conservatism which then dominated our lovely, slightly backward state. I wish that someone at that time had suggested to us that we were pioneering with forms of participatory democracy, but this was before we came to the era of the "politics of rhetoric." In any event, I learned about Congressional campaigns by working in four of them, first as a "helpful egghead," next as campaign manager and finally as Congressional candidate.

During the 1957–1958 period while serving as Maine's Democratic State Chairman, I met and discussed political matters with a considerable number of practitioners, large and small, good, bad, and indifferent. There were conversations with Senator John F. Kennedy whose drive for the Presidency began in 1957 and with a number of his closest political associates. These were invariably "practical" conversations having to do with advancing the Kennedy cause. During the same period, I was privileged to have an uninterrupted two-hour relaxed conversation with Speaker Sam Rayburn, a man of great political wisdom, dignity and candor. In 1958 Governor Muskie asked me to serve as his campaign manager in his race for a seat in the United States Senate. Following this, I served as Senator Muskie's Administrative Assistant in Washington for three years. From 1962–65 I served as Special Assistant to W. Willard Wirtz, Secretary of Labor, and remained interested in Congress as viewed from the special vantage point of a Cabinet officer's office.

My views about Congress have been greatly influenced by these experiences as participant-observer in Congressional politics. It goes without saying that I have also read virtually everything that has been written about Congress during this long period of time.

4. Samuel P. Huntington, "Congressional Responses to the Twentieth Century," in *The Congress and America's Future,* David B. Truman, ed. (Englewood Cliffs, N. J.: Prentice-Hall, 1965), p. 9.

5. See Rowland Evans and Robert Novak, *Lyndon B. Johnson* p. 364; and see also Alan Otten, *Wall Street Journal,* Oct. 19, 1967.

6. See John F. Manley, "Wilbur D. Mills: A Study in Congressional Influence," *American Political Science Review,* 63, (June 1969), pp. 442–464. This should also be compared with Manley's earlier article, "The House Committee on Ways and Means: Conflict Management in a Congressional Committee," *American Political Science Review,* LIX, 1965, pp. 927–39. Mills may turn out to be not very typical of the Coalition chieftains. He is believed to have developed an ambition for the Speakership. If so, he will find it increasingly necessary to respond to interests far more cosmopolitan in nature than would be customary for an entrenched Congressional oligarch content with his committee chairmanship. I personally expect that Mills will prove increasingly more flexible on a number of issues. He is never opposed in a general election at home and only rarely meets a weak challenge in the party primary. If he wishes to be a national legislator, clearly he is not severely limited by constitu-

ency constraints. See also Ralph K. Huitt, "Democratic Party Leadership in the Senate," *American Political Science Review*, Vol. LV, No. 2 (June 1961), pp. 333–44 and "The Outsider in the Senate: An Alternative Role," *American Political Science Review*, Vol. LV, No. 3 (September 1961), pp. 566–75.

7. For a sharp critique of the seniority system by an "insider" who now has considerable seniority see Richard Bolling, *House Out of Order* (New York: Dutton, 1965).

8. See Richard E. Neustadt, "Politicians and Bureaucrats," in *The Congress and America's Future,* Truman, ed. Neustadt suggests: "Bureaucracy has brought a new contestant into play: the great prospective struggle is between entrenched officialdom and politicians everywhere, White House and Hill alike." I find that Congress is controlled by an entrenched leadership group of its own which is largely cut off from competitive politics. Neustadt is justifiably concerned about "a great confusion" concerning "who is fighting whom and who is winning in our government." So am I, but I also fear the confusion may be confounded by political analysis which does not focus on the reality that Congress has been dominated for the greater part of the past thirty years by conservative, provincial, narrow-gauged men. On this point, Roger H. Davidson has argued that: "In many respects, the civil service represents the American people more comprehensively than does Congress." This appears in his essay, "Congress and the Executive: The Race for Representation," in *Congress: The First Branch of Government,* Alfred de Grazia, ed. (New York: Doubleday-Anchor, 1967), p. 383.

9. Seymour Hersh has listed the incredible array of defense establishments located in Rep. Rivers' district in his essay, "The Military Committees," which appeared in *The Washington Monthly,* April 1969.

10. See Davidson, "Congress and the Executive," p. 386, for the perception that Federal civil servants need the psychological capacity to function within large complex organizations. Presumably this capacity, if present, would be little stimulated during a long Congressional career. Davidson finds that as average Congressional tenure lengthens and hence as "insularity" and "stability" are built into Congress as an institution, there is a tendency for Congress to reenforce its "local" rather than its "national" orientation. Interestingly enough, Davidson's more recent *The Role of the Congressman* (New York: Pegasus, 1969) draws the opposite conclusion, unless I misread him. In any event, I prefer the original view, which seems justified in the case of most of the Coalition leaders whose careers I am familiar with.

11. I am in complete agreement with Nelson Polsby when he writes: "It is a cliché of political science that in legislative matters it is the President who initiates policy, and Congress which responds, amplifying, and modifying and rearranging elements which are essentially oriented in the Executive branch. Not much work has been done, however, on following

this river of bills-becoming and not-becoming-laws back to its source. Where do innovations in policy come from *before* the President 'initiates' them?" See his "Policy Analysis and Congress" which has been reprinted in *The Analysis and Evaluation of Public Expenditures: The PPB System,* as put together by the staff of Senator William Proxmire's Subcommittee on Economy in Government in the 1st session of the 91st Congress.

See also James L. Sundquist, *Politics and Policy,* especially Chapter XI, for a similar view.

12. We are beginning to have the benefit of a really superlative study of the Ways and Means Committee from John F. Manley whose articles on the subject were cited above. For a brief analysis of Congress and Medicare see Theodore R. Marmer, "The Congress: Medicare Politics and Policy," in *American Political Institutions and Public Policy,* Allan P. Sindler, ed. (Boston: Little, Brown, 1969). For more detail one should read Eugene Feingold, *Medicare: Policy and Politics* (San Francisco: Chandler, 1966).

13. Richard Fenno, *The Power of the Purse* (Boston: Little, Brown, 1966). It seems almost impossible to exaggerate the importance of Fenno's study for our understanding of how one of the most significant Congressional subsystems works. Fenno and Lewis Anthony Dexter rank high among political scientists who have added most to our knowledge of the workings of Congress in recent years. Yet, oddly enough, each came close to the conservative Coalition without saying very much about it.

Chapter Four

1. Adam Yarmolinsky, "Ideas Into Programs," *Public Interest,* Vol. II, No. 2, Winter 1966, p. 72.

2. See Sundquist, *Politics and Policy.* Sundquist shows in elaborate detail how great domestic programs evolved during the Eisenhower, Kennedy and Johnson years to meet these problems.

3. President Kennedy was speaking at the opening session of a White House Conference on National Economic Issues, May 2, 1962. He is quoted in Schlesinger, *A Thousand Days,* pp. 644–5.

4. *Ibid.*

5. As quoted by Daniel P. Moynihan, who developed the theme more fully in "The Professionalization of Reform," *Public Interest,* (Fall 1965), Vol. I, p. 8.

6. Daniel P. Moynihan, *Maximum Feasible Misunderstanding.*

7. See "The Negro Family: The Case for National Action," (Washington, D. C.: U. S. Government Printing Office, March 1965); E. Franklin Frazier, *The Negro Family in the United States* (Chicago: University of Chicago Press, 1966) and Kenneth B. Clark, *Dark Ghetto* (New York: Harper and Row, 1965).

8. Lee Rainwater and William L. Yancey, *The Moynihan Report and The*

Politics of Controversy (Cambridge, Mass.: MIT Press, 1967). For Moynihan's view of the controversy see "The President and the Negro: The Moment Lost," *Commentary,* February 1967.

9. The sharpest critique I have seen of the kind of instrumentalism which shaped official Washington thinking in the 1960s appears in Noam Chomsky, *American Power and the New Mandarins* (New York: Pantheon, 1969).

10. See Edward S. Flash, Jr., *Economic Advice and Presidential Leadership* (New York: Columbia University Press, 1965).

11. Robert Lekachman, *The Age of Keynes* (New York: Random House, 1966) is the clearest and simplest introduction to the Keynesian full-employment revolution for the non-specialist.

12. See Walter Heller, *New Dimensions of Political Economy,* (Cambridge, Mass.: Harvard, 1966).

13. An influential voice urging increased public expenditure for domestic purposes was that of John Kenneth Galbraith, who ran inches ahead of Leon Keyserling. Within the Kennedy administration Heller's most persistent adversary on this and related issues was W. Willard Wirtz, the Secretary of Labor. The Heller-Wirtz debate started early. Its main outlines were revealed in addresses each man delivered at a Conference on Fiscal and Monetary Policy sponsored by the President's Advisory Committee on Labor-Management Policy, Washington, D. C., Nov. 14 and 15, 1962.

14. One should especially expect to find a number of excellent examples of the influence of professionals and technicians in those policy areas most directly affected by the physical sciences. I sincerely regret that my own experience in these policy areas is deficient and my understanding of natural-science policy developments is not sufficient to enable me at this point to deal with what must certainly prove to be a most fruitful area for further examination.

15. This brief description of the origins of the Manpower Development and Training Act is based upon Sundquist's marvelously detailed account. I also rely, but to a lesser extent, on my own involvement (1962–65) with Merrick and March in a number of matters of public policy.

Chapter Five

1. Aaron Wildavsky, *The Politics of the Budgetary Process* (Boston: Little, Brown, 1964), p. 13.

2. Charles E. Lindblom, *The Policy-Making Process* (Englewood Cliffs, N. J.: Prentice-Hall, 1968), pp. 26–27.

3. *Ibid.*

4. See Charles E. Bohlen, *The Transformation of American Foreign Policy* (New York: Norton, 1970). This brief survey of American policy toward the Soviet Union shows clearly how official American thinking has been limited by the basic assumption that the Soviet Union can only be dealt with effectively through ever-increasing military power.

5. Mr. X, "The Sources of Soviet Conduct," *Foreign Affairs,* July 1947.

6. George F. Kennan, *Memoirs: 1925–1950* (Boston: Little, Brown, 1967). See especially pp. 320–23.

7. *Ibid.,* p. 356.

8. Eugene Eidenberg, "The Presidency: Americanizing the War in Viet Nam," in *American Political Institutions and Public Policy,* Sindler, ed., p. 117.

9. As quoted in interview with Gloria Emerson in New York *Times,* April 2, 1969.

10. See Jean La Couture, *Ho Chi Minh* (New York: Vintage, 1968) for the kind of assessment which should have made its way into official American thinking.

11. Eidenberg interviewed McGeorge Bundy, William Bundy, Walt W. Rostow, Senator J. William Fulbright, the late Senator Everett Dirksen, John Roche and eight other individuals in the executive and legislative branches who preferred remaining anonymous. Eidenberg reports: "The escalation of American policy on Viet Nam was supported by virtually every senior national security adviser to the president." ("The Presidency," p. 117) Cf. Townsend Hoopes, *The Limits of Intervention,* (New York: David McKay Co. Inc., 1969).

12. For more detailed background on our involvement in Vietnam one could read almost endlessly. For a start I would suggest Theodore Draper, *Abuse of Power* (New York: Viking, 1967); Bernard B. Fall, *The Two Viet Nams,* rev. ed. (New York: Praeger, 1964); David Halberstam, *The Making of a Quagmire* (New York: Random House, 1965); Roger Hillsman, *To Move a Nation* (New York: Doubleday, 1967); Robert Shaplen, *The Lost Revolution* (New York: Harper and Row, 1965).

13. See Theodore Roszak, ed. *The Dissenting Academy* (New York: Random House, 1968), for a series of biting essays on the failure of the academic community to find an alternative.

14. James C. Thomson, Jr., "How Could Viet Nam Happen?," *Atlantic Monthly,* April 1968, vol. 221, no. 4, pp. 47–53. For a different view see Tom Wicker, *JFK and LBJ: The Influence of Personality Upon Politics* (New York: Morrow, 1968), who feels that Mr. Johnson's personal hardline cold-war attitudes were of decisive importance. Wicker, of course, is one of our most perceptive political reporters. But it is a curious fact that American journalists ordinarily overstress the role of individual personality. We have learned very little indeed from even our best journalists about the cold-war technocrats and their influence in keeping the containment doctrine supreme for two decades.

15. Enthoven so testified in 1967 before the Subcommittee on National Security and International Organizations, Government Operations Committee, U. S. Senate. See p. 91 of the Hearings, Part 2, 90th Congress, first session. The subcommittee is chaired by Senator Henry Jackson, Dem., of Washington, and is largely populated by Senators of "moder-

ate-to-liberal" persuasion. Other members include: Senators Edmund S. Muskie, Abraham Ribicoff, Fred Harris, Lee Metcalf and Jacob Javits. Robert Kennedy was a member of the subcommittee as well. The subcommittee also includes Senator Karl Mundt, one of the most conservative men in American public life, and Howard Baker, Jr., who is not easily labeled. The Jackson subcommittee has done an outstanding job in its searching review of the Program-Planning Budgeting System. See its initial memorandum *PPBS: Selected Comment*, Hearings Parts I and II, 90th Congress, 1st session. These were followed by Interim Observations and Part III of the Hearings in the 2nd session of the 90th Congress.

16. See the Jackson subcommittee's print, "Official Documents," 90th Congress, 1st session, for the President's statements, and Bureau of the Budget bulletins which universalized PPBS throughout the Federal executive branch. In the first session of the 91st Congress the subcommittee printed an article by Prof. Aaron Wildavsky entitled "Rescuing Policy Analysis from PPBS." The article also appeared in *The Public Administration Review*, March–April 1969.

17. *PPBS: Selected Comment*, Part II, p. 69.

18. For more detail on this version of the contrast between Defense budgetmaking before and after McNamara and for a more complete presentation of the "theory" behind PPBS by one of its principal architects see Charles Hitch, *Decision-Making for Defense* (Berkeley: University of California Press, 1965).

19. "Rescuing Policy Analysis from PPBS," p. 5.

20. For an excellent statement of the budgetary framework within which national priorities are established and a clear picture of the way in which military values predominate over nondefense considerations see testimony of Charles Schultze, Senior Fellow, Brookings Institution, Professor of Economics, University of Maryland, and former Director of the Bureau of the Budget, as it appears in the Congressional Record of June 4, 1969, H4509–4514. Schultze was one of the first to make detailed projections showing that deescalation in Vietnam was not likely to provide a huge "surplus" for nondefense purposes.

21. Compare Schultze's statement, *ibid.* Schultze does not think that the "problem" of military budgets is primarily attributable to the military-industrial complex but to the general public's uncritical acceptance of cold-war dogma. Nor is he inclined to think that the fact that the Defense budgets of the 1960s were produced using special procedures in which Secretary McNamara rather than the Director of the Budget Bureau made the final recommendations to the President had more than a "relatively modest importance."

Chapter Six

1. See Aaron Wildavsky, *Politics of the Budgetary Process,* for a perceptive guide to the world of big-time governmental budgeting as practiced
   in Washington, D. C., by men who know that budgeting in government
   establishes public priorities and hence is too important to be left to cost
   accountants.
2. The basic budgetary facts used in this chapter are drawn from nothing
   more complicated than *The Budget in Brief* for each of the fiscal years
   under examination. This small booklet may be obtained in the spring of
   each year from the Superintendent of Documents, Government Printing
   Office, Washington, D. C., for 45 cents. President Truman thought the
   booklet ought to be required reading in our colleges and universities. Mr.
   Truman was right although a little naive perhaps on this point.
3. For an intelligent and warmly favorable view of President Johnson as
   Chief Legislator see Howard K. Smith, "Prologue: A Strong Thread of
   Moral Purpose" in *To Heal and Build: The Programs of President
   Lyndon B. Johnson,* James MacGregor Burns, ed. (New York: McGraw
   Hill, 1968).
4. The words quoted are those of an anonymous Presidential adviser cited
   by Eugene Eidenberg, "The Presidency," p. 110. The failure of Johnson's advisers to assess the probable costs of their group decision to
   escalate the Vietnam War is thoroughly probed in Eidenberg's study.
5. Eidenberg, "The Presidency," p. 111.
6. Quoted in *ibid.,* p. 113.
7. Moynihan's reflections on the Howard University address and the lost
   opportunity which followed are presented in "The President and the
   Negro: The Moment Lost," *Commentary,* Vol. 43, (February 1967), pp.
   31–45.
8. Edwin L. Dale, Jr., "Uncle Sam's 50 Billion Dollar Surplus," New York
   Times Sunday Magazine, (November 7, 1965) pp. 32–33.
9. Schultze's anonymous friend was quoted to this effect by Hobart Rowen
   in the Washington *Post,* (January 25, 1966).
10. *Ibid.*
11. New York *Times,* (December 8, 1966).
12. New York *Times,* (January 28, 1967). See also the Committee for Eco-
    nomic Development's report, "The National Economy and the Vietnam
    War," which appeared in April 1968. The CED report noted the failure
    of government policy makers to perceive early and clearly what the
    general economic impact of the Vietnam buildup would be. The lack of
    candid communication between Pentagon and the Council of Economic
    Advisers is referred to rather delicately in the CED report which said in
    part: "The economic decision-makers did not correctly foresee what the
    size of the Viet Nam effort would be. To some extent this kind of error
    in forecasting is inevitable when military objectives are subject to change
    and enemy responses are uncertain. *However, it seems also to have*

been true that the possibilities which the managers of the military effort had in mind were not always made clear to the managers of official economic policy." p. 25. (Italics mine.)

Chapter Seven

1. See statement by John K. Galbraith in *Congressional Record,* June 2, 1969, H4381, Vol. 115 No. 90, 91st Congress. Professor Galbraith was one of several individuals who prepared statements for the Congressional Conference on the Military Budget and National Priorities which was held in Washington, March 28–29, 1969. The Conference report and various proposals put forth at the Conference were placed in the Congressional Record by Rep. Robert Kastenmeier, D. of Wisconsin, a leading figure in organizing the Conference, and a leading member of the Democratic Study Group.
2. Since leaving the Pentagon Charles Hitch has become President of the University of California, our largest multiversity, while Dr. Alain Enthoven has taken a position as Vice President of Litton Industries. The ease with which the leading proponents of cost-benefit systems analysis have moved from the RAND Corporation to the Defense Department to the multiversity and major defense corporations does not seem likely to lessen the apprehensions of those who fear the emergence of a power elite within the military-industrial-educational establishment.
3. As quoted by Richard F. Kaufman in "As Eisenhower Was Saying . . . We must Guard Against Unwarranted Influence by the Military-Industrial Complex," New York *Times* Sunday Magazine, June 22, 1969, p. 72. Mr. Kaufman served as staff economist to the Joint Economic Subcommittee on Economy in Government chaired by Senator William Proxmire, D. of Wisconsin, a leading critic of Pentagon procurement practices.
4. See Seymour Hersh, "The Military Committees," *Washington Monthly,* Vol. I, No. 3, April 1969, pp. 84–85.
5. As quoted in *Congressional Quarterly, Special Report, Weekly Report,* May 24, 1968, entitled "The Military-Industrial Complex", p. 1158.
6. Lewis Anthony Dexter, "Congressmen and The Making of Military Policy," in *New Perspectives in the House of Representatives,* Robert L. Peabody and Nelson W. Polsby, eds., 2nd ed. (Chicago: Rand McNally, 1969) p. 181.
7. Quoted by Hersh, "Military Committees," pp. 84–85.
8. Dexter, "Congressman and Military Policy."
9. Quoted by Hersh, "Military Committees," p. 87.
10. This analysis of the Democratic Study Group draws upon the excellent brief account which appears in John Bibby and Roger Davidson, *On Capitol Hill: Studies in the Legislative Process* (New York: Holt, Rinehart and Winston, 1967) especially pp. 156–57. For more recent data I am indebted to a Bowdoin College senior honors paper prepared by

Peter DeTroy, '69, which was prepared under my supervision. I have also discussed the DSG with a number of Congressmen who have been active in the group at one time or another. In addition, I relied on DSG material in a Congressional campaign in which I was engaged in 1960. *Congressional Quarterly, Inc.,* whose reports are indispensable for the serious student of Congress, keeps close tabs on the DSG. See especially Congressional Quarterly Weekly Report, October 10, 1969, "Democratic Study Group Shifts Role in 91st Congress," pp. 1940–1945.

11. Rep. Smith, who had been a member of the Rules Committee since 1933, assumed the chairmanship in 1955. According to Professor James A. Robinson, Smith's years of service on the Rules Committee marked him as the member with the longest tenure on the Committee after it was reconstituted in 1910. Robinson also rated Smith as one of the two or three ablest House parliamentarians in modern times. I am convinced that most close Washington observers of Congress during the period of Judge Smith's career would agree with this assessment. See James A. Robinson, *The House Rules Committee* (Indianapolis: Bobbs-Merrill, 1963). Professor Robinson seems to me to have established himself as one of the two or three most knowledgeable experts on Congress among academic political scientists. My perspective on the role of the Rules Committee in the 1960s has been sharpened by reading an excellent brief review entitled, "The House Rules Committee and The Programs of the Kennedy and Johnson Administrations," unpublished manuscript, 1969, by Assistant Professor Douglas Fox and Charles H. Clapp, an undergraduate, Bowdoin College.

12. This sense of frustration is not necessarily limited to young House "liberals." See Richard E. Neustadt, "Politicians and Bureaucrats," in *The Congress and America's Future,* Truman, ed. Neustadt offers the following observation about serving in the House of Representatives: "It may well be the most frustrating place to work in Washington. It certainly ranks high among such places." (p. 117)

13. See Milton C. Cummings, Jr., and Robert L. Peabody, "The Decision to Enlarge the Committee on Rules: An Analysis of the 1961 Vote," in Peabody and Polsby, eds., *New Perspectives in the House,* pp. 253–81.

14. I was one of the Democratic "hopefuls" running in Maine's old 2nd Congressional District, which disappeared when the State was redistricted following the 1960 Census. The Maine 2nd Congressional District seat had been a Democratic seat, 1956–1960. It was one of the twenty House seats lost in the narrow Kennedy victory over Nixon. (Nixon received 57% of Maine's popular vote in 1960.) The material sent by Bill Phillips on behalf of the DSG was far more useful than that which I received from the House Democratic campaign staff, a notoriously ineffectual operation. By the end of the 1960s the DSG's research operation was the best partisan research activity in the Democratic party.

15. New York *Times,* January 8, 1967 and *Congressional Quarterly Weekly Report,* Vol. 25, January 13, 1967, p. 39.

16. See Don Larrabee, "Hathaway Leads Attack on Pentagon Spending," Maine *Sunday Telegram,* June 15, 1969, p. 7D.
17. The Jackson subcommittee study of PPBS has been cited previously in Chapter 5.
18. I base this assessment of Senator Muskie not only on what has been written about him by other observers, but also upon my own awareness of what he has written, said, and done since he was first elected Governor of Maine in 1954. Since I was closely associated with Senator Muskie from 1957 to 1962, I am not unmindful that my judgment of him is inevitably subjective. I do not think it is inaccurate or extreme, however.

Chapter Eight

1. Richard Hofstadter, The Age of Reform (New York: Vintage Books, 1955), p. 23
2. See Max Frankel, "The Moon and Politics," New York *Times,* July 21, 1969.
3. The figures on the black migration come from William K. Stevens, "Farm-to-city Migration is Nearing End," New York *Times,* (March 23, 1969). For the earlier immigration movement which started "in the peasant heart of Europe" see Oscar Handlin, *The Uprooted* (Boston: Little, Brown, 1951).
4. For a sympathetic appraisal of the urban machine see "Local Politics: The Functions of Urban Machines" Chapter Four of Fred I. Greenstein's *The American Party System and the American People* (Englewood Cliffs, N. J.: Prentice-Hall, 1963).
5. The projections referred to are summarized in a United States Department of Labor Press Release, USDL 7399, September 14, 1966. The detailed projections may be found in the September 1966 issue of the *Monthly Labor Review.*
6. See Daniel P. Moynihan, "The Crisis in Public Welfare," *Public Interest,* Winter 1968, No. 10.
7. Message from the President of the United States Relative to Welfare Reform, Document No. 91–146, House of Representatives, 91st Congress, 1st Session, August 11, 1969.
8. The figures appeared in the *Christian Science Monitor,* January 17, 1970, in an article entitled, "Finch Takes Offensive For Welfare," by Richard L. Strout, the Monitor's veteran Washington correspondent and one of the ablest political reporters in the country.
9. Udall and Califano were quoted in an Associated Press dispatch which appeared in the Portland (Maine) *Press Herald,* June 7, 1969.
10. Samuel Huntington, *The Common Defense* (New York: Columbia University Press, 1961), p.42.
11. Aaron Wildavsky, "The Two Presidencies," *Transaction,* (December 1966) p. 7.

12. *Ibid.*, p. 11. The Curtiss-Wright Export Case sets forth an extreme form of the scope of Presidential authority in the realm of foreign affairs.
13. See John C. Donovan, *Congress and the Making of Neutrality Legislation, 1935–1939,* unpublished doctoral dissertation, Harvard University, 1949.
14. Wildavsky *Op. cit.,* p. 12.
15. *Ibid.,* p. 14.
16. See US Senate, Permanent Subcommittee on Investigation of the Committee on Government Operations, *The TFX Contract Investigation: Hearings,* 88th Congress, 1st Session, 1963, for a full exposure to Secretary McNamara as a cabinet officer quite capable of defending his own position. One should also read Robert J. Art's case study, *The TFX Decision* (Boston: Little, Brown, 1968), in order to understand why McNamara made his decision and how he was able to enforce his decision when the traditional arrangements had left the final authority for selecting sources for weapons development in the hands of the military chieftains.
17. Wildavsky *Op. cit.,* p. 14.
18. See James C. Thomson, Jr., "How Could Viet Nam Happen?" *Atlantic Monthly,* April 1968, Vol. 221, No. 4, pp. 47–53.
19. Schattschneider, *Semi-Sovereign People,* p. 102.
20. For more detail on this trend see James M. Burns, *The Deadlock of Democracy* (Englewood Cliffs, N. J.: Prentice-Hall, 1963).
21. The best-known electoral studies have been those undertaken by the Columbia University Bureau of Applied Social Research and the University of Michigan Survey Research Center. The principal Columbia studies are: Paul Lazarfeld, et al., *The People's Choice* (New York: Columbia University Press, 1948), and Bernard Berelson, et al., *Voting* (Chicago: University of Chicago Press, 1954). Of the various Michigan studies, two seem to me to have the greatest significance. They are: Angus Campbell, et al., *The Voter Decides* (Evanston, Ill.: Row, Peterson, 1954), and *The American Voter* (New York: Wiley, 1960).
For a different view of voting behavior, one that preceives more "rationality" in the data, see V. O. Key, Jr., *The Responsible Electorate* (Cambridge: Harvard University Press, 1966), the last book by a great political scientist.

Chapter Nine

1. This paragraph is based on views expressed by Ladd in a letter to the author in January 1970. Professor Ladd was commenting on an earlier draft of this chapter. I am enormously indebted to him for helping to clarify my thinking on these important points, as I am for his warm encouragement throughout the writing of this book.
2. Ladd, *Ideology in America.* A brief summary statement of Ladd's thesis appears in his essay, "The Changing Face of American Political

Ideology," *Massachusetts Review,* Vol. 8, No. 2, Spring 1967, pp. 251–66.

3. David Apter, *Ideology and Discontent* (New York: Free Press, 1964) pp. 31–33.
4. Ladd, "Changing Face", p. 261.
5. See Moynihan, *Maximum Feasible Misunderstanding.*
6. James L. Sundquist, who served on the Shriver Task Force, has shown that the sources of program ideas were quite diverse. The Budget Bureau became the principal sponsor of Community Action before Shriver was chosen to head his since-famous task force. Shriver originally was skeptical of Community Action and actively sought other theories and approaches to the problem. Here is an excerpt from Sundquist's account: "Not only were the departments and agencies given a chance to resurrect all of the proposals the Budget Bureau had buried . . . but Shriver encouraged them to do so. Meanwhile, he cast a dragnet out to the business community, to the intellectual world, to state and local governments, and to private organizations of all kinds in the search for additional suggestions. People who might have ideas were brought in for conferences with the task force staff. . . . And if a new idea was presented, the burden of proof was upon any listener who said it might not work." *Politics and Poverty,* p. 143.
7. In *ibid.,* p. 120, Sundquist quotes David Hackett, the executive director of the Presidents Committee on Juvenile Delinquency and a close personal friend of Attorney General Robery Kennedy, as follows: "I quickly learned that you can't get consensus among professionals, so I had to pick one of the best and rely on his judgment". He picked Ohlin.
8. See Eugene Burdick, "Political Theory and the Voting Studies," in Eugene Burdick, and Arthur Bradbeck, eds. *American Voting Behavior,* (Glencoe, Ill: The Free Press, 1959). A vigorous dissent from the concord theory of nonparticipation appears in Schattschneider, *Semi-Sovereign People.*
9. *Observer,* October 12, 1969.
10. Schlesinger, *Thousand Days,* p. 709. Schlesinger discusses Kennedy's relations with Congress in some detail, emphasizing his cautious approach, pp. 707–13.
11. Barrington Moore, *Political Power and Social Theory,* (Cambridge, Mass: Harvard University Press, 1957), p. 183.
12. Seymour Martin Lipset, *Political Man* (Garden City, New York: Doubleday, 1960) p. 406.
13. Daniel Bell, *The End of Ideology* (New York: The Free Press, 1960. New York: Collier Books, 1962).
14. John K. Galbraith, *The Affluent Society* (Boston: Houghton Mifflin., 1958)
15. *Ibid.,* p. 323.
16. All of the quotations from *The Affluent Society* which appear in this

paragraph and in the following four paragraphs are taken from Chapter 23, "The New Position of Poverty," 1st ed.

17. The second revised edition of *The Affluent Society* appeared in 1969. I have used the revision as it was published by Hamish Hamilton, London. The quotation comes from Galbraith's Introduction, p. xxiv. The second edition, needless to say, has been significantly strengthened in the discussion of race and poverty. Evidently, Galbraith has changed his thinking about revised editions. In his preface to the Pelican edition written while he was in New Delhi as US Ambassador 1962, he put it this way: "The author should give his best in the first round. Then, if time shows he has been wrong, he should count on the reader to see the mistake and make the necessary correction."

Chapter Ten

1. Gunnar Myrdal, *An American Dilemma* (New York: Harper, 1944)
2. See Jack Newfield, *A Prophetic Minority: The American New Left* (New York: New American Library, 1966).
3. Compare, for example, the statement by Senator Edmund S. Muskie speaking in Oakland, California: "We can never again afford to play politics as though it were a game of playing one group off against another." Portland (Maine) *Evening Express,* November 15, 1969.
4. Bertram M. Gross, *Social Intelligence for America's Future* (Allyn and Bacon: Boston, 1969). The quotation comes from the preface written by Gross and Michael Springer, p. vii.
5. *Ibid.* p. viii.
6. *Ibid.*
7. Schattschneider, *Semi-Sovereign People,* p. 141.

1. Fenno, *Power of the Purse.*
2. Richard E. Neustadt, "Presidency and Legislation: The Growth of Central Clearance," the *American Political Science Review,* XLVIII (September 1954) 641–2, 654–71.
3. Wildavsky, *Politics of the Budgetary Process.*
4. See Townsend Hoopes, *The Limits of Intervention* (New York: McKay, 1969) and Henry Brandon, *Anatomy of Error* (London: Andre Deutsch, 1970). Clark Clifford became Secretary of Defense on March 1, 1968. On March 31, President Johnson announced a unilateral limited bombing halt and his own intention not to serve beyond his term of office.
5. Washington *Post,* August 15–16, 1969.
6. Ralph K. Huitt, "Democratic Party Leadership in the Senate," *American Political Science Review,* LV, number 2 (June 1961), 333–44. R. K. Huitt, "The Outsider in the Senate: An Alternative Role," *American Political Science Review,* LV, number 3 (September 1961), 566–75. Manley, "Wilbur Mills: A Study in Congressional Influence," *American Political Science Review,* 63 (June 1969), 442–64. Manley, "The House Ways and Means Committee: Conflict Management in a Congressional Committee," *American Political Science Review,* LIX (1965), 927–39.
7. Fenno, *Power of the Purse.* James A. Robinson, *The House Rules Committee* (Indianapolis: Bobbs-Merrill, 1963). Lewis A. Dexter, Part V in Raymond Bauer, Ithiel de S. Pool and L. A. Dexter, *American Business and Public Policy* (New York: Atherton Press, 1963). Roger Davidson, *The Role of the Congressman.*
8. Lazarsfeld, et. al., *The People's Choice.*

INDEX

Adams, John, 24, 61
  on power, 21–22, 26–27
Adams, Sherman, 40, 41
Affluent Society, The (Galbraith), 207–210
Agnew, Spiro T., 163
Aid to Families with Dependent Children, 174, 210
Aiken, George, 161
Alinsky, Saul, 81
American Political Science Association, 211
American Presidency (Rossiter), 35
American Vocational Association, 95
Anderson, Clinton P., 159
Anti-ballistic missile system, 26, 36, 147, 158, 183, 187
Appropriations Committees, 142–146, 154
Apter, David, 192–193, 194, 197
Area Redevelopment Act of 1961, 42, 71, 93
Aristotle, 19
Armed Services Committees, 142–146, 147, 148–149

Bailey, John, 202
Ball, George, 134
Bates, William, 68, 69
Bay of Pigs, 31–33, 36, 41–42, 44, 221
Bayh, Birch, 159, 162
Bell, Daniel, 39, 206, 207
Bissell, Richard, Jr., 31–32
Blacks, *see* Negroes
Blatnik, John, 150, 156
Bolling, Richard, 65, 150, 152, 156
Boone, Richard, 54

Bow, Frank T., 68, 69
Bowles, Chester, 108–109
Brademas, John, 156
Brooke, Edward W., 160
Brown, Clarence, 153–154
Brownlow, Louis, 37, 39
Budget, 23, 25–26, 112–115, 118–138, 175–177
  Johnson, 119–135; black commitment, 123–124, 133; early, 120–122; 1965, 122–123
  Kennedy, 119–120
  New Deal, 38–39
  Vietnam War, 46, 88, 119, 123–126, 129–135, 137, 140
Bundy, McGeorge, 43, 47, 109, 122, 123, 202
Bundy, William, 109, 110, 122, 123
Burdick, Quentin N., 159
Bureau of the Budget, 25, 38, 39, 42, 43, 79–80, 95, 96, 97, 128, 133–134
  as policy-maker, 51–56
  relationship with Department of Defense, 140–141
  in the war on poverty, 49–51
Bureau of Labor Statistics, 89
Burr, Aaron, 27
Byrd, Senator Harry, 54, 67, 87, 88, 120
Byrnes, John, 68, 69

Califano, Joseph A., 176
Cannon, William, 52, 54
Carroll, Lewis, 188
Carswell, Judge G. Harrold, 163
Case, Clifford P., 159
China, 105, 106, 107, 117

Church, Frank, 159, 162
Civilian Intelligence Agency (CIA), 22, 31, 32, 33, 123
Clark, Clifford, 41
Clark, Joseph, 93
Clark, Kenneth, 82, 83
Clifford, Clark, 134
Cloward, Richard, 51, 80, 83, 91, 97, 196
Coffin, Frank M., 156
Cohen, Benjamin, 41
Colmer, William, 67, 69, 154
Communism, 100–117
Community Action, 33, 50, 51–56, 64, 80–82, 97–98, 128, 196
Congress, 20, 37, 38, 42–43
    Coalition in, 57–75, 92, 121, 140–147, 150–151, 153, 158, 161, 162, 186, 199
    control of the administration by, 72–75
    Johnson and, 44–46, 55, 56, 62–64
    parochial aspect of, 57–75
    party representation (1958–1968), 60–61
    presidential relationship, 57–75
    social reform and, 91
Conlon, Richard, 151
Constitution, 20–21
    eighteenth-century background, 20–22
Containment in the sixties, 100–117
    alternatives, 108–110
    analytical defects, 105–108
    the double standard, 113–117
    the Program-Planning-Budgeting systems, 110–117
    world view, 102–105
Cook, Marlow W., 160
Cooper, John Sherman, 159
Corcoran, Thomas, 41
Council of Economic Advisers, 39, 42, 43, 50, 77, 79, 84–88, 89, 98, 119–120, 129, 133–134, 217, 218
Cranston, Alan, 160
Cuba, 31–33, 36, 41–42, 44, 221

Dale, Edwin L., Jr., 124–125, 129
Daley, Richard, 202
Defense contracts, 141–147

Democratic Study Group, 146, 149–158, 189, 219
Department of Defense, 139, 141–147
    relationship with Bureau of the Budget, 140–141
Department of Health, Education and Welfare, 59, 72, 73
Department of Labor, 73, 89, 94
Dexter, Lewis Anthony, 146, 147
Dirksen, Everett, 69, 162
Dodd, Thomas J., 161
Domestic Council, 79–80
Dominican Republic, 117, 122
Douglas, Paul, 65
Dulles, Allen, 31–32
Dulles, John Foster, 48, 104, 182

Eagleton, Thomas F., 160
Easton, David, 211
Economic Opportunity Act of 1964, 33–34, 49–51, 54, 63–64, 71, 81, 110, 121, 174
Economy
    employment, 84–91
    Gross National Product, 30, 85–86, 98–99, 126, 207
    Heller on, 84–88
    Kennedy on, 77–78
    recessions, 84–88
Education, 42, 45, 122, 132, 207–208
    college and university enrollment, 169
    vocational, 42, 45, 71, 93–96
Eidenberg, Eugene, 108, 110
Eisenhower, Dwight D., 42, 43, 48, 59, 62, 71, 102, 176, 205
    as an institutionalized president, 39–40
    on power, 23
Ellender, Allen J., 166
Employment, 84–91
    full, 89–91
Employment Act of 1946, 84, 218
End of Ideology, The (Bell), 206
Enthoven, Alain, 111–112, 114, 139.
Evans, Rowland, 55, 63

F-111, 26, 115, 182
Factions
    liberty and, 27–28

Madison on, 27–28
power of, 27–30
Fairbank, Professor John K., 106
Federalist papers, 27–28
Feldman, Myer, 51
Fenno, Richard, 72, 73
Flemming, Arthur, 33
Fogerty, John, 73
Foreign Affairs, 103–104
France, 104–105, 182
Fraser, Donald, 156–157
Frazier, E. Franklin, 82
Fulbright, J. W., 148

C-5A Galaxy cargo plane, 142, 148–149
Galbraith, John Kenneth, 28, 138, 202, 207–210
Glazer, Nathan, 78
Goldberg, Arthur, 94
Goldwater, Barry, 60, 61, 63, 121, 152, 153, 164, 199, 202
Goodell, Charles E., 160
Goodwin, Richard, 24, 124
Gore, Albert, 159
Great Britain, 103, 105, 170, 200–201
Great Society, 64, 124
Greece, 103
Griffin, Robert P., 160
Gross, Bertram M., 218–219
Gross National Product, 30, 85–86, 98–99, 126, 207
Groups, *see* Factions
Gulf of Tonkin resolution, 121

Hacker, Andrew, 58–59
Hackett, David, 50, 51, 54, 97
Halleck, Charles A., 151
Hanna, Mark, 204
Harris, Fred, 160, 163, 164
Hart, Philip A., 159, 164, 165
Hartke, Vance, 159, 162
Hartz, Louis, 21
Hatfield, Mark O., 160
Hathaway, William D., 156–157
Hayden, Carl, 142
Haynsworth, Judge Clement F., 163
Hechler, Ken, 156
Heller, Walter, 42, 50, 77, 98, 119, 204
on the economy, 84–88

Hersh, Seymour, 142
Hillsman, Roger, 109
Hitch, Charles, 111–112, 139
Ho Chi Minh, 105, 106–107, 122, 124
Hofstadter, Richard, 169
Holifield, Chet, 150, 151, 156
Holland, Elmer, 93
Hoover, J. Edgar, 23, 32
Hopkins, Harry, 37, 41
House, Edward Mandell, 37, 41
House of Representatives, 44, 58–62, 63, 64
Coalition in, 57–75
parochial aspect of, 57–75
party representation (1958–1968), 60–61
See also Congress
Howard University, 56, 124, 133
Hughes, Harold, 160, 163, 164
Hughes, Philip S., 141
Huitt, Ralph K., 65
Humphrey, George, 199
Humphrey, Hubert, 65, 164, 201
Huntington, Samuel P., 24, 61, 65, 139, 176, 179, 180

Ideology, 188–210
the change of generations, 202–204
the end of, 204–206
faulty analysis, 206–210
the presidency as a cosmopolitan office, 194–198
the scientific culture, 192–194
voting, 198–201
Income taxes, 128–129
Inouye, Daniel K., 160

Jackson, Henry M., 114, 159, 161
Japan, 170
Javits, Jacob K., 159
Jefferson, Thomas, 202
Johnson, Ben, 30
Johnson, Lyndon B., 60, 65, 67, 74, 83, 87–88, 94, 102, 107–108, 110, 142, 152, 164, 177, 178, 181, 194–196, 203–204, 221
budgets, 119–135; black commitment, 123–124, 133; early, 120–122; 1965, 122–123

Congress and, 44–46, 55, 56, 62–64
as an institutionalized president, 44–56
power role of, 22
the Program-Planning-Budgeting System, 112–113, 116, 123
the war on poverty, 33–34, 36, 49–56, 63–64, 80–81, 121
the Welfare State and, 39
Judd, Walter, 157

Kastenmeir, Robert W., 156
Kefauver, Estes, 65
Kennan, George, 103–104
Kennedy, Edward, 147, 159, 162, 163, 164
Kennedy, John F., 23, 31–33, 45, 49–51, 54, 55, 62, 63, 71, 83–88, 98, 102, 108, 119, 151, 152, 164, 177, 186, 196, 200–205, 221
budget, 119–120
on the economy, 77–78
as an institutionalized president, 40–49
manpower training bill, 42, 71, 93–96
Nuclear Test Ban treaty, 42, 178–179
tax reform, 87–88
Kennedy, Robert, 50, 80, 97, 189, 196
Keynes, John Maynard, 99
Korean War, 103, 181

Ladd, Everett, Jr., 190–194, 197, 215
Laird, Melvin, 26, 73
Landrum, Phil M., 64
Lapp, Ralph E., 145
Laski, Harold, 74
Leadership in the institutionalized presidency, 35–56
Eisenhower, 39–40
Johnson, 44–56
Kennedy, 40–49
Roosevelt, 36–38, 39, 41
Truman, 39, 41
Liberty, factions and, 27–28
Life, 104
Lindblom, Charles, 100, 101, 118
Lipset, Seymour Martin, 205–207

Litton Industries, 146
Locke, John, 20, 21, 90
Lomasney, Martin, 172
London Observer, 200–201
Long, Russell, 67, 68, 161
Lowi, Theodore, 29

McCarthy, Eugene, 22, 35, 94, 100, 150, 152, 155, 156, 159, 163, 164, 165, 189, 200
McClellan, John L., 166
McCormack, John, 153, 154, 155, 158
McGee, Gale W., 159
McGovern, George, 156, 160, 163, 164, 216
McIntire, Clifford, 157
McIntyre, Thomas J., 159
McKinley, William, 204
McLuhan, Marshall, 35
McNamara, Robert, 47, 122, 131, 139–140, 175, 179, 180, 181, 182, 202
as a centralizing force, 23–30
the Program-Planning-Budgeting System (PPBS), 111–116, 122
Madden, Ray, 154, 156
Madison, James, 26, 27–28
on factions, 27–28
Magnuson, Warren, 161
Mahon, George H., 67, 68, 69, 72, 146
Manpower Development and Training Act of 1962, 42, 72, 93–96
Mansfield, Mike, 69, 159, 163, 165
Mao Tse Tung, 106, 107
March, Michael, 94–96, 97
Marshall, George C., 103
Martin, Joseph W., Jr., 151
Marx, Karl, 214
Mathias, Charles, 160, 162
Medicare, 42, 45, 67, 100, 122, 126
delays in the program of, 71–72
Merrick, Samuel V., 94–96
Metcalf, Lee, 150, 151, 156, 159
Michigan Survey Research Center, 199
Mills, Wilbur, 65, 67, 68, 69, 71–72, 87, 100, 154
Mobley, M. D., 95, 96
Mondale, Walter, 151, 160
Montesquieu, Baron de, 20
Montoya, Joseph M., 160
Moore, Barrington, Jr., 205, 207

Moss, Frank E., 159
Moynihan, Daniel P., 33, 34, 50, 51, 52, 53, 80, 124, 218
    on the professionalization of reform, 78, 79
Moynihan report, 82
Muskie, Edmund S., 159, 161–162, 163, 164, 165, 200, 201, 216
Myrdal, Gunnar, 211

National Security Council, 39, 79
"Negro Family, The," 82, 124
Negroes, 53, 56, 67, 70, 82, 190, 192, 193, 208–209, 212
    Johnson commitment, 123–124, 133
    migration, 170–172
    unemployment, 90–91, 209
    the youth, 173–175
Nelson, Gaylord, 160
Neustadt, Richard, 36, 37, 44, 92, 133
New Deal, 41, 44–45, 60, 69–70, 121, 173, 193, 204
    budget, 38–39
New Dimensions of Political Economy (Heller), 87
New Economics, 126–128
New Frontier, 40–41, 204
New York Times, 125
Nixon, Richard M., 36, 42, 62, 70, 78, 79–80, 83–84, 163, 164, 183, 184, 195, 218
    power role of, 22
    on welfare, 174–175
North Atlantic Treaty Organization (NATO), 117
Novak, Robert, 55, 63
Nuclear Test Ban treaty, 42, 178–179

Office of Economic Opportunity, 73, 79
O'Hara, James G., 156
Ohlin, Lloyd, 51, 80, 83, 91, 97, 196
Otten, Alan, 63

Pastore, John O., 159
Pearson, James B., 160
Pell, Claiborne, 159
Percy, Charles H., 160
Phillips, William G., 151, 152

Plato, 19
Pogo (comic strip), 168
Policy
    Bureau of the Budget in, 51–56
    containment in the sixties, 100–117; alternatives, 108–110; analytical defects, 105–108; the double standard, 113–117; the Program-Planning-Budgeting System 110–117; world view, 102–105
    politics and, 180–183
    power and leadership, 19–34; McNamara as a centralizing force, 23–30
Policy-Making Process, The (Lindblom), 118
Political Man (Lipset), 205–207
Politics and Policy (Sundquist), 93
Population
    Negro migration, 170–172
    statistics, 169–170
Power
    Adams on, 21–22, 26–27
    controlling, 19–23
    eighteenth-century view of, 21–22, 23
    Eisenhower on, 23
    of factions, 27–30
    Johnson's role, 22
    Nixon's role, 22
    policy leadership and, 19–34; McNamara as a centralizing force, 23–30
    twentieth-century view of, 22–23
Presidency
    as an arrangement of agencies, 19
    congressional relationship, 57–75
    as a cosmopolitan office, 194–198
    institutionalized, 35–56; Eisenhower, 39–40; Johnson, 44–56; Kennedy, 40–49; Roosevelt, 36–38, 39, 41; Truman, 39, 41
    legislation established by, 70–71
    social reform and, 91–93
    two major aspects of, 177–180
President's Committee on Administrative Management, 37
President's Committee on Juvenile Delinquency, 50–51, 53–54, 80–81, 97

Program-Planning-Budgeting System (PPBS), 110–117, 122, 123, 161, 181
Proxmire, William, 26, 65, 150–151, 159, 164, 165

Rainwater, Lee, 82
RAND Corporation, 111–112, 116
Randolph, Jennings, 159, 164
Rayburn, Sam, 150, 151, 152, 156
Reader's Digest, 104
Reagan, Ronald, 164
Recessions, 84–88
Reischauer, Edwin O., 106
Reuss, Henry, 156
Ribicoff, Abraham A., 160
Rivers, Mendel, 67, 68, 69, 142, 146
Rockefeller, Nelson, 164
Romney, George, 164
Roosevelt, Franklin D., 44–45, 46, 47, 63, 64, 69–70, 121, 122, 179, 202, 203
    as an institutionalized president, 36–38, 39, 41
Roosevelt, Theodore, 41
Rossiter, Clinton, 35
Rostow, Walt, 109, 122
Rowen, Hobart, 128
Rusk, Dean, 47, 122
Russell, Richard, 67, 68, 69, 72, 84–85, 142–146, 147, 165, 166
    as a shaper of military policy, 148–149

Salinger, Pierre, 41
Saxbe, William B., 160
Schattschneider, E. E., 57, 184
Schlesinger, Arthur M., Jr., 32, 40, 41, 42, 76, 202, 221
Schultze, Charles L., 52, 54, 125, 128, 136
Schweiker, Richard S., 160
Scott, Hugh, 69, 156, 162
Semi-Sovereign People, The (Schattschneider), 57
Senate, 45, 158–167
    Coalition in, 57–75
    parochial aspect of, 57–75
    See also Congress
Shriver, Sargent, 49, 50, 53, 54, 55, 64

Smith, David G., 27
Smith, H. Allen, 68, 69
Smith, Howard, 67, 150, 151, 153–154, 155
Smith, Margaret Chase, 67, 68, 161
Social reform, 76–99
    the Congress and, 91
    diverse patterns in, 96–99
    the Presidency and, 91–93
    professionalization of, 78–80
    social action theories, 80–84
Social Security, 136–137
Sorensen, Theodore C., 32, 34, 41, 51, 98, 221
Sparkman, John J., 161
Springer, Michael, 218–219
Staats, Elmer B., 54
Stennis, John, 67, 68, 146, 148, 166
Stevenson, Adlai, 164
Sundquist, James L., 93
Symington, Stuart, 159

Taxes, 42, 45, 126
    income, 128–129
    Kennedy reform, 87–88
Technology, 2, 31, 79, 111–113, 137, 170, 191
    manpower training, 93–96
Thompson, Frank, 150, 156
Thomson, James C., Jr., 108–109, 134
Thoreau, Henry David, 213
Thousand Days, A (Schlesinger), 76
Through the Looking Glass (Carroll), 188
Tocqueville, Alexis, 19
Tonkin Gulf Resolution, 178
Toynbee, Arnold, 107
Trade Adjustment Act, 42
Truman, David, 36
Truman, Harry, 100, 102, 164
    as an institutionalized president, 39, 41
Truman Doctrine, 102–104
Turkey, 103
Tydings, Joseph, 160, 162

Udall, Stewart, 175–176
"Uncle Sam's $50 Billion Surplus" (Dale), 125–126
Unemployment, 84–91

manpower training, 93–96
  necessity of, 89
  Negroes, 90–91, 209
Union of Soviet Socialist Republics, 103, 105, 106, 170
Urban Affairs Council, 79

Vanderbilt, Commodore, 29
Vietnam War, 26, 30, 31, 46–49, 56, 64, 74, 101–117, 137, 162, 163, 179–183, 194, 199, 200, 220, 221
  budget, 46, 88, 119, 123–126, 129–135, 137, 140
  cost of, 105
Vocational education, 42, 45, 71, 93–96
Vocational Education Act, 45
Voting, 122, 184, 198–201
Voting Rights Act, 122

Wallace, George, 164, 201
War on poverty, 33–34, 36, 49–56, 63–64, 80–81, 121
  Bureau of the Budget in, 49–51
  political objectives of, 53
Washington *Post*, 127, 128
Watson, Albert W., 153

Ways and Means Committee, 154
Weapons Culture, The (Lapp), 145
Welfare, 38, 39, 70, 88, 132, 173–175, 183, 210
  Nixon on, 174–175
White, Lee C., 51
White, William S., 65
White House Conference on National Economic Issues, 77
Wildavsky, Aaron, 100, 113, 116, 177–183
Williams, H., 159
Williams, John Bell, 153
Williams, John J., 67, 68
Williams, Roger, 213
Wilson, Woodrow, 37, 66, 122, 203
Wirtz, Willard, 89
Woodlawn Organization (Chicago), 81
World War II, 38–39

Yancey, William L., 82
Yarborough, Ralph W., 159, 162
Yarmolinsky, Adam, 64
Ylvisaker, Paul, 51
Young, Milton, 67, 68
Young, S., 159